D0163145

7/11

Privatize This?

Privatize This?

Assessing the Opportunities and Costs of Privatization

Richard A. McGowan, SJ

PRAEGER

AN IMPRINT OF ABC-CLIO, LLC
Santa Barbara, California • Denver, Colorado • Oxford, England

Copyright 2011 by Richard A. McGowan, SJ

Library of Congress Cataloging-in-Publication Data

McGowan, Richard, 1952–
   Privatize this? : assessing the opportunities and costs of privatization / Richard A. McGowan.
     p. cm.
   Includes bibliographical references and index.
   ISBN 978-0-313-37586-6 (hard copy : alk. paper)—ISBN 978-0-313-37587-3 (ebook)
  1. Privatization—Case studies. I. Title.
   HD3850.M34   2011
   338.9′25—dc22   2010049765

ISBN: 978-0-313-37586-6
EISBN: 978-0-313-37587-3

15 14 13 12 11   1 2 3 4 5

This book is also available on the World Wide Web as an eBook.
Visit www.abc-clio.com for details.

Praeger
An Imprint of ABC-CLIO, LLC

ABC-CLIO, LLC
130 Cremona Drive, P.O. Box 1911
Santa Barbara, California 93116-1911

This book is printed on acid-free paper ∞

Manufactured in the United States of America

Contents

Preface

Throughout my academic career, I have analyzed the relationship between the business and public policy processes. Up to now, this interest has focused on interactions between the various "sin" industries (gambling, alcohol, and tobacco) and government. I have always been intrigued by the fact that government maintains control and ownership of some segments of these industries while permitting private ownership in other segments. In the U.S. gambling industry, for example, state governments operate their own lotteries while they permit private casinos. Meanwhile, our Canadian neighbors insist that lotteries be operated by private firms while provincial governments own casinos. Recently there has been a movement in the United States to privatize lotteries, yet in New Hampshire, there has been a proposal that the state operate its own casino. Hence I have a growing interest in the whole privatization process.

This book is not a traditional text written by an economist or a political scientist on the growing popularity of privatizing government enterprises. Rather, reflecting my own training in the business strategy field, it focuses on the strategic advantages and disadvantages for government and private firms of engaging in the privatization process.

The first chapter, entitled "A Brief History of the Nationalization versus Privatization Debate," focuses on the period after World War II, when governments became much more involved in providing services. Public transportation and health care are just a few of the services that government started to provide in place of the private sector. Then, in the 1980s, the neoliberal tradition, symbolized by Ronald Reagan and Margaret

Thatcher, attacked big government and the services that it provided. The question posed at the end of this chapter is: Where are we in the "issue life cycle" for privatization? Has the pendulum swung from privatization to more government involvement, or is the privatization movement just hitting its stride?

Chapter 2, entitled "Evaluating the Privatization Process: Making Sure the 'Game' Is Fair," develops a model that will serve two purposes. First, it allows the reader to evaluate why a privatization or nationalization occurred. Second, it gives the reader a "scorecard" to evaluate whether the process was a "success." The model includes all of the stakeholders in the privatization/nationalization decision and what "issues" and concerns set off the process. The "game" that needs to be played is to achieve a balance (establish a Nash Equilibrium) between the conflicting goals of equality and efficiency in both political and economic terms.

Part Two analyzes four very different international examples of privatization. All of the examples were controversial, and all of them involved tradeoffs between revenue (efficiency) and access to service (equality). Ironically, European countries, as well as South American countries, have been in the forefront of dealing with the privatization/nationalization question, well in advance of the supposed champion of free-market capitalism, the United States.

Chapter 3, entitled "Privatizing Sin: The 21st-Century Cigarette Industry," focuses on the unique situation faced by the Spanish government as it decides to exit a controversial industry. Clearly there are revenue issues connected with cigarette sales that need to be balanced by public health concerns. The other question that will be explored is the government's need to set up a regulatory process for a previously nationalized industry.

Chapter 4 studies Argentina's privatization of its oil industry. In the 1980s, Argentina's government was facing a fiscal crisis as well as high inflation. Meanwhile, its nationalized oil industry was failing to keep up with demand for its products. The government firm was also woefully inefficient because of underfunding for its maintenance. One way of resolving two problems for the Argentine government was to privatize its oil industry. The chapter explores two questions: Did the privatized oil industry become more efficient? What happened to the price of gasoline and oil products as a result of this privatization?

Chapter 5, on Venezuela's oil industry, offers a contrasting point of view. In February 1999, Hugo Chávez became president of Venezuela, and one of his first acts was to nationalize the Venezuelan oil industry. This chapter attempts to ask the same questions as the previous chapter but in reverse order. Did gasoline and oil products become much more accessible to the people of Venezuela? On the other hand, did this nationalization cripple the long-term prospects of the oil industry in Venezuela?

Finally, Chapter 6 is entitled "Public Good or Inefficiency? Port Facilities in the United States and Canada." Canada and the United States operate some of the biggest port facilities in the world. These facilities are vital in maintaining their export industries. Yet in the United States, government owns and operates most port facilities, whereas in Canada, the private sector owns all of the ports. The advantages and disadvantages of both approaches are explored in this chapter.

Part Three examines state-operated industries that were once private enterprises. These chapters analyze why governments operate monopolies for certain industries while allowing the private sector to own and provide goods and services in other sectors of the economy.

In two cases, government has decided to operate a service or a good that other governments have turned over to private firms. These cases are explored in Chapters 7 and 8, which investigate state-controlled liquor stores from two states: Pennsylvania and New Hampshire. One of the more interesting results of the Prohibition experiment was how states reintroduced alcohol consumption. In New Hampshire and Pennsylvania, the sale of wine and distilled spirits became state-run operations. These chapters explore how this approach affects consumers in both of these states. Has the existence of "state stores" made wine and distilled spirits less accessible to the public? What about the pricing structure of these products for the public? Has there been a movement to privatize these stores? What are the revenue concerns of each of these states? The two chapters come to very different conclusions and discuss the "ideology" behind them.

Finally, Chapter 9 examines the phenomenon of regional transportation authorities such as the MTA, MBTA, and SEPTA. Between 1945 and 1965, cities such as New York, Boston, and Philadelphia started to acquire the various private firms that constituted their public transportation network. The first part of this chapter chronicles how these transit authorities were assembled, highlighting the similarities along with their differences. The second part examines the current status of these authorities with a special emphasis on their relationship with their respective state legislatures.

Part Four analyzes various proposals to privatize goods and services that are still being operated by government—in particular, how the stakeholders are "satisfied" so that the privatization might eventually be realized. The chapters draw on financial data to discuss the many aspects of privatization.

Chapter 10 is concerned with the privatized prison industry. The movement toward the privatization of prisons in the United States is a result of the convergence of two factors: the exponential growth of the U.S. prison population and the resulting explosion in the costs of trying to maintain correction facilities. In 1984, the first private prison was opened, and by 1997, the privatized prison industry had gross revenues exceeding $1 billion. This chapter examines the growth of private prisons as well as their current scope. It addresses the question of whether the gains in "efficiency" that proponents claim for private prisons outweigh the public values of safety, justice, and legitimacy, which opponents say are lost with private prisons.

Chapter 11 illustrates all of the issues involved in privatizing a lottery, using Illinois's attempt to privatize its lottery as an example. This chapter gives the reader an opportunity to experience firsthand the dilemmas that confront public policy officials as they attempt to ramp up the revenue from an enterprise that has always been operated by state government. What would be the "correct" asking price? What would be the appropriate rate of taxation on profits? Finally, what type of regulatory commission would need to be established to oversee this new private enterprise?

The book concludes with the controversial relationship between the U.S. government and General Motors (GM). In many quarters, the bailout of GM was labeled as the "nationalization" of the U.S. auto industry. Using the previous criteria established in the book, this chapter discusses whether the bailout of GM may be described in this way.

Overall, it is my hope that this book will enable the reader to analyze the many complex issues that privatization represents and, at the same time, show that it is possible to predict the success or failure of a proposed privatization of a governmental service.

Acknowledgments

As with my previous five books, I owe a debt of gratitude to many students at Boston College. Over the many years of teaching my business policy course, I have "pretested" a number of the case studies described in this book. Students made many helpful suggestions on how to improve the cases and gave useful insights into the privatization process.

A number of students also served as research assistants for this volume. Without their contributions, it would not have been possible. First, I would like to thank Steve Twomey and Pat Bianchi for their efforts in researching the state liquor chapter. Andreas Tsitos did yeoman work on the privatized prisons chapter, and Meghan Skira did invaluable research on the oil industry chapters. Matt Raffol helped to revise the cigarette chapter and did the research on the General Motors chapter. Finally, I need to thank Mike Gordon for doing the research on the public transportation chapter and also for developing the index for each chapter. Without all of these contributions, this book would not have been written. Of course, any mistakes in the book are attributed solely to me. It is my hope that the book will inspire others to further analyze and contribute to the debate over privatization.

Part One

Introduction

Chapter 1

A Brief History of the Nationalization versus Privatization Debate

The landscape of the air travel industry in the United Kingdom (UK) has changed dramatically over the past three decades, and the major changes have nothing to do with recently imposed fees for checked bags, blankets, or bottles of water. Instead, the main shift relates to the transfer of ownership of aviation-related companies from the British government to the private sector. Two of the most prominent examples of this type of change are the divestitures of airline giant British Airways and BAA Limited, self-identified as the "world's leading airport company"[1] and owner and operator of seven airports in the UK.

British Airways was formed on March 31, 1974, through the merger of the British Overseas Airways Corporation (henceforth identified as "BOAC") and British European Airways ("BEA"). Both BOAC and BEA were state-owned at the time of the merger, and consequently, the newly formed enterprise was also owned by the British government. In 1979, as the political scene in Britain began to shift when the Conservative Party led by Margaret Thatcher came into power, the business setting experienced significant change as well.

British Airways, however, was not an immediate target for privatization, although it clearly required change. The airline was stuck in a rut of unprofitability, sustaining losses as great as $170 million in 1982.[2] Therefore, the government needed to prepare for the company's privatization. As Ellen Pint points out in her 1990 article published in the *Journal of Public Policy*, "the [British] Government needed to improve [the airline's] profitability to make it saleable."[3] Consequently, over 20,000 of the 58,000 BA personnel were cut, leading to a $217 million profit in 1984, just two years after the aggravating loss.[4] The airline was finally privatized on February 11, 1987, and as recent analysis suggests, the privatization has yielded a successful result, at least from a financial standpoint. Between fiscal years 1996 and 2008, British Airways earned a pretax profit in all but one year.

The story of BAA Limited is similar to that of British Airways. At its inception, the British Airports Authority—which would later become BAA Limited—was a government-owned enterprise established under the Airports Authority Bill passed in 1965. It endured as a nationalized company until the late 1980s, during which time Thatcher's government pushed to privatize the company. The Airports Act of 1986 officially dissolved the authority, and a new company, BAA, was formed. Then, in 1987, BAA was privatized and undertook an initial stock offering, with a capitalization of just under $2 billion.

As is apparent from the two aforementioned examples, privatization can effectively boost profits or raise funds on the capital market. However, privatization does more than simply raise revenue; in fact, it is often pursued so that the previously state-owned companies will "become less politicized, more efficient, and [ultimately] provide higher quality products and services."[5] But despite the fact that privatization seems to pose a simple and adequate solution to the problems encountered with nationalized enterprises, it is often difficult to achieve. Obstacles at the policy, administrative, logistical, and planning levels all abound. Moreover, even if these barriers did not exist, many countries would still choose to maintain state-owned rather than private companies. In some countries, some companies that are currently *privatized* are targets for nationalization or renationalization. Clearly, the options to nationalize or to privatize are controversial.

The remainder of this chapter will scrutinize in depth the arguments both for and against the two policies. It will also briefly outline the history of the nationalization versus privatization debate, beginning with an examination of the period immediately following World War II, then looking at the shift that occurred during the 1980s, and finally analyzing the current state of affairs.

THE ARGUMENT FOR NATIONALIZATION

To "nationalize" something, according to the *Merriam-Webster* definition, is to "invest control or ownership of in the national government."[6] Nationalization is generally pursued for economic, political, or social reasons.

Economically speaking, nationalization may be the best option (principally in developing countries) to accelerate development. This is a key motive behind the nationalization of many industries in Africa, Asia, and Latin America. The state is able to undertake projects that may otherwise be deemed too risky by private investors but are seen as necessary for national growth. The government may also nationalize "necessary" projects with significant capital requirements when private funding is insufficient. In this case, privatization would be impossible and thus nationalization is the only alternative. The government can, of course, easily raise funds by increasing taxes or borrowing both within its own borders as well as abroad. Multiple nations, for example, have nationalized their airline industries in order to promote development; for instance, Air India is currently fully state-owned.

Another economic motivation for nationalization is the desire of the national government to gain control of certain profitable industries; this secures the revenue that the industry generates, rather than allowing private or foreign investors to cash in on the industry. For this reason, Chile nationalized the copper industry under Salvador Allende in 1972. The government derives the right to take over the industry based on the idea "that underground assets belong to the public and should not be eligible for private exploitation."[7]

Nationalization may be advantageous from a governmental standpoint for political reasons as well. This "political" category contains many facets. For example, a government may nationalize a company in order to rescue it from bankruptcy. Such was the case with the Conrail enterprise in the United States:

> Congress approved the Nixon administration's proposal for a federal government takeover of seven bankrupt railroads in the northeast United States in 1974. The policy was a response to a crisis brought on by the bankruptcy of the Penn Central Railroad in 1970. The firms were consolidated into a single entity, Conrail, which was established as a government-sponsored corporation, but intended to be private and profit-seeking. However, the government eventually became the only "shareholder" in Conrail because of legislative provisions that made it virtually impossible for Conrail to be profitable.[8]

Additionally, a government may nationalize an industry for security reasons, fearing that some sort of safety hazard would occur if the firm were to be privatized. For example, some companies in Argentina create military goods and other items considered to be of interest to national security, and hence this industry is considered "untouchable";[9] as a result, these types of companies have been nationalized. In the United States, in response to the terrorist attacks of September 11, 2001, the federal government created the Transportation Security Administration (TSA). The formation of the TSA resulted in government regulation of all airport security checkpoints instead of private firms regulating these checkpoints as in previous years. Currently, security checkpoints at a limited number of U.S. airports are operated by private firms, but these are still overseen by the TSA under the Screening Partnership Program.[10]

Often, the goal of nationalization is socially related: to create equity. The term "government-owned" is usually synonymous with "publicly owned," and thus it is easy to see why a nationalized firm is equitable. When a company or industry is nationalized, the public has easy and equal access to the goods and services that it provides. For example, public transportation systems and utilities are commonly nationalized. These types of enterprises are vital for the public good, but they may not be sufficiently rewarding to attract private entrepreneurs.

Aside from providing equal access for consumers, nationalization may also appease workers. Labor unions are some of the principal interest groups that tend to favor nationalization, because the government is able to provide more jobs with fair wages and working conditions under this policy. As evidenced by the British Airways path to privatization, company employees are often the first group to suffer when the privatization of a nationally owned entity is on the horizon. This is an especially critical issue in developing countries with a less than stable political environment, as a large divestiture of a state-owned enterprise and the resulting job loss could cause massive political upheaval.

In conclusion, then, the motives for nationalization are varied. Usually, they are economic, political, or social in nature. The national government must ultimately be able to justify its nationalization policy and operate the state-owned enterprises well if it wishes to avoid future takeover by the private sector.

NATIONALIZATION FOLLOWING WORLD WAR II

Government ownership of various industries increased after the second World War. Although all of the previously mentioned motives for nationalization could have played a role in this trend, the driving force behind the surge in nationalized industries was probably the economic and infrastructural devastation facing many nations following the war. Unfavorable postwar economic conditions probably discouraged private investment. In addition, some industries, such as the railroad industry in many countries, had been nearly destroyed by the war and required government intervention to rebound successfully.

Great Britain was one of the many countries that experienced a substantial increase in government ownership after World War II. The Labour Government nationalized various industries, including transportation, utilities, banking, and natural resources, during the six years following the war. Ellen Pint both details and examines the effects of the nationalization policy in her article cited earlier. Specifically, she looks at the effects of the policy on four particular groups: shareholders, employees, consumers, and the Treasury.

The fact that Britain is a democratic nation affected the government's approach to nationalization. Since elections had to be held at minimum every five years, the Labour Government wanted to ensure that it was politically efficient in executing its policy. It wanted to be as effective as possible in a short period of time, as well as please the interest groups that it thought to be most influential, so that the party would be reelected. Thus, the British government aimed to please company shareholders. In some other countries, the government nationalized industries through a process known as "expropriation," in which no compensation was paid to existing shareholders. However, the British government had previously decided that "the policy of outright confiscation will not be adopted."[11] It valued most companies according to the stock market valuation, which shareholders generally found acceptable. The one exception was the acquisition of utilities companies, which were "taken over on the basis of 'net outstanding debt,' "[12] an approach that benefited the government.

As one would expect, British nationalization policy aimed to improve the "status and condition of workers,"[13] but this was not entirely the case. The government did not generally grant wage increases because they would have allegedly resulted in "higher prices or operating losses, which may have made the nationalization policy unpopular."[14] Even though overall employment increased, company employees were probably less than satisfied following the nationalization.

Consumers, on the other hand, applauded this governmental policy. Lower prices allowed wider access to the good or service, increasing customer satisfaction. It was important to maintain this level of consumer satisfaction to prevent the nationalization policy from being easily overturned when the Labour Party did not hold power. Furthermore, as Pint points out, "Nationalization was . . . one of the distinguishing features between Labour and Conservatives. If it were widely perceived to be merely a means of shifting income from consumers to workers, the popularity of the policy would be greatly reduced."[15]

Finally, the Treasury likely suffered from the policy of nationalization. After all, the government was probably forced to nationalize because the affected industries were not sufficiently profitable for the private sector. Therefore, one could infer that the Treasury would struggle with profitability as well, since it funded the state-owned enterprises.

In addition to the effects on each interest group in developing nationalization policy, the government also needed to consider the degree of difficulty in reversing its policy in the future. Various financing structures each affected differently the ease of reversibility. Consolidating smaller, private firms into one larger, nationalized firm helped the government make its policy more irreversible. It is also interesting to point out that differences in political systems affect the reversibility of nationalization policy. For example, the complex political system in the United States of a bicameral legislature and a three-branch setup makes it more difficult to pass a nationalization policy than it would be in Britain. However, policy in the United States is also more difficult to reverse after being passed.

Nationalized enterprises were also quite prevalent outside Europe during the second half of the 20th century. As of 1986, for example, several nations had a significant nationalization component to their respective economies:

> In Mexico, the number of state-owned enterprises increased from 180 to over 500 in the 20 years between 1960 and 1980; those 500 companies accounted for 10 percent of GDP in 1980 . . . 75 percent of Brazil's state-owned enterprises have been established since 1960. . . . In just 15 years, the number of state enterprises in Tanzania grew from around 50 to over 400, and presently [fall 1986] account for 15 percent of its GDP. . . . Between 1974 and 1982, the Portuguese government nationalized over 60 percent of the nation's productive capacity equaling 15 percent of its GDP.[16]

Despite the prominent presence of nationalized industries in many countries around the globe, economic problems actually increased in many nations during the 1980s. Successful state-owned companies were quite rare. Simply stated, many nationalized enterprises had become financial losers. According to a 1985 article published in *The Economist*, for instance, the Japan National Railway lost nearly $20 million daily during that time.[17] Not only were most nationalized firms unable to meet their economic, political, and social goals, but furthermore, they were often accused of being inefficient or producing low-quality goods and services. The need for change had become strikingly apparent, and that change would take the form of widespread privatization.

THE ARGUMENT FOR PRIVATIZATION

Privatization, defined by *Webster*'s as the process undergone "to change (as a business or industry) from public to private control or ownership,"[18] is essentially the inverse of nationalization. Privatization is often economically motivated. It is interesting to note that even though privatization would seemingly be more popular in countries with a capitalistic economy, "even countries without a capitalist predisposition, such as China and Hungary, have expressed favorable attitudes towards privatization [in the 1980s]."[19]

The fundamental argument in favor of privatization is that privatization increases economic efficiency and ultimately leads to more potential for long-term economic growth than nationalization. The driving force that brings about this efficiency is competition. It is easy to see why competition is so vital when examining what occurs when it is absent. Without competition, nationalized industries often become "privileged deadbeats,"[20] according to the Council on Foreign Relations book *The Promise of Privatization: A Challenge for U.S. Policy*, and among nationalized industries, "cases of gross incompetence, padded payrolls, and even outright looting . . . have not been hard to find."[21] Under state ownership, companies are subject to both corruption and bureaucracy. Corruption is common because the state has nobody else to regulate the companies and decisions are often made for purely political reasons. Bureaucracy is problematic because the government is often unwilling to improve or advance a good or service unless the industry's performance is so poor that it reflects negatively on the administration. Ideally, competition eliminates these elements.

Competition under privatization also typically yields a greater revenue stream. Managers of a privatized industry may be more specialized or better equipped to run the industry than their government-appointed counterparts, thus enhancing the business. Also, state-owned enterprises do not exist to generate profits, whereas privately held corporations do.

Consequently, state-owned enterprises are often frivolous when it comes to spending money. For example, nationalized companies typically employ many more workers (which would explain why labor unions favor nationalization), but consequently, the workers are less productive and thus the real cost of the good or service is higher. Additionally, the government can raise taxes or issue debt to fund a failing industry, even if it does not make economic sense to let the industry persist. A private company, on the other hand, must fund its operations by either attracting private investors or using its own previous revenue; therefore, a private company has a greater incentive to create high-quality goods and services and is better from an economic standpoint. Finally, the revenues generated by private enterprises are taxed, and hence the public Treasury will still benefit from this privatization.

State governments do have alternatives that allow them to enjoy the benefits of privatization without completely privatizing an industry. One common alternative is governmental outsourcing of a particular good or service to the private sector. The aforementioned TSA situation is a good example of this type of outsourcing. Another example of a service that has been contracted to the private sector around the globe is garbage collection. This allows for a more efficient team of managers and employees to manage the trash collection, while the service is still "publicly owned" and funded by the government. Outsourcing to the private sector can be especially important when the good or service to be produced requires extensive managerial or technical knowledge, in which case the private sector can often provide better resources than the government.

Another effective alternative to privatization may be "to allow private firms to enter into competition with the public enterprises."[22] An example would be allowing a private airline to enter into direct competition with a state-owned airline. Alternatively, the government could allow for *multiple* state-owned companies to compete against one another, as was the case in the 1980s in China, when the government allowed for the creation of a new state-owned airline when a state-owned air transport company already existed. The bottom line is that all of these options allow for competition, which in turn helps to realize the benefits of privatization.

It is generally acknowledged that not *all* industries should be privatized. The most noteworthy example of a time in which privatization is generally considered not to be beneficial is in the presence of a natural monopoly. A natural monopoly, according to the dictionary of terms on the *economist. com*, is "when a monopoly occurs because it is more efficient for one firm to serve an entire market than for two or more firms to do so, because of the sort of economies of scale available in that market."[23] A utility is often a natural monopoly; because the principal cost is the setup cost, it is typically more efficient for one firm to dominate the market, as this will keep the average cost to the customer lower. In a situation such as this, the enterprise is often publicly owned.

Under the argument for privatization, competition is the key that can lead to economic efficiency and long-term growth. Evidently, that was the thought process of countries around the globe as the 1980s approached and a need for change was necessary.

THE 1980s: A SHIFT TOWARD PRIVATIZATION

The push for privatization was strong in the 1980s, sweeping across countries regardless of their political ideologies and at all levels of economic development. The inefficiencies of state ownership had been exposed and economies globally were suffering, both of which weakened faith in national governments. The skeptical public turned to the private sector for the solution.

A whirlwind of varying conditions set up the perfect storm for privatization during this time period. *The Promise of Privatization* cites several circumstances that favored a move toward privatization, emphasizing both the rise of a managerial class and changes in market structures.[24] The former refers to the arrival of managerial and technical knowledge that did not exist before, accompanied by financial resources, which allowed those in the private sector to take over and successfully manage a recently divested industry. The latter refers to developments in technology that allowed for the development of "an international capital market in which developing countries could raise capital for the financing of their public enterprises."[25]

Great Britain and Chile were two of the most notable nations leading the privatization crusade. In Britain, Thatcher and her Conservative Party proposed broad privatization changes when they entered office just before 1980. Thatcher was convinced of the efficiency argument outlined previously in this chapter, and she wanted to lessen the size and power of the state. She seemed to think that a bigger government meant a weaker economy, and she wanted a strong economy so that Britain could emerge as a leader in the global economy. After all was said and done, the following firms in the UK had been privatized: British Telecom, British Airways (as previously noted), British Petroleum, Cable and Wireless, Rolls-Royce, British Gas, British Steel, and "the 10 regional water authorities of England and Wales."[26]

A major effect of the British privatization has been more widespread share ownership, which was one of the original goals. This is considered to benefit shareholders, the first interest group Pint examines in her article. The public Treasury also benefits from the privatization, at least in the short term, because the disposal of some ailing industries and the increase in revenue from their sales put the Treasury in a stronger financial position. The new privatization policy likely hurt employees of state-owned companies, mainly because privatization substantially reduced both employment and the power of labor unions. However, the government did initiate some transfer payments to new employees and gave in to some less significant union demands in an effort to appease workers. Finally, consumers experienced mixed results. Most privatized industries were competitive, and those that were not—such as the utilities or other natural monopolies—were carefully regulated by the government. Hence, as Pint points out, "consumer protection has not been an issue."[27] However, although the prices of the monopolized industries were regulated, product and service quality purportedly declined. This was one key flaw in allowing privatized monopolies to exist.

In Chile, a large number of enterprises in nearly all sectors of the economy were privatized between 1973 and 1990.[28] While the dynamics differed in regards to the type and size of the enterprises being sold and the implications for the role of the government, Chile's shift toward privatization made it a leader in privatization advancement among developing nations. From 1973 to 1981, the Chilean government began selling firms and banks that had been both illegally and legally nationalized under the Allende government. The number of enterprises owned by the state decreased from 270 in 1973 to 47 in 1983. However, the rapid privatization over this decade led to the concentration of ownership of these enterprises under large conglomerates. With the privatization of banks occurring as well, the conglomerates became highly indebted, and ultimately became insolvent as Chile slipped into a recession in the end of 1981. Of the enterprises and banks that were privatized, 70 percent became insolvent.

The period from 1984 to 1986 marked the reprivatization of these enterprises, with a focus on avoiding indebtedness as previously nationalized firms left the soft financing hands of the government. This round of privatization utilized much more foreign investment than the privatization of the 1970s. In addition, in 1985, the government declared that it would start a new privatization program that included core state-owned enterprises, including telecommunication, power supply companies, water purification units, and steel mills. By 1988, almost all of the enterprises were going to be fully privatized, and in total, 39 enterprises were included in the program. The support for this round of divestitures was much more ideological, as some of the enterprises were among the largest in the country and accelerated the country's development in their respective industries. Hernán Büchi Buc, Chilean minister of finance at the time, cited the importance of private property as the foundation for a market economy, the gains in efficiency as a result of privatization, the reprivatization and recapitalization of the banks affected by the financial crisis, and the stabilizing effect on the capital market by deepening the stock market as reasons supporting this rapid shift toward privatization.

CONCLUSION

The cases in Great Britain and Chile provide examples of shifts toward privatization, including the motives or goals, the process by which the governments handled the divestitures, and the resulting consequences. In order to accurately analyze these actions and evaluate their effectiveness, it is necessary to develop an analytical framework that can work with all privatization versus nationalization debates. The next chapter will outline fundamental elements of the privatization "game" and provide an initial presentation of the consequences of privatization for the various stakeholders.

NOTES

1. BAA, "Who We Are," http://www.baa.com (accessed May 20, 2009).
2. J. Vickers and G. Yarrow, "Regulation of Privatised Firms in Britain," *European Economic Review* 32:2–3 (1988): 465–473.
3. Ellen Pint, "Nationalization and Privatization: A Rational-Choice Perspective on Efficiency," *Journal of Public Policy* 10 (1990).
4. Vickers and Yarrow, "Regulation of Privatised Firms in Britain."
5. Vickers and Yarrow, "Regulation of Privatised Firms in Britain."
6. *Merriam-Webster Dictionary*, http://www.merriam-webster.com/dictionary/nationalize (accessed May 20, 2009).
7. Vickers and Yarrow, "Regulation of Privatised Firms in Britain."
8. Pint, "Nationalization and Privatization."
9. Vickers and Yarrow, "Regulation of Privatised Firms in Britain."
10. Transportation Security Administration, "Screening Partnership Program," http://www.tsa.gov/what_we_do/optout/index.shtm (accessed May 20, 2009).
11. Pint, "Nationalization and Privatization."

12. Pint, "Nationalization and Privatization."

13. Pint, "Nationalization and Privatization."

14. Pint, "Nationalization and Privatization."

15. Pint, "Nationalization and Privatization."

16. Vickers and Yarrow, "Regulation of Privatised Firms in Britain."

17. Tokyo Correspondent, "Japan; A Voice from the Past," *The Economist* (December 7, 1985).

18. *Merriam-Webster Dictionary*, http://www.merriam-webster.com/dictionary/privatization (accessed May 20, 2009).

19. Vickers and Yarrow, "Regulation of Privatised Firms in Britain."

20. Raymond Vernon, ed., *The Promise of Privatization: A Challenge for U.S. Policy* (New York: Council on Foreign Relations Books, 1988).

21. Vernon, *The Promise of Privatization.*

22. Vickers and Yarrow, "Regulation of Privatised Firms in Britain."

23. *Economist*.com Dictionary, http://www.economist.com/research/economics/searchActionTerms.cfm?query=natural+monopoly (accessed May 20, 2009).

24. Vernon, *The Promise of Privatization.*

25. Vernon, *The Promise of Privatization.*

26. Pint, "Nationalization and Privatization."

27. Pint, "Nationalization and Privatization."

28. Barry Bosworth, Rudiger Dornbusch, and Raúl Labán, *The Chilean Economy: Policy Lessons and Challenges* (Washington, DC: Brookings Institution Press, 1994).

Chapter 2

Evaluating the Privatization Process: Making Sure the "Game" Is Fair

During the past decade, one of the more interesting developments in the evolution of strategic management literature has been the introduction of game theory. The founders of game theory have won a series of Nobel Prizes in mathematics and economics (John von Neumann, a mathematician; Oskar Morgenstern, an economist; and John Nash of *A Beautiful Mind* fame). At first glance, however, the introduction of the rather esoteric concepts of game theory would seem to run contrary to strategic management's traditional stress on being useful to "practicing" managers or public policy makers as they decide how to provide a service or product to the general public. Yet the concept of a "game" provides some tools for guiding one's thinking in public policy situations and can provide a broad overview that is extremely useful.

In the strategic management context, game theory has been used to describe how managers need to think about how their competitors will respond to the actions they take. In other words, there is a strategic interdependence among the various participants or stakeholders. In traditional economic theory, each individual makes choices in isolation, unaware of what other competitors are doing. However, in game theory, two or more participants try to maximize their utility, knowing that competitors are aware of what they are doing.

But what makes game theory even more revolutionary in the development of economic theory (and in turn strategic management) is that it takes into account the risk preferences of the various participants. No longer is it assumed that every competitor wants to maximize profits or have perfect information about the market; rather, competitors will act to bring about the most preferred possible outcomes for themselves and other players. In this environment, strategy is important, but perhaps more important is signaling one's intentions and behavior to other players in the game in order to achieve the most preferred outcomes.

Information for game theory decisions is probabilistic in nature, and every participant has a different risk preference. The source of uncertainty is the intentions of other players. Risk structures and the use of the mean and variance (in order to determine probabilities) help to identify how participants in the game will respond to uncertain prospects. Participants then use marginal analysis to make optimal decisions given the constraint that other players are acting in the same manner.

But although game theory has become an integral part of the business strategy curriculum, it is almost totally neglected in privatization literature. This chapter is a first step to remedy this deficiency. Just as game theory has redefined what the "rational" actor is in a microeconomic setting, it might provide the opportunity for privatization scholars to reevaluate how government, firms, and various stakeholders deal with political economy questions such as privatization.

To accomplish this introductory task, this chapter is divided into three parts. The first part describes the characteristics of a "game," emphasizing those features that have to do with "fairness," since this characteristic has the greatest influence on the outcome of political economy dilemmas such as the decision to privatize or nationalize. The second section develops a model, entitled the "Arena for Privatization Games," that will attempt to give readers a framework for cataloging the various types of "games" they could encounter as part of the "privatization" process. The third section applies this model to develop possible strategies in dealing with various dilemmas that managers might confront.

CHARACTERISTICS OF A GAME

How many times as children did we hear the phrase "It's only a game"? The phrase was used to calm the player who was taking the game "too seriously." Every summer, there are numerous reports of parents who have interfered with Little League baseball games. An example occurred in a suburb of Philadelphia a few years ago, when the manager of a Little League team (a policeman) paid his pitcher to hit the best hitter of an opposing team in the head. Unfortunately, the pitcher was successful, and the hitter was hospitalized. But the pitcher felt such remorse over the incident that he told authorities that his manager had paid him to aim at the head of the opposing player. The public reaction to such stories is: "Isn't it a shame that adults can't just let the kids play the game?" The emphasis on "winning" at all costs is decried, and there is a nostalgic yearning for simpler times when adults would not interfere in kids' games. So what have these adults done that has violated our sense of a "game"? Adults certainly regulate every other aspect of a child's life, so why shouldn't they interfere in a child's game?

The objection to adult interference in games is that games are a special world in which children are protected against the reality of the adult world. In fact, all games are construed as occasions that operate outside of the "normal" world. What makes the world of a game so unique? The French sociologist Roger Caillois proposed that the following three characteristics separate games from reality: (1) a game must be voluntary; (2) a game must have boundaries; and (3) a game must have uncertain outcomes.[1]

A Voluntary Activity

A "game" certainly must be defined as a free and voluntary activity (otherwise the dynamics of the game and its outcomes are very different; as an example, consider the ancient Roman coliseum and its "games"). When a game begins, it is presumed that the game will be a source of fun and reward for the players, coaches, and audience. If any of the participants were forced to play, the game would lose its fun and its reward. The entertainment value of the game would disappear for everybody. Participants play a game only if and when they wish to, making the game a free or voluntary activity. Unfortunately, over time, the participants sometimes "forget" that the game is free and voluntary, and they thereby forfeit the ability to exit or withdraw. Clearly, in the case of privatizing a firm or industry, the voluntary aspect of the game can be violated, making the process much more controversial.

This desire to play a game is what makes it both entertaining and rewarding. The game's quality is judged by its ability to provide excitement and escape from the routine and to hold the attention of the audience and the participants. The chief reward of playing a game is recognition of the skill involved in playing the game. This sense of freedom also extends to "exiting" the game. A person playing a game has to be free to say, "I am not playing this game anymore." Finally, a game is something that creates neither goods nor wealth. It is unproductive activity in which participants play for the "love of the game" and in which the thrill of victory and the agony of defeat are the chief emotions. That is the reason why sports purists dismiss professional athletics: paid professionals no longer play just for the "love of the game."

In the example above concerning the Little League, the manager was willing to do anything to "win the game." He was not allowing his players "to be kids." His players were not having "fun" and, even worse, were not playing for the "love of the game."

Governed by Rules

A game is also an activity separate from the "real" world and isolated from the rest of life. What makes games different from the real world is that all games have precise limits of place and time. Players need a racetrack, a field, a ring, a stadium, or a board for checkers and chess. To leave the "place" where the game is played can disqualify the game's player.

There are also boundaries placed on the time in which the game needs to be played. A specific game has definite starts and conclusions, as does a season (the distinction being that a season encompasses a series of games and that the outcome of one game influences the performance during the season). All players have to follow the rules or at least pretend that they are following the rules. To move the "play" along, they agree to abide by the decisions of an umpire or referee, who generally interprets events according to preestablished rules. Every game is a restricted, closed, and protected environment, very unlike the "real" world. Games provide their participants a certainty that does not exist in the real world. To employ a person or thing that comes in from outside the ring or stadium is considered "bad" sportsmanship and usually disqualifies the player who brought in the outside influence.

Clearly, the manager who paid to have an opposing player hurt violated the rules of the game. Adults who inject themselves into a Little League game violate the "enclosed" and "protected" atmosphere that ought to characterize a game. By constantly challenging the umpire's calls and even threatening the umpires with violence, some Little League parents destroy the "safe" and contained world that a game is designed to provide the participants. Similarly, when parents badger the coach of a Little League team to win at all costs or to play their son or daughter at various times, this also violates the "sanctity" of the rules under which the game operates.

An Uncertain Activity

The characteristic that keeps a player playing a game is the uncertainty of results. The old baseball maxim "You never know until the last out" explains this facet of a game. Games are stopped once the outcome is no longer in doubt, or upon preestablished conditions. Every game of "skill" involves the uncertain risk of the player missing a shot or making a poor throw. If teams are unfairly matched, the game between them is boring, and both the players and the audience lose interest.

Even for "unskilled" games such as lotteries or roulette, a player has to be assured that there is a possibility that he or she can either win or not win. The entertainment value of a lottery game or a card game rests with the player's ability to believe or dream that every player has an equal chance of winning the game. Hence, the player of an unskilled game places a certain amount of trust in the operators of the game. If that trust is violated, then the game ceases to be played. (Applying the principle to the world of business and economics, the current "shake-down" in the Venezuelan oil industry attests to the fact that "players" [oil firms] will flee a "game" when they no longer trust that the rules will be enforced.)

Once again, the manager in our Little League example violated this fundamental gaming principle. Clearly, the manager's wish to win at all costs resulted in trying to remove "uncertainty" for his players. When adults are accused of taking the fun out of the game, it is precisely because they want to rig the results. If there is no doubt about the outcome of a game, then the game loses its joy and fun. We could argue that no game truly exists in these circumstances. The child in a Little League game is also not free to enter or leave the game if he or she wishes. (Again drawing a parallel to business and economics, one could say, for example, that monopolies cannot play the traditional "market" game because only one player exists and the outcomes are predictable in the long run.)

Although there are certainly other characteristics of games, these three characteristics seem to be universally a part of every game. They also correspond to a player's conception of a "fair" game. A game is considered "fair" if (1) the player is free to enter or leave a game; (2) the rules that govern the game apply to all players at all times, but "interpretations" of the rules by the umpires or referee can vary and impose an element of unpredictability not under the control of the players; and (3) the results of the game cannot be rigged beforehand.

The rules for "fairness" form the basis of a model that will be developed in the next section. This model is intended to be a "first look" at the various issues that confront public officials, managers of firms, leaders of public interest groups, or nongovernmental organizations as they play the "game" of privatizing a previously owned governmental enterprise.

THE ARENA FOR PRIVATIZATION "GAMES"

We now move to a more specific analysis of what will be termed "the privatization game."

The model or "arena" described in Figure 2.1, "The Arena for Privatization 'Games'," has three distinct parts. The first, the ring or field, is where the contest is played and includes the rules of engagement (specific procedures, processes, and the like) as well as the generally accepted rules of behavior (which are not necessarily written down but which every player knows). Players include individuals, organizations of every kind and variety, networked organizations, and the government (which can also play the curious role of "referee" here). This ring is the place in which the game is played.

The second part is the area of the audience and/or the contestants. The "and/or" choice is important because it reflects two key aspects of the game. The first is that, as in every game, there is an audience. The audience has the power to influence the outcome of the game by the nature and extent of its

Figure 2.1   The Arena for Privatization "Games"

involvement.[2] This does not mean that audience members must become actively involved as players or contestants, but rather that they can exercise influence by their choice of whom they support and the degree to which they support them. In a sports game, the "home team advantage" is considered important; in any game, the audience can provide psychological resources to the players that enable them to compete. The second aspect of the audience role is that audience members can become "contestants" and enter the ring or field as players. For organizations, it is important to understand the process and motivations for actual involvement of audience members in order to provide clues as to how they might act as they enter the game.

The third part of this model is the larger environment. The "game" area is separated from the larger environment by a permeable line. That is, it is very possible that other players (for want of a better term) can either enter as part of the audience or move directly into the field or ring of the game.

The following analysis will give managers and firms a sense of the various business and societal "games" they might encounter; will suggest strategies to deal with audience members who are not contestants; and will propose methods to deal with contestants in the ring or field. We begin by focusing more clearly on the ring or field of engagement.

THE RING OR FIELD

Before beginning a privatization "process" or "game," the players must decide and agree on the rules of the game and where it will take place. These conditions also mark the beginning of the "play." One player can even determine "where" the game is to be played initially, while tactics available to other players allow them to move the game to another arena. In essence, three questions need to be answered to determine the "ring" or "field":

1. What "level" will the game be played at?
2. Where will the game be initiated?
3. Who will serve as referee?

The Level of the Game

There are at least six levels at which the privatization/nationalization game can be played: the local, state, regional, national, transnational (but regionally based), and global levels. Each affords different levels of engagement for organizations to consider. In general, if the game involves contentious issues or "high" stakes, it will most likely be played at the federal level. Clearly, each player will try to pick the level that makes him or her feel most at "home," that is, wield the greatest power or have the greatest advantage over other competitors. But picking a level still contains some risk. One can overestimate one's strength at a particular level, underestimate the strength of competitors at that level, or misread the sheer amount and level of audience involvement and potential participation in the game itself. In baseball, the competition at the single-A, double-A, triple-A, and Major League levels is quite different.

Where Will the Game Be Played?

Once the level of the game has been determined, the next question is where the game will be played. For purposes of discussing privatization and nationalization, we offer alternative "playing fields" where the game can be played, each with its own rules and procedures, audiences, referees, and appeal processes. The potential fields are (at all levels noted above) (1) the legislative branch of government; (2) the judiciary branch (including here such areas as mediation and arbitration); and (3) the regulatory or executive branch.

Who Will Serve as "Referee"?

In all games and in many ways, the ultimate referee is the audience, especially where issues of fairness and equitability are raised. However, for the normal operation of the game, the selection of the ring presumes the existence of a referee acceptable to the players of the game. What makes games in the public policy arena such an interesting challenge is that government can simultaneously serve as a "player" and a referee in the game.

In the legislative game, the referee can be either the executive branch (in the form of a veto) or the committee system and leadership of the legislative bodies. The leadership plays a key role in selecting the issues and the agenda, presenting the issues, and determining which committees will consider the issues.[3] The committee system invests enormous power in the committee chair and in the individual members with regards to the consideration of issues and the form and manner in which they will be delivered (if at all) to the legislative body for consideration. There are also clear rules regarding what, how, and by whom a piece of legislation can be introduced, considered, and processed. If players are unhappy with the outcome of the game or a decision made in the game, they can appeal the referee's decision to the judiciary.

In the judicial game, the referee can be either the jury or the presiding judge. Either the jury or the judge makes the ultimate ruling on guilt or innocence and on the amount of damages or punishment to be awarded to the defendant(s). Like the legislature, the judiciary has a clear set of rules and processes for consideration of issues that come before it. Unlike the legislature, the judiciary is a reactionary game field: the judicial system awaits players to bring the game into this playing area. The legislature can select the game (issue) that is to be played in a more activist manner.

In the regulatory game, the referees are the members of the regulatory agency. The sitting commissioners (or whatever term is used) make the final decision and judgment; however, regulatory staff members have enormous unseen influence on the commissioners and how the issues are brought before them. Regulatory agencies lie between the legislature and the judiciary in terms of the game. That is, they can wait for issues to be brought to them or seek out issues on their own. They have their own rules and processes. Because of the nature of regulatory games, they receive far less publicity than games in the legislative or judicial ring and have smaller audiences, but the audience is usually very interested and knowledgeable about the game being played and often quite eager and willing to be involved. Decisions of regulatory agencies can be appealed to the judiciary or the legislature.

Based on significant empirical, practical, and theoretical experience in the United States, there are clear choices for organizations to consider when playing the game. The best set of rules in terms of clarity, consistent enforcement, and interpretability lies in the regulatory arena. That is, from a probability or uncertainty standpoint, engaging in the regulatory game is more predictable (although not certain) than in any other arena. Then, in order of increasing uncertainty, judicial games are next, followed by legislative games. Part of the reasoning relates to where decisions in the game can be appealed and under what "rules" such decisions can be appealed. In the court of public opinion, appeals can be taken to any of the other game fields; in the legislative game, for example, appeals can be taken to the judicial branch (but only a limited number of decisions can be appealed) or the executive branch (but with the potential override of a veto always a possibility).

Now that the framework for the game has been addressed and the elements of the game of privatization explicated, we can turn to evaluating how the various stakeholders will view a particular privatization process.

A STAKEHOLDER EVALUATION OF A PRIVATIZATION PROCESS

In the previous section, the word "fair" was mentioned frequently. There have been volumes written about "fairness." In the context of the privatization game, "fairness" is essentially a tradeoff between efficiency and equality.

Each of the stakeholders must be willing to compromise on one of these aspects for the privatization to be "successful." Clearly, the positives must outweigh the negatives, since the privatization game is *not* a zero-sum game. In other words, the gain of one stakeholder cannot be achieved at the expense of another stakeholder. A successful privatization has to be beneficial to all parties in both the short and long run. The rest of this section will delineate some of the efficiency and equality aspects that determine how a particular stakeholder might fare as a result of a privatization of a service or good previously provided by government.

Employees

As a general rule of thumb, this is the stakeholder group that is most vulnerable in a privatization process or game and the one that usually leads the charge against any change in the status quo of a state-operated firm or industry. Why? When "efficiency" becomes the rationale for a privatization, it usually implies that prices are too high. The service or good provided is deemed to be too expensive, often because of high costs, particularly labor costs both in terms of wages paid to workers as well as high administrative costs. Hence one of the "efficiencies" that privatization of a firm might accomplish would be to reduce labor costs to reduce prices, even though this would hurt employees as a group.

So it appears that employees (both blue and white collar) might be incurring a substantial part of the costs of a privatization. This could be true, but employees in the long run might preserve more jobs, especially if the firm or industry has been experiencing no growth or even a long-term decline. If so, the newly privatized firm might achieve economies of scale or expand into other growing and more profitable markets. A case in point would be public utilities that provide electricity, water, or natural gas. After a privatization process, these firms might be able to vertically integrate and provide consumers with one-stop shopping, thereby preserving jobs and actually expanding opportunities for employees. However, the example of Enron certainly shows that the outcomes of the privatization "game" are uncertain.

Public Interest Groups

These groups also tend to oppose a privatization process, usually because they have more political influence than they have economic influence. But the intensity of this opposition is also dependent upon how "ideological" the opposition to a firm or industry has become. For example, we will later examine the privatization of the Spanish and French cigarette industry.

Although this privatization has enormous economic implications, the chief interest of antismoking groups is not economic at all. Clearly, they are not interested in an "efficient" cigarette industry, and certainly not in lowering cigarette prices. Their goal is the death of the cigarette industry. The stance that an ideological group takes on a proposed privatization would greatly depend on whether the privatization would hasten the demise of the industry or firm. Environmental groups often fall into this category because they are quite ideological in their outlook toward any privatization.

Other public interest groups have more of an economic focus. For example, we will also examine the privatization of a public utility that provides natural gas to a region. Public groups affected by this development might focus on the access to or price of the good or service being provided, making economic power their primary concern. They may not initially oppose the privatization, favoring the long-term survival of the private enterprise. Classifying the true interest of a public policy group will determine not only the strategy of how the privatization might take place, but also how the various stakeholders will decide if the privatization might be labeled a "success."

Potential Shareholders

Here the question is not whether the privatization should take place but who will own the newly privatized firm or industry. Should the ownership be widely dispersed among the citizens of the country or among potential customers? Should ownership be concentrated in the firm and be a "national" champion? How would the public feel about ownership that is outside the country?

The answer to these questions depends on a few factors. If the previously nationalized firm is operating below industry standards or if it needs a great deal of investment to meet environmental requirements, then the large amount of investment necessary would usually preclude wide ownership.

Another series of questions would involve economies of scale and scope. Does the privatized firm need to achieve greater size to achieve economies of scale? For example, suppose a country decided to privatize its national champion airline. Would this airline be able to have the necessary routes and support to fly on its own? If it needs to find a merger partner, what sorts of restrictions would the government put on this merger? In general, are economies of scale necessary to achieve the efficiencies needed to lower prices to consumers?

As far as economies of scope are concerned, does the newly privatized firm require the ability to expand into new but related markets? Does a natural gas utility need to vertically integrate backwards to own natural gas supplies in order to become more efficient? Does that firm need to offer repair services or equipment, thereby competing with other firms offering those services? Should a privatized lottery be able to offer other gambling products such as Internet gaming or sports gambling? Should a previously government-run enterprise be allowed to "morph" into a firm that has little or nothing to do with its original product or service?

Finally, who should decide whether the ownership of a privatized firm is restricted because of security or "national" pride issues? Would foreign ownership of a privatized firm pose a threat in times of war? For example, if an airline had been utilized to transport troops in times of war, how would this play out with a privatized airline that is no longer operated by the government?

Customers

In general, consumers or customers are enthusiastic about any proposed privatization. They are promised better products or services as well as lower prices. But they also have to be concerned with access to the product or service in the long run. This access is usually determined by the following scenarios:

1. Was the privatized firm given the monopoly position that it enjoyed as a nationalized firm?
2. What sort of regulatory framework was set in place by either the executive or legislative branch of government? Are the regulatory bodies composed of independent regulators or a combination of industry and political appointees?
3. Did the newly privatized firm dominate the regulatory body, or did the regulatory commission keep a firm handle on pricing and accessibility?

Ultimately, the customer's reaction to the policies and strategy of the newly privatized firm or industry will determine its "success." All of the other stakeholders will attempt to influence the customer's or consumer's reaction to a privatization.

Another measure of "success" regards the government use of funds from a privatization. Did the government use the proceeds to pay off debt with no investment in the future growth of the economy? Particularly in the case of privatizing a natural resource, did the government reinvest to diversify the economy and thus expand opportunities for employment and economic growth?

CONCLUSION

This book will show that many strategic interdependencies exist between stakeholders and other "players" when dealing with the privatization process or game. In such situations, the reader must try to determine how these stakeholders will act and how they will react to the actions taken by other stakeholders, especially when interactions unfold over time.

The model developed in this chapter will hopefully allow the reader to simplify and sharpen the analysis of the privatization process. Decision makers rarely have enough information, and the "issue" can seldom be adequately simplified. Therefore, a formal game theory model can provide an absolute guide as to what action to take. In the many privatization arenas, the concept of a "game" provides a framework for logical reasoning and a structured lens to examine business and societal phenomena such as signaling, commitment, and reputation. In this sense, the concept of a "game" provides decision makers with a useful tool for focusing on the intuition and reasoning that they need to employ as they enter the privatization arena.

NOTES

1. Roger Caillois, *Man, Play and Games* (New York: Schocken Books, 1979).

2. E. E. Schattschneider, *The Semi-Sovereign People: A Realist's Guide to Democracy in America* (New York: Holt, 1960).

3. Roger Cobb and Charles Elder, *Participation in American Politics: The Dynamics of Agenda Building* (Baltimore, MD: Johns Hopkins University Press, 1981); John Mahon and Richard McGowan, *Industry as a Player in the Political and Social Arena: Defining the Competitive Environment* (Westport, CT: Quorum Books, 1996); John Mahon and Richard McGowan, "Modeling Industry Political Dynamics," *Business and Society* 37 (December 1998): 390–413; John Mahon and Richard McGowan, "How Legislation, Regulation, and Society Change Competition," in *1999 Handbook of Business Strategy*, ed. P. Goett (New York: Faulkner and Gray, 1999), 211–222; Richard McGowan and John Mahon, "Corporate Political Competitive Analysis," in *2000 Handbook of Business Strategy,* ed. P. Goett (New York: Faulkner and Gray, 2000), 189–203.

SOURCES

American Gaming Association. *State of the States: The AGA Survey of Casino Entertainment*. Washington, DC, 2009.

Cobb, R. W., and M. H. Ross, eds. *Cultural Strategies of Agenda Denial: Avoidance, Attack, and Redefinition*. Lawrence: University Press of Kansas, 1997.

Ibarra, P. R., and J. I. Kitsuse. "Vernacular Constituents and Moral Discourse: An Interactionist Proposal for the Study of Social Problems." In *Constructionist Controversies: Issues in Social Problems Theory*, ed. G. Miller and J. A. Holstein. New York: Aldine de Gruyter, 1993.

Mahon, J. F. "Corporate Political Strategy." *Business in the Contemporary World* 2:1 (1989): 50–63.

McGowan, R. *States Lotteries and Legalized Gambling: Painless Revenue or Painful Mirage.* Westport, CT: Quorum Books, 1994.

McGowan, R. *Business Politics and Cigarettes: Multiple Levels, Multiple Agendas.* Westport, CT: Quorum Books, 1995.

McGowan, R. *The Search for Revenue and the Common Good: An Analysis of Government Regulation of the Alcohol Industry.* Westport, CT: Quorum Books, 1997.

Merrill Lynch. "Gaming Industry: Uncertainty Is the Only Sure Thing." 1999.

Mitnick, B. M. "The Uses of Political Markets." Paper presented at the National Meeting of the Academy of Management, August 2001, Washington, DC.

Stone, D. *Policy Paradox and Political Reason.* Glenview, IL: Scott, Foresman, 1988.

U.S. Bureau of Economic Analysis. "Recreation Expenditures." 1999.

Part Two

International Examples

Chapter 3

Privatizing Sin: The 21st-Century Cigarette Industry

Few industries have undergone the rapid change that the cigarette industry has during the past 30 years. The industry has been consolidated to such a degree that there are only four major worldwide players: Philip Morris, British American Tobacco (RJR), Japan Tobacco, and Imperial Tobacco. But this is clearly a very recent phenomenon. Up to the 1980s, the industry was a mixture of private firms such as Philip Morris, RJR, American Tobacco, and British American Tobacco, but the predominant purveyors of cigarettes were nationalized firms such as Tabacalera (Spain) and Seita (France).

Most governments (except the United States and Great Britain) preferred to operate their own cigarette firms and establish a monopoly on cigarette sales within their borders. The production, distribution, and sale of cigarettes were strictly controlled by a government monopoly. These firms produced their own brands and also "licensed" popular U.S cigarette brands such as Marlboro, but in no way were American cigarette makers permitted to control the distribution and pricing of their brands. In fact, American brands sold at a premium price along with a higher ad valorem sales tax. So the domestic brands were cheaper, and the excise tax rate on the domestic brands was lower than on the American brands.

These nationalized cigarette firms were extremely profitable. While the U.S cigarette firms utilized their very substantial cash flows to diversify into other consumer products (for example, Philip Morris bought Miller Beer and General Foods as well as Kraft), part of these cash flows, as well as substantial tax revenues, also went directly into the Treasury. The cigarette industry was a cash cow for many governments. So why would governments be willing to privatize these firms that were such a lucrative source of revenue?

The primary reason is certainly the smoking and health issue. In 1964, the first warnings appeared that cigarette smoking was associated with increased risk of developing cancer and heart disease. In the 1980s, second-hand smoke proved to be an issue that the cigarette firms found very difficult to overcome. Now nonsmokers could petition government to forbid cigarette smoking in most public places because the cigarette smoke would harm not only the smokers, but also the nonsmokers. Clearly there is a conflict here between the health of its citizens and a government's need for revenue. As the dangers of cigarette smoking became more evident, antismoking groups were able to put pressure on governments to not only exit the industry, but also to enact legislation to curb cigarette use.

Just how a nationalized cigarette firm eventually became part of one of the four remaining giants of the cigarette industry will be illustrated by the evolution of the Spanish cigarette industry.

IN THE BEGINNING

In 1492, Columbus brought tobacco from America into Spain. Although he brought it as a gift to the king and queen, tobacco soon became scrutinized during the Inquisition. Rodrigo de Jerez, a Spanish sailor who actually traveled with Columbus, was persecuted in 1501 for smoking in public. Yet by this time, smoking was extremely common among sailors, merchants, and soldiers. In time, the hysteria of the Inquisition gave way; by the 1530s, the pipe had become popular, and among the lower classes, the use of rolled leaves had become widespread. Over the next few decades, tobacco became part of Spanish culture and eventually was even regarded as "virtuous and full of medicinal effects."[1]

In 1620, the first tobacco-processing plant was constructed in Seville, and in 1636, the general of Spain established a government monopoly over the production and sale of tobacco in the kingdoms of Castilla and León. Several years after the announcement of this monopoly, the Spanish government built the Royal Factory of Seville. This factory was the world's largest producer of tobacco products for almost 200 years.

In 1817, the tobacco industry—growing, processing, and selling—was deregulated, which caused the emergence of new products and packaging. Manufacturing plants began processing snuff, and the sale of cigarettes developed into singles and rolls. This quickly caused the cigarette to become the new way of smoking. To manage the revenue from tobacco products and stamps, the Compañía Arrendataria de Tabacos (CAT) was incorporated in 1887 as a limited-liability lending company.

TABACALERA (1945 TO 1985)

In 1945, the Spanish government took control of the tobacco industry and incorporated Tabacalera, essentially a government tobacco monopoly that allowed the Spanish government to quickly enjoy the profits. By 1984, Tabacalera accounted for almost 4 percent ($2.5 billion) of all the revenue the Spanish government received. In 1986, Spain took the huge step of joining the European Economic Community (EEC), the forerunner of the European Union (EU). But in order to meet the legal requirement of entry into the EEC, the Spanish passed legislation in November 1985 that had the following provisions:

1. As of December 31, 1985, the Spanish government would sell 51 percent of its interest in Tabacalera and allow management to make all operational and marketing decisions.
2. Tabacalera would continue to maintain its monopoly on the manufacturing of tobacco and the distribution of non-ECC manufactured tobacco products.
3. Taxes on products of EEC members would be the same as those on Tabacalera products.
4. The Spanish government would maintain its monopoly on the retail selling of tobacco products.[2]

TABACALERA (1986 TO 1999)

Besides adjusting to a new ownership structure, the management of Tabacalera was also facing a much different cigarette market than it had throughout its history. Traditionally, Spanish cigarette smokers had preferred "black" cigarettes, which used Turkish tobacco that had a much stronger taste as well as higher nicotine content. But with the coming of the smoking and health issue, younger Spanish cigarette smokers were searching for a "healthy" cigarette, known as the "blond" cigarette, which up to this point only American cigarette firms had supplied.

Tabacalera had two options. It could continue its policy of licensing American cigarettes and promote these cigarettes as a way of assuring itself of this fastest-growing segment of the Spanish cigarette market, or it could develop its own "generic" blond cigarette brands. Although clearly this was risky strategy, it would permit Tabacalera to achieve three goals:

1. Because Tabacalera would no longer have to share its profits with American firms, it would increase its profit margins on blond cigarette sales.
2. With its entrance into the European Union (EU), Tabacalera could export its cheaper generic blond cigarette to other EU members without a licensing agreement.
3. This cheaper generic blond cigarette might enable Tabacalera to gain a foothold in the potentially lucrative export markets of Africa and South America.

The newly privatized Tabacalera developed a strategy that mimicked the one used by American cigarette firms: it developed a variety of brands that would appeal to various niche markets. Tabacalera also invested its excess cash flows from its cigarette operations to purchase various Spanish food concerns, much as Philip Morris had purchased Miller Beer, General Foods, Krafts, and Suchard Chocolate and RJR had purchased Nabisco. And as with its American cousins, this diversification strategy proved to be highly unsuccessful. In 1995, 91 percent of Tabacalera's profits were still tobacco-related.[3] But the diversification strategy did permit Tabacalera to claim that it was no longer a cigarette firm but a consumer product company. This claim was particularly useful for its largest shareholder: the Spanish government.

SPANISH GOVERNMENT (1986 TO 1999)

Spanish public policy makers had two goals during the period when Tacabalera transitioned from a nationalized cigarette firm to a privatized firm: (1) to ensure that revenue from tobacco operations would remain the same or increase; and (2) to respond to the demands of antismoking groups to curb the use of tobacco.

On January 1, 1987, the Spanish excise tax on cigarettes was increased by 5 percent, and additional increases were promised in the future. So clearly the Spanish government was looking to increase tobacco revenue. But with the privatization of Tabacelera, the government was also collecting revenue from corporate taxes, dividends, and rents on facilities. Hence, the revenue that the Spanish government received from Tabacalera's operations increased by 32 percent throughout the period of 1986 to 1999.[4] It appeared that the Spanish government was doing quite well while distancing itself from its tobacco operations.

Starting in 1988, the Spanish government enacted a number of antismoking bans. First, cigarette smoking was banned in the workplace and then banned from various public places to protect nonsmokers from second-hand smoke. Ironically, this ban has never applied to bars or restaurants. In 1990, Spanish lawmakers outlawed all advertising of cigarettes, including in TV and radio as well as the print media. The Spanish government seemed to be much more willing to enact most of the antismoking agenda after the privatization of Tabacalera.

BIRTH OF ALTADIS

With the onset of the antismoking movement, countries with nationalized cigarette firms faced three options. One, of course, was to maintain the status quo. Although this would ensure that the revenue stream from cigarette sales would continue, it had a distinct disadvantage: government officials would be accused of putting revenue concerns over health concerns. But how could government regulate an industry that was so profitable to it? However, if a government could suppress any such criticism, then this strategy could be implemented. China National Tobacco is the prime example of this strategy and is currently the largest tobacco firm by volume in the world.

Of course, the other option was to privatize. But there are two ways to privatize a cigarette firm. We have just seen how the Spanish government decided to have its own national champion cigarette firm. But there is another way. The government of a nationalized cigarette firm could sell the entire firm to a foreign firm. This has turned out to be the most common way of dealing with this issue. Examples of countries that have followed this strategy are Italy, Hungary, the Czech Republic, Lithuania, Ecuador, and Malaysia.

Obviously, with this solution, governments could claim that they were now totally free to enact any antismoking measures, including a huge increase in the cigarette excise tax rate. The other appealing aspect of this sale was the substantial one-time payment for the sale of the nationalized firm.

But who would buy these nationalized cigarette firms? The vast majority were sold to Philip Morris (Altria), British American Tobacco (RJR), Japan Tobacco, or British Imperial. Ironically, then, one of the unforeseen consequences of the antismoking movement is the consolidation of the cigarette industry. Given the increasing power of the antismoking movement, no firm would ever want to enter this industry, and as we have seen, the antismoking movement has forced government to exit the industry. So when government wants to sell its cigarette industry, in reality it is forced to sell to one of the big four cigarette firms.

Hence, by 1999, both the Spanish and French governments were faced with a dilemma. Both governments had created national champion cigarette firms: Tabacalera (Spain) and Seita (France). While they dominated their home markets, both firms found it increasingly difficult to increase revenue. So to compete with the "Big Four" of the cigarette industry and maintain their independence, the two national champions agreed to join their firms in an attempt to capture the European market. Thus, we have the birth of Altadis.[5]

With unlimited access to the EU markets, the Altadis Group became the third-largest cigarette firm in Western Europe. By 2000, total sales reached 1.6 billion euros (a 3.8 percent increase), and the group's total cigarette sales exceeded 100 billion cigarettes. Of these sales, international distribution provided 32 percent of the volume and 26 percent of the value.[6]

In order to continue this growth and success, Altadis realized the need to invest in research, development, and product quality. It believed that by linking the knowledge and methods used by France and Spain, it could reinforce and optimize its R&D activities. Its R&D platform and innovations lab therefore focused on a twin mission of improving different kinds of tobacco and their treatment and lowering the tar and nicotine content. Altadis also hoped to improve product quality by streamlining manufacturing. It underwent a major industrial reorganization, both in France and in Spain, to improve productivity. But the question remained: Were these measures radical enough not only for the economic survival of Altadis, but also for the continuing protection of both the French and Spanish governments?

LEGAL ISSUES

When speaking of the tobacco industry, the primary focus is not lack of competition, but rather the emphasis is on the many legal battles that the industry faces. This is obvious if you have ever tried to find economic statistics on the global economy of the tobacco market. Instead of Web pages that describe the organization and market breakdown of tobacco sales, health and death statistics fill the screen. Antismoking, anti-advertising, and legal sites bombard you with tar and nicotine effects, as well as the tobacco scandals of every company out there. It has been proclaimed that "the globalization of tobacco marketing, trade, research, and industry influence represents a major threat to the public health worldwide."[7] In an industry that is filled with international powerhouses, a new threat flexes its muscle and attacks them all: lawyers.

While tobacco companies boast growth in revenues and net income, the reality is that, as each day passes, "smoking becomes a thing of the past."[8] The number of smokers declines every year, in tandem with an increase in efforts by government and health activists to tighten up restrictions on the sale and use of tobacco. Today, smoking has been banned from offices for some time, but the focus has now moved to bars, restaurants, and other public places. Some cities have prohibited smoking outright, shutting down even separate smoking rooms. In 2001, a bill was proposed that is considered the "most restrictive anti-smoking measure" ever witnessed. If the bill had been passed, the legislation would have set fines of up to $750 for people who smoke in their homes if the smoke crossed property lines and offended neighbors.[9]

Although this bill seems rather restrictive, it does not appear to be such a far-fetched idea when one examines the current antismoking legislation occurring in Canada. On January 1, 2002, a law was passed that banned any indoor smoking where minors were present. Several months later, another law was passed that prohibited smoking in all workplaces and public spaces, with no allowance for designated smoking rooms. In Quebec, it is against the law to sell tobacco by mail order, over the Internet, on school grounds, or in health care, social services, or child care facilities. While all of these laws have been passed in Canada, the rest of the world is catching up.

In May 2008, the European Union gave its final approval to legislation that would ban the use of the terms "light" and "mild" for advertising cigarettes, and would allow for graphic pictures of diseased lungs and hearts on cigarette packs.[10] Currently, the government of Hong Kong is considering banning smoking in offices, shops, and factories. There has even been talk of setting up no-smoking zones in public indoor entertainment establishments, including karaoke bars and parlors. Large restaurants in Hong Kong have already designated a third of their floor space as "non-smoking." As of March 2009, Israel banned smoking in all public areas, including hospitals, shopping malls, and restaurants. (The government has permitted, in certain cases, separate smoking rooms if proper ventilation is established.) While other governments have created laws to make smoking more difficult, the Catalonia region of Spain has created monetary incentives to quit smoking. For those citizens who quit for at least six months, the government reimburses them nearly $400 for anti-addiction treatments.

Many parts of the world have already enacted smoking restrictions and have now shifted the focus to prevention by examining the advertisement of tobacco. In April 2009, Egypt banned cigarette advertising on state-run television. Health officials from several Asian countries, including Indonesia, Thailand, and Nepal, agreed to support a proposal that would totally ban cigarette advertising. While this is a rather radical movement, other countries, including China and the Philippines, have taken smaller steps, such as the banning of tobacco advertisements on one media. In Russia, where it is already illegal to have television tobacco ads, the Duma is currently examining legislation that would ban cigarette advertising using printed media, on street billboards, and in public transportation. While these countries are using the law as a means to prevent smoking, the Malaysian government has turned to an even higher power, asking the country's top Islamic body to declare smoking an official sin. (Alcohol and drugs are already condemned.)[11]

THE FATE OF ALTADIS

With the fierce competition that Altadis faced from other firms and the overwhelming presence of the government, both locally and internationally, the board of directors of Altadis was faced with the question: Where do we go from here?

Altadis had evolved into a global company. It had grown considerably, especially in the last decade, by pursuing its strategy of growth and investment in new markets and acquisitions. The company had the brands, the people, and the focus to deliver sustainable growth and long-term shareholder value. While it clearly had the potential to succeed in the global arena, many questions had to be answered. Are there still areas of possible global growth? With antismoking legislation becoming even stronger and more prevalent in the media, how can sales be generated? How will advertisement of new brands be dealt with? What is the main goal for the company, and how can it achieve that goal?

In 2007, Altadis found itself in a weak position among the major competitors in the tobacco industry. How did this happen? Altadis had a steep decline in profits and was forced to cut costs as core Spanish and French cigarette markets were hard hit by tougher antitobacco regulations, cutthroat price competition, and higher taxes. Imperial Tobacco Group PLC was able to capitalize on the company's vulnerability. After the board of directors of Altadis rejected numerous buyout offers from other tobacco companies, Imperial Tobacco offered the Altadis shareholders €50 per share. According to the Spanish Securities and Exchange Commission, a minimum of 80 percent is needed to accept the conditions of the offer. Shareholders controlling approximately 95.81 percent of the shares accepted the terms of the offer, which made the offer unconditional and the takeover bid for Altadis successful. Imperial Tobacco used the squeeze-out process to obtain all of the outstanding Altadis shares and thus to remove Altadis from the stock exchanges of Madrid, Barcelona, Bilbao, and Valencia as well as from Eurolist by Euronext Paris. Today, Altadis is a wholly owned subsidiary of Imperial Tobacco.[12]

Soon after the takeover of Altadis, Imperial Tobacco made an offer to buy out the logistics subsidiary of Altadis, Compañía de Distribución Integral Logista, S.A. When Imperial Tobacco took control of Altadis, it also gained 56.92 percent of Logista's shares. Imperial Tobacco offered the rest of Logista's shareholders €52.50 per share. Approximately 37.30 percent of Logista's shareholders accepted the offer. In the end, Imperial Tobacco collected 96.92 percent of Logista's shares.[13] Imperial Tobacco intends to use the squeeze-out process to take over Logista and then buy out the rest of its outstanding shares. Much like Altadis, Logista will become a wholly owned subsidiary of Imperial Tobacco.

The acquisitions of Altadis and Logista put Imperial Tobacco in a great position to be a dominant player in the tobacco industry. Already strong in areas such as the Netherlands, Belgium, the Republic of Ireland, and France, Imperial Tobacco has increased its dominance in France, Spain, and other Spanish-speaking countries through the purchase of Altadis. This now presents a problem for the French and Spanish governments. Imperial Tobacco has nearly complete control of these markets and has gained the power to dictate the prices for the tobacco products in those areas. The acquisition of Logista presents another problem for the Spanish government. When the squeeze-out is finished, Imperial Tobacco will gain possession of one of the leading logistics companies in Europe. What was once a primarily Spanish-French company is now part of a global tobacco giant. Overall, the purchases of these two companies allow Imperial Tobacco to challenge Philip Morris as the leader in the tobacco industry. This certainly was not the outcome envisioned by the proponents of the privatization of either the Spanish or French nationalized cigarette firms.

NOTES

1. Nicolas Monardes, "De Hierba Panacea," 1571.

2. Richard McGowan, *Business, Politics, and Cigarettes* (Westport, CT: Quorum Books, 1995).

3. McGowan, *Business, Politics, and Cigarettes.*

4. Altadis, http://www.altadis.com/en/quienes/nuestrahistoria.html#beggining (accessed January 8, 2007).

5. Altadis, http://www.altadis.com/en/quienes/perfilgrupo.html (accessed January 8, 2007).

6. Yahoo! Finance, http://biz.yahoo.com/p/i/ity.html (accessed April 3, 2008).

7. Derek Yach, "Globalization of Tobacco Industry Influence and New Global Responses," *Tobacco Control* 9 (2000): 206–216.

8. Lisa Khoo, "Banning the Butt: Global Anti-Smoking Efforts," *CBC News Online* (May 2001).

9. Khoo, "Banning the Butt."

10. Joe Becker, "Global Ridicule Extinguishes Montgomery's Anti-Smoking Bill," *The Washington Post* (November 28, 2001), A11.

11. Lisa Khoo, "Banning the Butt: Global Anti-Smoking Efforts" *CBC News Online* (May 2001).

12. Santiago Perez, "Imperial Tobacco Secures 93.5% of Altadis Shareholders (50% of Habanos)," *Havana Journal* (July 21, 2008), http://havanajournal.com/forums/viewthread/792/.

13. Perez, "Imperial Tobacco Secures 93.5%."

Chapter 4

Privatize or Nationalize? Argentina's Privatization of Its Oil Industry

Throughout the past two decades, governments in the developing world (as well as those in developed economies) have used the privatization of state assets as a key tool of economic policy. One of the more unique privatizations took place in 1993, when the president of Argentina, Carlos Saúl Menem, offered a landmark initial public offering (IPO) for the state-owned oil company, Yacimientos Petrolíferos Fiscales (YPF). Since its creation, YPF has always operated on the forefront of the public-private ownership debate in Latin America.

While many countries in Latin America had privatized state-owned industries, such as the telecommunications and airline industries, Argentina was the first to privatize a state oil company. State-owned oil companies in Latin America are different from any other state-owned industry because they provide a nationally controlled link to oil, the key resource for industrialization and competition in the global market. The goal of this chapter is to assess the wider economic and political benefits and the limitations of oil privatization, using YPF as a case study.

BACKGROUND

As discussed in the first chapter, privatization can be defined as any movement toward a market-driven economy or any increase in private ownership and control. Today, elements of privatization and free-market orientation can be seen in almost every economy in the world, from the mixed markets of Europe and the United States to the former communist economies of

Eastern Europe and even communist China, which is gradually opening up to private enterprise. Privatization, however, is no longer considered a panacea for economic problems.

During the post–World War II period, state-controlled industries guarded socialist and mixed-market economies from foreign investors and interests, especially in the oil industry. In the case of newly independent nations, the government often formed state companies in an attempt to sever itself from a resented colonial power. With the prevalence of the state-controlled industries, politicians quickly found that they could control the economy for numerous political uses. Consequently, they encouraged the use of state companies while claiming that they benefited public welfare, even though these companies actually resulted in weakened competitive abilities and decreased economic efficiency. By the 1970s, however, many state companies had become synonymous with bloated bureaucracies, wasteful cost inefficiencies, and corruption.[1]

HISTORY OF YACIMIENTOS PETROLÍFEROS FISCALES

The history of YPF includes several economic and political problems, such as the capital shortages and heavy government taxes that faced state oil companies across Latin America. Unlike other Latin American state oil companies, however, YPF never attained anything more than marginal operational or financial success. As Latin America's oldest state oil company with the region's third-largest oil reserves, YPF is a perfect case for examining the costs and benefits of privatization.

In 1907, government construction workers discovered oil in Comodoro Rivadavia, Patagonia. The 1853 Argentine Constitution allowed the government to claim ownership of subsoil materials only on lands located in the national territories (which includes Patagonia), but not in the provinces. Consequently, the government quickly declared this area a state oil reserve and began preliminary attempts at exploration and drilling. However, many of the Argentine elite struggled with the idea of a state-owned oil company, since they were used to a model of private foreign capital financing like they had in England. This ideological struggle between provincial elites and Buenos Aires nationalists has been present since the beginning of YPF's history and foreshadowed its eventual privatization.

In 1910, President Roque Sáenz Peña established the Petroleum Bureau, the predecessor to YPF, under the Ministry of Agriculture to revitalize the state's oil operations. This decision was supported by the populist belief that national control of oil was necessary to support a growing middle class, as well as the growing suspicion of foreign oil companies in Latin America (Standard Oil of New Jersey, in particular). Nationalist sentiment increased as a result of World War I, since in war, Argentina could no longer rely on cheap coal and other key imports from its economic benefactor, England.

On June 3, 1922, President Hipólito Yrigoyen announced a reorganization of the country's oil industry and replaced the Petroleum Bureau with the newly created Yacimientos Petrolíferos Fiscales. Shortly after the creation of YPF, Marcelo de Alvear won the 1922 presidential election and backed an aggressive oil policy. Alvear was determined to encourage industrialization and to protect Argentine oil from export by the many companies that had expanded in the provincial territories through bilateral agreements with the provincial elites. To this end, Alvear appointed Colonel Enrique Mosconi, a man adept in public relations and with previous civil and military engineering experience, to head YPF.

Mosconi was a staunch nationalist who believed that the development of Argentina's oil industry was the highest national priority, but he was also a realist. He understood the political difficulties involved in a complete nationalization of the oil industry, which would require expropriation of fields already legally held by foreign oil companies. More practical would be to nationalize all remaining oil fields located within national territories, thereby limiting the foreign companies to their current, marginal holdings. Alvear followed Mosconi's advice, and by 1927, oil exploration in the national territories had been restricted to the state.

Mosconi built a refinery and expanded drilling in Comodoro Rivadavia, and YPF was profitable in its early existence. However, Argentina's demand for oil was growing faster than anywhere else in Latin America, and to meet this demand and remain profitable, Mosconi knew that YPF needed to expand its exploration and production. Exploration, however, is a highly capital-intensive activity, which YPF could not yet support from its earnings alone. When Mosconi approached the government seeking additional capital, he was denied. This exemplifies how the Argentine government often supported oil nationalism ideologically but sometimes failed to support it fiscally.

Without the government financially backing exploration in the national territories, Mosconi knew that YPF could only survive if it gained monopoly access to the provinces, where foreign companies had already discovered oil. The elites of provinces like Salta and Jujuy had already granted concessions to foreign oil companies, and Mosconi feared foreign domination. To improve YPF's public image in preparation for the upcoming political battle for national control of provincial oil fields, Mosconi cut oil prices below market levels.

Mosconi was wary of completely alienating the provinces, and he did not want to turn YPF into an inefficient bureaucracy. He continued to advocate simply limiting foreign oil companies to their current concessions, and he also advised changing YPF's ownership structure to a joint venture: 51 percent state-owned and 49 percent owned by private Argentine investors. YPF, however, was a permanently weakened institution, short on finances, undermined in administrative capability, and with no chance for long-term growth. This meant that the only way to slow Argentina's oil imports (and bolster foreign reserves) was to allow private capital into its oil industry. During the 1940s and 1950s, Presidents Juan Perón and Arturo Frondizi attempted to open the oil industry to private capital, but the opposition from oil nationalists was too strong. Consequently, Argentina had to rely on oil imports.

In 1976, a military coup led by General Jorge Videla took over the Argentine government. The military government was run by staunch conservatives eager to reduce government control of business and encourage foreign investment. Continuing the previous governments' trend of using YPF as a source of funds, Videla set a tax rate as high as 69 percent of sales revenue in the late 1970s.[2] The government also continued the old practice of setting domestic oil prices below the world market rate.

The next military dictator, General Leopoldo Galtieri, continued these oil policies. By the beginning of Galtieri's regime in 1981, YPF had accumulated $4 billion of debt, and with the extra burdens of the government's oil policy, the investment and expansion necessary for YPF to become self-sufficient were impossible. In 1982, a new hydrocarbons law was proposed that would limit YPF to its present concessions and open the rest of the country for private investment. This was thought to be the first step toward privatizing YPF. Military defeat in the Falklands War with England, however, brought great public dissatisfaction with the military regime, and civil rule returned to Argentina. YPF barely survived before the new hydrocarbons law could take effect.

Sixty years after its creation, YPF controlled the rights to produce the majority of oil in Argentina. However, years of bureaucracy, political meddling, and financial mismanagement left YPF without the financial and human capital to exploit this right. Consequently, from the 1930s onward, YPF could never even fully supply Argentina's national demand for oil. Costly oil imports filled this gap and contributed to Argentina's financial woes by depleting foreign reserves.

THE PRIVATIZATION OF YPF

When Carlos Saúl Menem became president in 1989, Argentina faced severe economic problems. The previous populist and military regimes left a legacy of hyperinflation, inefficient bureaucracies, and state-owned companies dependent on subsidies for survival. The 13 largest state-owned companies carried a total debt of $11 billion and had operating deficits of $3.8 billion.[3] Inflation rates had grown to 200 percent a month.[4]

Menem and his finance minister, Domingo Cavallo, declared a two-part economic program to reduce inflation and revive the Argentine economy. The first part was a currency convertibility plan that pegged the peso to the dollar. The second part was an aggressive privatization program. Menem hoped to use the proceeds from selling large state companies to pay off external debt, as well as $2 billion of retirement bonds owed to retired Argentine workers.[5]

Menem made it known that he wanted oil as an "economic resource," not a "sovereign resource," and this approach culminated in YPF's candidacy for privatization. However, there still remained the difficulty of winning support from the nationalists who opposed privatization. The stakeholders who supported a state-owned YPF included YPF employees, unions, the Peronist Justicialista Party (of which Menem was ironically a member), and private Argentine businesses that sold supplies to YPF.

In 1990, Menem started a two-year plan to prepare YPF for a public share offering. The program replaced and restructured management in order to put YPF into the best possible financial and administrative order before the sale.[6] Menem appointed Jose Estenssoro, the former president of Hughes Tool Corporation, to implement this program. To put YPF on a par with the global oil industry, Estenssoro mandated cost controls, management incentives, and the use of English in the workplace for the administration. Service-related segments like drilling rigs, transportation equipment, and seismic survey equipment were sold to former employees on favorable terms. Finally, Estenssoro trimmed YPF of outdated or non-core business segments like marginal oil fields, old shipping tankers, hospitals, and movie theaters.[7]

Finally, in July 1993, YPF shares were offered to private investors on stock exchanges in Buenos Aires, New York, and London. YPF's sale of

$3.04 billion marked both the largest privatization to date in Argentina and, more importantly, the first privatization of a state-owned oil company in Latin America. The Argentine government retained 15 percent of the shares, and former YPF employees and creditors retained 40 percent of shares. The remaining 45 percent of shares were sold to public investors, of which 46 percent were American, 25 percent Argentine, and 29 percent international.

Soon after privatization, YPF attracted attention from Repsol, the formerly state-owned Spanish oil company. Early in 1999, Repsol bought the Argentine government's remaining 15 percent holdings in the privatized YPF. Then in April 1999, Repsol made a $13.4 billion tender offer to buy out the other shareholders at $44.78 per share. Prior to the tender offer, YPF stock had been trading at around $30 per share. On May 10, the YPF board of directors accepted the acquisition offer for a final sale price of $16 billion.[8]

The new Repsol-YPF entity continued to aggressively expand its operations, with plans to invest $6 billion in Argentina between 2007 and 2009.[9] In 2000, Repsol-YPF acquired rights to an oil concession in the Santa Cruz province and has continued investing in exploration and production in the Mendoza province.[10] Repsol-YPF has outmaneuvered competition and dominates the downstream oil industry in Argentina, accounting for about half of the country's total refining capacity. By 2002, Repsol-YPF was producing 45 percent of the oil in Argentina.

EVALUATING THE PRIVATIZATION PROCESS FOR YPF

A framework for evaluating privatization involves a four-step process. The framework evaluates the economic and political effects of privatization over the short and long term, forming a two-by-two matrix, as shown in Figure 4.1.[11]

A major issue was the ownership structure that resulted from YPF's privatization. Following privatization in 1993, YPF was owned by a diverse group of small shareholders. In 1999, it was acquired by a single oil corporation, Repsol. Therefore, Repsol's acquisition of YPF will serve as the marker between the short- and long-term periods.

Cell (1): Economic Effects in the Short Run

Did privatization enable YPF to develop business strategies that could lead to increases in market share and/or profits? Is YPF better able to achieve operating economies and to reduce its overall cost structure?

	Short Run	**Long Run**
Economic	(1) Business efficiency	(3) Corporate options
Political	(2) Effects on various stakeholder groups	(4) Stakeholder options

Figure 4.1   A Framework for Evaluating the Privatization Process

The privatization of YPF has allowed it to pursue a number of business strategies that were unavailable throughout its history because of financial or political restrictions. For example, privatization directly influenced YPF's ability to achieve strategic growth. Although the state-owned YPF had the exclusive exploration rights over much of Argentina's oil reserves, the company lacked the capital necessary to exploit these resources. After privatization, YPF finally had access to this capital, and it was freed from the burdens of inefficiency due to government ownership. The additional capital allowed the privatized YPF to increase exploration, and oil production grew by 60 percent between 1990 and 1996.[12] Rapid growth in the short term helped the privatized YPF consolidate its strong market position against competitors.

The capital flows from privatization also allowed YPF to pursue growth opportunities throughout Latin America and the world. Before privatization, YPF only had domestic operations. In 1994, it started two major international projects along Argentina's northwestern borders. First, YPF built a $200 million pipeline into Chile, where it supplied 40 percent of that country's oil market.[13] Second, YPF formed a joint company, Yacimientos Petrolíferos Fiscales Bolivianos (YPFB), with the Bolivian state oil company, which explored oil resources along the border of Argentina and Bolivia. In 1995, YPF significantly expanded its foreign operations by acquiring an independent American oil exploration company, Maxus Corporation, for $1.7 billion. By the time Repsol made its tender offer in April 1999, YPF was producing 17.5 percent of its oil reserves in foreign locations.[14]

Privatizing YPF drastically improved the cost of operations and labor efficiency. After a $56 million overhaul of YPF's La Plata refinery in 1995, the cost of processing a barrel of oil dropped from $4.69 to $2.66. The number of workers needed to run the refinery operations dropped from 1,350 to 690.[15] Production levels also increased from 483,000 barrels per day in 1990 to 700,000 barrels per day in 1994.[16] YPF also increased efficiency during the privatization process by selling off the unprofitable, noncore business segments, including hospitals and movie theaters.

Cell (2): Political Effects in the Short Run

The key questions addressed in the second cell are: Did the Argentine government receive more revenues than it had from the state-owned YPF? Were unions and other interested parties satisfied that their interests were not discounted when short-term policy decisions were made for the newly privatized YPF?

As a result of the privatization, two forms of government revenue were generated: revenue from the sale of YPF and the future revenue from oil taxes on the new, private YPF. The government was far more concerned with the short-term goal of stabilizing Argentina's beleaguered economy, which was marked by hyperinflation and staggering debt (see Table 4.1). Consequently, the immediate proceeds of the sale were far more politically valuable than future tax revenues. Of the 90 percent of state assets that Menem privatized, YPF was the crown jewel, selling for $3.04 billion. From the government's perspective, the privatization alone represented a major political achievement, considering the historic controversy over YPF's ownership structure.

Oil tax revenue was not a short-term concern and could always be legislated in the future. In addition, it appeared that oil tax revenue would increase, because YPF was expected to become more efficient and profitable after privatization. A privatized YPF was expected to increase taxable profits and expand production capacity, which would then prevent the government's foreign reserves from being spent on oil imports.

In order to gain the short-term political support necessary to privatize YPF, Menem had to connect opposition stakeholders to the privatization process. These stakeholders included YPF employees, unions, the Peronist Justicialista Party, and private Argentine businesses that sold supplies to YPF. Menem built short-term political support using a variety of techniques that included selling YPF shares at below-market value to YPF employees, offering early retirement to YPF executives, providing government subsidies to the unions that would distribute new shares to YPF employees, and offering subsidized opportunities for employees to buy smaller, noncore YPF business segments. Menem also gained additional

Table 4.1   Inflation Rates in Argentina (1989–1995)

	1989	1990	1991	1992	1993	1994	1995
Inflation (%)	4,924	1,344	84	18	7.30	3.90	1.60

Source: Argentina Department of Statistics (http://www.indec.mecon.ar/).

political support from the traditional oil nationalists by selling YPF shares on the open market instead of selling them to a single corporate interest. After the initial public offering, the government retained a 15 percent interest in YPF, and private Argentine investors owned an additional 25 percent of the company.

Cell (3): Economic Effects in the Long Run

The key questions addressed in the third cell are: Did privatization aid in the development of a corporate strategy that will ensure continued profitability? Can the firm pursue a diversification strategy so that it no longer depends on just one source of revenue? Has privatization enabled the firm to compete in new markets outside those in which it has traditionally been present?

Over the long term, the privatization of YPF culminated in its acquisition by the Spanish oil company, Repsol. As a result of this merger, Repsol-YPF became Latin America's largest private energy company in terms of total assets. It was precisely this opportunity that Repsol-YPF was looking for: to use a foothold in the Argentine market to expand throughout Latin America. In 2000, Repsol-YPF gave a major presentation in Madrid that revealed its plans to spend $11 billion in Latin America over six years.[17] By 2002, Repsol-YPF dominated the local Argentine market, producing 45 percent of the country's oil and controlling 58 percent of retail gasoline sales.[18] Repsol-YPF continues to invest heavily to maintain its position in the Argentine market, earmarking 25 percent of its global investment budget, or about $5.67 billion, for Argentina.[19]

Repsol-YPF has established exploration and production operations all over the world. The company's oil and gas reserves are located in Argentina, Bolivia, Trinidad and Tobago, Venezuela, Brazil, Ecuador, Colombia, Peru, North Africa, Libya, Algeria, Spain, and the United States. As of December 2007, Repsol-YPF had oil and gas exploration and production interests in 27 countries, either directly or through its subsidiaries.

In 2000, to gain influence in the Brazilian market, Repsol-YPF swapped $1 billion worth of assets with Petrobras, the Brazilian state oil company. The swap also allowed Repsol-YPF to divest some of its Argentine assets that were threatening to provoke political problems due to domestic competition requirements. In July 2005, Repsol-YPF became one of the major oil and gas producers in the Caribbean when it exercised a call option for the purchase of three oil fields and one gas field in Trinidad and Tobago from BP. Investment in these fields is estimated to total $500

million by 2025. In July 2006, Repsol-YPF acquired 28 percent of the
Shenzi oil field, and in early 2007, the company acquired 28 percent of the
Genghis Khan oil field, both of which are located in the Gulf of Mexico.[20]
The company expects significant cost savings and improvements in oil and
gas exploitation through these acquisitions because the fields are adjacent
and share the same reservoirs.

Cell (4): Political Effects in the Long Run

Does the government still retain some measure of power or influence
over the future course of the product of the YPF privatization, Repsol-YPF?
What amount of freedom has the government given to the foreign-owned
Repsol-YPF entity?

Argentina's historic swings between populism and military government
have created groups of ideologically entrenched stakeholders concerned
with the privatization of YPF. The severely weakened Argentine economy
led many nationalist stakeholders to accept the privatization of YPF. Yet,
even after privatization, YPF remained a strong symbol of nationalism
for the Argentine people. When Repsol acquired YPF, old nationalist
fears about foreign domination of Argentina's oil resources and markets
returned.

Although exploration and production activity in Argentina is now
completely open to the private sector, Repsol-YPF has maintained a
position of control in the country. Almost immediately after Repsol
acquired YPF, the Argentine Congress passed an antimonopoly bill that
increased the powers of the courts to determine if mergers and acquisitions
violated fair trade practices.[21] This bill eventually forced Repsol-YPF
to divest some of its assets. Repsol-YPF used this divestment to its
advantage through regional expansion, swapping 700 gas stations with
Brazil's Petrobras in exchange for 300 gas stations and a refinery in
Brazil. Further divestment is expected, as one of the goals of Repsol-YPF's
2008–2012 strategic plan is greater diversification of the company's share
portfolio.

In March 2002, Finance Minister Roberto Lavagna implemented a 20
percent tax on crude oil exports and froze domestic oil prices in order to
generate capital to help the recovery of Argentina's failed bank system. In
May 2004, Argentina increased the duties on crude oil exports to 25
percent and established a progressive tax scheme on oil exports in August
2004, with rates ranging from 25 to 45 percent. The Ministry of Economy
and Production issued a resolution in November 2007 that again changed
the export tax structure. Under the new tax scheme, when the WTI (West

Texas Intermediate) international price exceeds the WTI reference price (fixed at $60.90 per barrel), the producer can collect $42 per barrel, with the remainder to be withheld by the Argentine government as an export tax. If the WTI price is below the reference price but over $45 per barrel, a 45 percent tax rate applies. Luiz Mendez, Repsol-YPF's spokesperson, stated, "This type of state intervention could create a dangerous situation because the oil producers will not want to sell crude to the refineries, which could cause supply problems."[22] In Repsol-YPF's 2007 Annual Report, the company identifies high export taxes that cannot be compensated by price increases as one of the main risks facing Repsol-YPF.[23]

Another policy that drew heavy criticism was the deregulatory law that allowed oil companies to repatriate up to 70 percent of their earnings. In October 2002, a federal prosecutor tried to overrule this law to keep more capital in Argentina's collapsed economy. Under intense pressure, in early 2003, President Eduardo Duhalde issued a decree restating the legality of an oil company's right to repatriate 70 percent of its earnings.[24] However, many oil companies remain nervous that the government could use the federal prosecutor's ruling as case law to change the repatriation quota in the future.

But although the Argentine government has been using Repsol-YPF's monopoly status to play on popular sentiments, there has been no statistically significant change in government tax revenues from oil since May 1999, after Repsol acquired YPF.[25]

In summary, the long-term political viability of the YPF privatization has proven a qualified success. The long-term economic benefits of government tax revenue from oil have been sustained since Repsol acquired YPF. However, the acquisition of YPF by a foreign company, Repsol, reignited nationalist tensions over oil, which has historically divided Argentina's politics. Argentina's economic collapse in 2001 put more pressure on the government to raise revenue and generate capital to revive the failed banking system. This placed Repsol-YPF in the public spotlight, leading to significant attempts by politicians to generate extra revenue by reregulating Repsol-YPF's monopolistic control of the Argentine oil industry.

CONCLUSION

This chapter has discussed the history of the oil industry in Argentina, from the formation of the state-owned oil company, YPF, to its privatization over 70 years later. Throughout this history, Argentina's fundamental lack of a political consensus has repeatedly hindered the success of YPF and interrupted the full exploitation of Argentina's oil resources.

Over the short term, the privatization of YPF has proven to be an economic and political success. Considering the years of political turmoil over oil nationalism, YPF's privatization is a landmark political achievement in Argentine history. The privatization has led to an increase in investment capital and operational efficiencies that has helped to fully develop Argentina's oil resources. YPF executives and unions received opportunities to benefit from the privatization, including subsidized shares in the privatized company and special opportunities to buy noncore business segments. The government generated capital immediately through the privatization by selling YPF, which then helped stabilize Argentina's hyperinflation in the late 1980s.

Over the long term, Repsol's acquisition of YPF has not affected the Argentine government's oil tax revenues to a statistically significant level. Oil privatization, even under foreign ownership, has proved politically sustainable, and there is no indication that the government would attempt to completely reverse the privatization process by renationalizing Argentina's oil reserves. However, the government has demonstrated that under political or economic pressure, it will try to meddle with the privatization process by raising taxes on the oil industry and by increasing regulation of the oil monopoly it helped create, Repsol-YPF.

Despite uncertainties about the future, Argentina possesses Latin America's third-largest oil reserves (after Mexico and Venezuela) and remains Latin America's most deregulated energy market. In 2004, Repsol-YPF invested $1 billion in Argentina and made an additional $6 billion of investment between 2007 and 2009. Repsol-YPF's long-term investment commitment to Argentina inspires confidence that the government has learned not to change industry regulations too quickly.

In conclusion, Repsol-YPF is a unique company in Latin America, where oil resources are typically monopolized by state companies. Repsol-YPF's perceived success in building a relationship with the Argentine government will undoubtedly serve as a model for oil privatization in the rest of Latin America. The continued economic benefits for Repsol-YPF will depend on its ability to develop a lasting, mutually beneficial political relationship with the Argentine government. Without cultivating a wider base of political support in the long term, Repsol-YPF will find its earnings and market share used against it politically. If Repsol-YPF wishes to benefit from Argentina's historically "national" oil resources, it must take steps to develop its public image as more national than foreign. Argentina's economic collapse has given Repsol-YPF a unique opportunity to improve its national image by taking a public role in the reconstruction of the Argentine economy.

RECENT DEVELOPMENTS

In December 2004, about a decade after privatization, the Argentine government created the state-owned company Enarsa to promote oil and gas exploration, extraction, and production in the country. The company was created in large part because of a steady decline in energy supply and infrastructure capacity that has recently led to shortages in Argentina. Enarsa works on its own and with other companies to develop oil and gas areas and build pipelines and power plants. Since its creation, Enarsa has been mostly involved in exploration and exploitation of offshore energy resources. It also collects data for the Argentine government to help it attract energy investment and set energy policies.

In addition, in December 2007, Repsol-YPF entered into a memorandum of understanding with Argentina's Petersen Energia in which Repsol sold a 14.9 percent stake in YPF to Petersen Energia and gave the company the option to increase its stake to 25 percent within the next four years. In addition, Repsol intends to float another 20 percent of the company to noninstitutional investors in the fall of 2008, but it plans to keep a majority stake in YPF.

NOTES

1. Daniel Yergin and Joseph Stanislaw, *The Commanding Heights: The Battle between Government and the Marketplace* (New York, Simon and Schuster, 2002).

2. Carl E. Solberg, *Oil and Nationalism in Argentina: A History* (Stanford, CA: Stanford University Press, 1979).

3. Myrna Alexander and Carlos Corti, "Argentina's Privatization Program: Experience, Issues, Lessons," World Bank (1993).

4. "Q&A: Argentina's Economic Crisis," *BBC News* (February 12, 2003), http://news.bbc.co.uk/1/hi/business/1721061.stm.

5. "Argentina's Superior Sales," *LatinFinance* (July 2003).

6. Graciana del Castillo, "Privatization in Latin America: From Myth to Reality," United Nations Economic Commission for Latin America and the Caribbean (1995), http://www.worldbank.org/wbi/publicfinance/publicresources/privatization%20in%20Latin%20America.pdf.

7. Clifford Krauss, "Argentina's Rapidly Rising Oil Fortunes," *The New York Times* (April 24, 1999), C1.

8. Beth Rubenstein and Ian Katz, "This Bid Breaks a Big Latin Taboo," *Business Week* (May 17, 1999).

9. "Repsol YPF to Invest US$700m in Mendoza from 2003–07," *Business News America* (February 16, 2004).

10. "Govt. Grants Repsol-YPF Hydrocarbons Concession in Santa Cruz," *ISI Emerging Markets Newswire* (March 27, 2000).

11. Richard McGowan and John Mahon, "A Framework for Evaluating Privatization Policy," *Business and the Contemporary World* 6 (1994).

12. "Argentina Industry: Petroleum Extraction Up 60%," *Economist Intelligence Unit* (January 28, 1998).

13. "Directory of Innovative Financing: Argentina," Inter-American Development Bank (October 1995), http://www.iadb.org/sds/publication/publication_47_e.htm#1.

14. Krauss, "Argentina's Rapidly Rising Oil Fortunes."

15. Krauss, "Argentina's Rapidly Rising Oil Fortunes."

16. "Privatization and the Globalization of Energy Markets: Argentina," United States Energy Information Administration (August 2000), http://www.eia.doe.gov/emeu/pgem/ch3a.html.

17. "Repsol-YPF Looks to Latins for Growth," *Energy Argus* (August 2, 2000).

18. "Privatization and the Globalization of Energy Markets: Argentina."

19. "Repsol-YPF to Invest US$1.2 billion in Neuquen," *Business News Americas* (November 14, 2003).

20. Repsol YPF's FY2007 Form 20-F filed with the United States Securities and Exchange Commission, http://www.sec.gov/ (accessed June 25, 2009).

21. Matthew Robinson, "Argentina: Giant Killer," *Energy Compass* (June 4, 1999).

22. "Government Threatens Oil Companies with Tax Increase," *Business News Americas* (February 24, 2003).

23. Repsol YPF Annual Report, http://www.repsol.com/imagenes/es_es/Form%2020F%20Repsol%20YPF%202007_tcm7-476684.PDF (accessed June 25, 2009).

24. Natalie Hoare, "Argentina to Maintain Oil Revenue Export Quota," *The Oil Daily* (December 20, 2002).

25. Richard McGowan, "Reevaluating the Privatization Process: An Analysis of the Privatization Process of Argentina's Oil Industry," *Economic Annals of the University of Craiova* (February 2006).

Chapter 5

The Never-Ending Cycle of Privatization and Nationalization: Venezuela's Oil Industry

Even before the Spanish Conquest, the indigenous people of Venezuela knew about the country's abundant oil supply. They used crude oil that seeped to the surface for medicinal and other practical purposes. It was not until 1913, however, that the Caribbean Petroleum Company drilled the first commercial oil field in Venezuela. Soon after, Royal Dutch Shell and Rockefeller's Standard Oil became the country's major producers of oil. By 1929, Venezuela was the world's second-largest oil producer after the United States, as well as the world's largest oil exporter. From 1926 to 1947, Venezuela produced more oil than the entire Middle East combined.[1]

Venezuela is now a world-class oil producer and holds what could be the largest oil province in the world, the Orinoco Oil Belt. (According to the U.S. Energy Information Administration, estimates of recoverable reserves from the Orinoco Belt range from 100 to 270 billion barrels.) In 2006, Venezuela was the world's sixth-largest net oil exporter, and oil accounted for more than 75 percent of the country's export revenues, half of its total government revenues, and about one-third of its total gross domestic product.[2] The oil industry is of central importance to the Venezuelan economy and has often been used as a foreign policy tool.

Since commercial oil activity began in Venezuela, the industry has experienced "on and off" nationalization. Foreign oil companies controlled almost all of Venezuela's oil industry until the 1960s, when the government gradually moved toward nationalization. Formal nationalization of the oil industry occurred in 1976 with the creation of the state-owned oil company Petroleos de Venezuela S.A. (PDVSA). Beginning in 1989, however, the

Venezuelan government followed an oil policy known as Apertura Petrolera and opened the country's marginal oil fields to foreign private investors. When Hugo Chávez became president in 1999, he set out to "renationalize" the oil industry and to regain the state's control of PDVSA. As discussed in Chapter 4, the Argentine government, in contrast, never attempted to renationalize YPF after privatizing it in the 1990s. Chávez, on the other hand, wanted to reverse the Apertura policy.

HISTORY OF VENEZUELA'S OIL INDUSTRY

Venezuela's oil history begins with the Caribbean Petroleum Company's discovery of the first major oil field in Venezuela in 1913; the company then sold a 51 percent shareholding interest to Royal Dutch Shell. In 1917, the first oil refinery was built in the country and the first shipment of oil was exported. After World War I, a surge of foreign oil companies arrived in Venezuela and made major oil discoveries. In 1929, Venezuela produced 137 million barrels of oil, making it the second-largest oil producer in the world after the United States.[3]

By 1935, Venezuela was truly an oil-producing country, with production totaling 400,000 barrels per day. There was, however, already a strong reaction against the foreign oil companies, which the Venezuelan people viewed as "heartless new conquerors."[4] In fact, from 1920 to 1940, Venezuelan novelists led this reaction against foreign capital. The resentment was based on the foreign companies' association with the dictatorial governments of Venezuela, their large profits, and their poorly maintained oil fields.

During the presidency of Isaías Medina Angarita, the government enacted the Hydrocarbons Act of 1943. This law transformed old concession titles into new titles valid for an additional 40 years but with more favorable conditions for the Venezuelan government. It also established a royalty rate of 16.6 percent for each barrel of oil that a foreign company extracted and increased the tax rates on concession areas. These new taxes soon became the main source of revenue for the state. In 1945, a radical political party called Acción Democrática overthrew Angarita and appointed Juan Pablo Pérez Alfonzo as the minister of development. In an effort to increase the state's control over the oil industry, Alfonzo pressed for a 50–50 split of oil profits between the state and the foreign companies. In 1948, the government passed a law known as the Fifty-Fifty Agreement that made the state a partner in all the major oil companies' activities.

In 1956, in contrast with the policies of Acción Democrática, President Marcos Pérez Jiménez offered the foreign oil companies low taxes, little government interference, and high profits. Jiménez wanted to continue promoting the growth in Venezuela's oil production and exports and to generate revenue for his large building projects. Under Jiménez, the government granted about 1.6 million acres of new lands to 14 foreign oil companies, and oil production and exports grew significantly.[5] In addition, the new concessions generated about $600 million for the Venezuelan government. Following the Jiménez presidency, the democratic governments of Venezuela followed an oil policy intended to increase the government's revenue from the industry.

Acción Democrática returned to power in 1958 with a clear oil policy known as Pentágono Petrolero. The new government stopped granting oil concessions to foreign companies, and this immediately resulted in the reduction of exploration in Venezuela and the deterioration of its oil-producing capacity. In 1960, the government created the state-owned oil company Corporación Venezolana del Petroleo (CVP), the Venezuelan Oil Corporation, to participate in all oil-related activities and produce greater benefits for the country from oil exploration. But the CVP did not became the strong national oil company that the government envisioned. Instead, it operated like a small company and never produced more than 100,000 barrels per day.[6] In the same year as CVP's creation, Venezuela led the formation of OPEC to coordinate major oil-exporting countries' policies and defend oil prices.

Throughout the 1960s, the Venezuelan government increased its share of oil company profits and strengthened its ability to control oil prices for export purposes. In 1971, the government passed the Hydrocarbons Reversion Law in an early shift toward nationalization. According to this law, all the assets, plants, and equipment belonging to the foreign oil companies within or outside the concession areas would be returned to the state without compensation in 1983.[7] Decree 832 of December 1972 required the foreign companies to submit their exploration, production, refining, and export plans to the government for approval each year. By early 1973, "for all practical purposes, the Venezuelan oil industry was in the hands of the state."[8]

By March 1974, there were two different drafts of an oil nationalization bill in the Venezuelan Congress. In May of that year, President Carlos Andrés Pérez created the Nationalization Commission to analyze what was necessary to successfully nationalize the oil industry. Pérez asked the commission to create a formula that would determine the compensation paid to concessionaries, a plan to operate the industry during the transition to state ownership, and procedures to ensure the legal payments and funds of workers. Pérez made it clear that the object of nationalization was the companies' assets, not the companies themselves. New companies would be created, and the Venezuelans who currently managed the multinational companies would retain their management positions to ensure continuity.

The nationalization law was declared in August 1975 and became effective in January 1976. Petroleos de Venezuela S.A. (PDVSA) became the owner of every share of the 14 operating companies, the inheritors of the former foreign companies. Administratively, these new companies remained identical to the previous concessionaries. Permitting the companies to continue working under their existing management structures allowed PDVSA to avoid production disruptions that could have arisen with immediate consolidation. Over time, however, PDVSA reduced the number of operating companies to four.

After nationalization, the organizational structure of the oil industry changed. The Ministry of Energy and Mines (MEM) became responsible for setting broad policy rules and goals. PDVSA created the specific programs and plans to achieve these goals and to oversee their implementation by its subsidiaries, and the operating companies were tasked with their execution. However, the lack of clarity regarding administrative responsibilities often led to conflicts between the MEM and PDVSA.

When PDVSA was created, it was given the right to operate as a private, profit-oriented company without political interference. However, from the company's early existence, PDVSA and the Venezuelan government have frequently had incompatible business and political goals. This became a problem in September 1982 when the bankrupt government of Luis Herrera Campíns violated the agreement reached by all parties at the time of nationalization and confiscated the company's $18 billion of investment funds,[9] effectively ending PDVSA's self-financing.

Oil production in Venezuela declined steadily each year from 1973 until 1985, and it became clear (especially after the confiscation of its investment funds) that PDVSA did not have enough capital to develop the country's reserves. As a result, PDVSA made exploration and exploitation of marginal and inactive oil fields a top priority in the early 1990s. To accomplish this goal, PDVSA needed capital, but funding through reduced taxes and royalties or through increased borrowing was impossible because of the company's tense relationship with the government. Consequently, in the late 1980s and early 1990s, PDVSA followed a policy known as Apertura Petrolera, or "oil opening," to attract foreign investment.

The Apertura policy resulted in 33 operating service agreements with 22 different foreign oil companies and four strategic associations to produce extra-heavy crude oil in the Orinoco Oil Belt.[10] For some of these marginal oil fields and projects, PDVSA negotiated with the MEM that the foreign companies pay only a 1 percent royalty rate instead of the customary 16.6 percent rate.[11] Since the operating contracts minimized the tax burden that fell on private investors, most of the profits generated by the new investments did not accrue to the state. However, the projects implemented as a result of Apertura reversed the decline in oil production and increased reserves.

Throughout the 1998 Venezuelan presidential campaign, Hugo Chávez criticized PDVSA's performance and the government's squandering of oil revenues. Chávez won the election and appointed Alí Rodríguez as the minister of energy and mines to reverse the Apertura policy and to achieve understanding among OPEC members regarding quotas and prices. During the Apertura years, PDVSA had changed its focus from fiscal revenue to production, concentrating on quantities and not prices. As a result, from 1994 to 1999, Venezuela did not abide by OPEC quotas.[12] Upon taking office, Chávez required PDVSA to implement output cuts and follow OPEC quotas.

In 2001, the new Hydrocarbons Law was enacted, replacing the 1943 Hydrocarbons Act and the 1975 nationalization law. Under the new law, royalties paid by private companies increased from 1 percent (or sometimes 16.6 percent) to 20 to 30 percent. In addition, the law required that all future foreign investment take the form of joint ventures with PDVSA instead of operating service agreements, profit-sharing agreements, or strategic associations.[13] Lastly, the law guaranteed PDVSA a majority stake in any new oil projects.

One year after the new hydrocarbon legislation, Chávez appointed a new board of directors to PDVSA that violated the company's traditional meritocracy process. This change, along with Chávez's new oil policies, provoked a PDVSA worker strike that lasted for two months beginning in December 2002. Before the strike, output was about 3.2 million barrels per day, while at one point during the strike, production measured less than 40,000 barrels per day.[14] The government fired 18,000 PDVSA workers, resulting in a loss of production, oil revenue, and technical knowledge and expertise.

In 2006, Chávez announced the state takeover of several major oil operations that had been controlled by foreign companies (as a result of the Apertura policy). Under the new contracts with the foreign companies, income tax rates on windfall profits increased from 34 percent to 50 percent. In addition, Chávez mandated that PDVSA have at least 60 percent ownership of these operations and any new projects. Continuing his renationalization plan, Chávez announced in January 2007 that the government would take control of the heavy-oil projects in the Orinoco Belt. The move allowed the foreign companies currently working on the projects to become junior partners.[15] Of the six major companies involved in the Orinoco projects, Total and Statoil reduced their holdings to allow for PDVSA's enlarged share, Chevron and BP kept their previous stakes, and ConocoPhillips and ExxonMobil left the projects completely.

EVALUATION OF THE NATIONALIZATION PROCESS

The matrix used to evaluate Argentina's privatization of the oil industry (see Figure 4.1) will also be used here to determine the short-term and long-term economic and political effects of the nationalization of Venezuela's oil industry. Although both short- and long-term effects can be evaluated, Chávez's renationalization policy only began in 1999 and continues today, making short-term effects easier to identify and discuss. We will see that Venezuela has repeatedly faced a tradeoff in the short run and the long run. When the government strengthened its control over the oil industry, as in 1976 and 1999, it did so to achieve the short-run goal of securing more oil revenue. In the long run, however, the country has struggled to diversify and develop the economy, growing increasingly dependent on oil dollars.

Economic Effects in the Short Run

Upon nationalization of the oil industry in 1976, the MEM and PDVSA set some short-term goals, which included finding new reserves, increasing production potential, modernizing refineries, and obtaining new export markets. The industry succeeded in meeting some of these goals. Work done at the refineries gave PDVSA more flexibility to operate at different levels of output. Huge Orinoco Belt heavy-oil projects began and new international clients were acquired. However, new reserves were mostly gas and heavy crude, and production potential did not increase. Increased spending was also a concern, as production expenditures rose from $1.21 per barrel in 1976 to $2.12 in 1979 (see Table 5.1). (According to a 1991 interview conducted by Terry Lynn Karl with a PDVSA official, one barrel of oil cost $1.80 to produce in 1976, over $3.00 in 1979, and reached $6.00 by the late 1980s; despite the discrepancies in the actual figures, costs clearly increased over those years.) The rise in expenditures

Table 5.1   Early Results for Nationalized Venezuelan Oil Industry

	1976	1977	1978	1979
Wells repaired	876	916	1,079	1,470
Operational expenditures (millions of bolívares)	2,322	2,835	3,259	3,883
Production cost per barrel ($/barrel)	1.21	1.48	1.92	2.12
Productivity per well drilled (barrels per day)	430	390	350	310
Time spent on repairs (days per well)	6	7	8	9
Production potential of light/ medium crude (thousand barrels per day)	1,879	1,733	1,789	1,631

Source: *The Nationalization of the Venezuelan Oil Industry* (Lexington, MA: Lexington Books, 1983), p. 74.

can be explained by the fact that several oil wells needed repair (about 1,500 wells repaired in 1979, compared to 876 in 1976) and more time was needed for those repairs (an average of nine days in 1979, compared to six days in 1976).[16] In addition, the technology needed to extract heavy crude was very costly.

Keeping production stable proved to be a difficult task for the newly created PDVSA because most oil fields were mature and exploration and investment had declined prior to nationalization. Production potential had a high decline rate of about 25 percent a year. As a result, the cost of maintaining production at 2.2 million barrels per day continually increased. The industry, however, managed to maintain this production level with some difficulty from 1976 to 1979.[17] Both the natural decline in the productivity of the fields and an influx of younger, untrained personnel into the oil industry contributed to this struggle to maintain production levels.

Prior to nationalization, the foreign oil companies knew they would face the reversal of their concessions in 1983, so they refrained from investment and exploration, focusing instead on producing at the lowest cost. From 1970 to 1975, investment in Venezuela's oil industry was at the low level of $1 billion per year. This lack of investment and exploration made it difficult to keep the country's oil industry modern and efficient. Technical knowledge and expertise declined as well. In the 1950s, about 800 geologists and geophysicists worked in Venezuela's oil industry, but in 1976, less than 40 were still engaged in exploration.[18]

After the state gained control of the oil industry, investment in production and exploration increased rapidly. In the first year after nationalization, investment remained at the same level as that of the prenationalization years, but in 1977, investment doubled, and in 1978, it doubled again. Investment levels in 1981 were higher than those of 1976 by a factor of 13.[19] The increased investment played a critical role in PDVSA's operational expansion. However, expansion also meant increased expenditures and operating costs. In fact, in absolute terms, operating costs were three times greater in 1980 than in 1975.

Political Effects in the Short Run

Throughout the nationalization process, the interests of many different stakeholders were considered. The Nationalization Commission was composed of people representing the cabinet, political parties, labor unions, universities, and economic groups. In the fall of 1974, a survey of oil industry workers was conducted on behalf of the commission. A majority of the workers reported that they were willing to stay in the industry after nationalization, since most agreed with the basic concept of nationalization (but not all the procedures). Oil company employees formed a group called Agrupación de Orientación Petrolera (AGROPET) to participate actively and cooperatively in the nationalization process. In early 1975, AGROPET presented several reports on nationalization to President Pérez and his cabinet. This critical event gave the government important information on how to structure the industry after nationalization.

The Venezuelan government and the Nationalization Commission knew that the nationalization debate needed to be a participatory process to be successful. By including workers and other interested parties in the nationalization process, they made the transition to a state-owned oil industry relatively smooth. The articles of the nationalization law stated that oil industry workers would retain all previously acquired benefits and privileges, which satisfied the workers. In addition, the oil industry was staffed mostly with Venezuelans who politically supported the nationalization decision, which eased the transition to state ownership.

The Venezuelan government rapidly reached agreements with the foreign oil companies during the nationalization process. Talks with the companies about compensation and possible technological and marketing agreements had been in progress for months before the nationalization law took effect. However, the government negotiated from a position of weakness regarding marketing and technology. Multinational companies initially controlled the marketing for the most part, and Venezuela needed their trading channels to continue oil exportation. Yet by 1979, more than half of Venezuelan oil exports were marketed outside the foreign companies' trade systems. In addition, the foreign companies possessed the technical knowledge necessary for the smooth and efficient operation of the industry. Through agreements, about 300 foreign specialists stayed in the nationalized oil industry as advisory staff.

In the late 1970s and early 1980s, control issues began to surface. The oil industry continued to generate income for the government, but its operational costs and expenditures increased. The government grew worried about the amount of control it should have over PDVSA. During Pérez's presidency, the industry had almost complete autonomy, but his successor, Calderón Berti, rapidly returned more control to the MEM. In addition, congressional committees and task forces increased their monitoring of the industry's activities, projects, and decisions.

Even before nationalization, the Venezuelan government was very dependent on oil revenues. The big oil crises of 1973 and 1974 generated a surge of income for Venezuela, prompting the Pérez government to begin a program of economic development. This program, however, led to inflation, balance-of-payment deficits, a huge national debt, and the deterioration of social services. Already the economy showed signs of distortion because of oil revenues. Government spending and borrowing continued until the government lost control, plunging the economy into a recession in 1980 and 1981. It became clear that oil income alone could not cover increased fiscal spending. In these years, the Venezuelan government faced a dilemma: the development of the heavy-oil deposits in the Orinoco Belt was essential to ensure that the industry could generate the income the country needed, but this development required investment that would be diverted from other sectors of the struggling economy.

Upon nationalization of the oil industry, the Oil Industry Fund was created to ensure the self-financing of PDVSA. The nationalization law required that 10 percent of the net value of oil exports be given to PDVSA for financing projects. By 1981, the fund had grown to $8 billion, and political leaders began to look to this monetary resource as a solution to the government's money problems. Initially, the fund remained untouched by the political sector partly because of Acción Democrática's defense of PDVSA's self-financing mechanism. Gonzalo Barrios, president of the party, believed "it was highly dangerous for the country to utilize financial resources of the oil industry to cover the waste and inefficiency of the government entities in debt."[20]

By August 1982, the economic crisis had deepened as Venezuela's international reserves plunged and capital rapidly exited the country.

On September 28, the Venezuelan Central Bank took over PDVSA's oil investment fund, ending the company's self-financing. This takeover exemplified the extreme dependence of public expenditure on oil income. Since the 1960s, the government had almost always spent all the money derived from oil and had established a spending pattern that was hard to change. For example, in 1974, when oil revenue tripled, expenditures tripled as well, but when oil revenue fell in the early 1980s, the government did not curb its spending.

Economic Effects in the Long Run

By the late 1980s, oil revenues were no longer sufficient to fund PDVSA's investments and various other state investments. PDVSA did not have enough capital to develop the country's reserves or engage in exploration, nor did it have the capital to fund the badly needed economic development of the country. The oil industry required constantly increasing investment to maintain production levels, and the logical alternative to increasing state revenues through petroleum was domestic taxation. However, the dependence of previous Venezuelan governments on oil dollars weakened the country's ability to develop a domestic tax base and extract revenues from the population. The Venezuelan people believed that oil revenues could adequately provide for their needs and opposed any increase in taxes. Knowing this, PDVSA advocated the Apertura policy, which allowed private foreign companies to develop the country's energy resources.

The projects implemented during the Apertura years reversed the decline in the country's oil production. Between 1989 and 1998, Venezuelan oil production increased nearly 70 percent, from 2.02 million barrels per day in 1989 to 3.41 million barrels per day in 1998.[21] Production levels during these years often violated OPEC quotas. While production rose, PDVSA's operating costs increased by 175 percent during the Apertura years, and so the company achieved almost no increase in profits.[22]

Apertura resulted in operating contracts and strategic associations with 22 different oil companies. Initially, the opening policy generated $2 billion in foreign investments for the country's oil industry. Much of this investment was concentrated in exploration, resulting in a huge spike in Venezuela's oil reserves. Proven reserves rose from 25 billion barrels in 1987 to 71.7 billion barrels in 1998—a 187 percent increase.[23]

When Chávez became president, he immediately ordered PDVSA to cut production by 525,000 barrels per day and abide by OPEC quotas. (PDVSA has not filed financial statements with the U.S. Securities and Exchange

Commission since 2004; recent production levels therefore are subject to debate among economists and industry analysts.) The December 2002 strike severely impacted Venezuela's oil production capacity, and many industry analysts identify the strike as a contributing factor to recent declines in production. As a result of the strike, production dropped from almost 3 million barrels per day to less than 500,000 barrels per day in January 2003. According to PDVSA, total loss in sales reached about $14.43 billion because of the strike. Between the fourth quarter of 2002 and the first quarter of 2003, Venezuela's gross domestic product fell by approximately 24 percent.[24]

According to industry estimates, the Venezuelan oil fields operated by the recently formed joint ventures produce about 400,000 barrels per day.[25] Many of these fields, however, are marginal, with very steep decline rates. In the coming years, Venezuela plans to more aggressively develop the energy resources in the Orinoco Belt. The country created a program called Magna Reserva to increase the amount of proven reserves in this region. PDVSA has joined with other national oil companies for this program, including Brazil's Petrobras, Iran's Petropars, China's CNPC, and India's ONGC, and estimates that the program could certify 260 billion barrels of oil.

In 2004, PDVSA recorded higher profits than had been forecasted, which meant that revenue was available to support public spending and fund projects. Using some of this income, the government created three trusts for public investment as part of its national development plan. One of the trusts (with funding up to $2 billion) was designated for the construction of hydro- and thermoelectric power plants and the funding of a national airline. Another trust was created for investment in housing and infrastructure developments, and the third trust was designated for investment in agricultural development projects. In addition, the Social Development Management Department of PDVSA financially supports state education, health care, and production programs. PDVSA supplies billions of dollars to these funds each year, which diverts large amounts of money away from oil-related activities and investment.

In 2007, Venezuela had 80 billion barrels of oil reserves, the largest amount in South America. In 2006, the country net exported about 2.2 million barrels of oil per day, the sixth-largest amount in the world.[26] In recent years, however, the country has struggled to maintain production levels because of the natural decline at existing oil fields and the lasting effects of the December 2002 strike. Most of PDVSA's oil fields experience annual decline rates of 25 percent, and industry analysts estimate that the company must spend about $3 billion a year to maintain production levels at those fields. Since Chávez took office, production has ranged from a low of 2.58 million barrels per day in 2003 to a high of 3.46 million barrels per day in 2000.[27]

Political Effects in the Long Run

One of the most significant long-run political effects of the 1976 nationalization of the oil industry stems from Article 5 of the nationalization law, which was added to the original draft and stated, "In special cases, and when it is convenient to the Public Interest, the National Executive Board or the aforementioned entities will be allowed to sign association agreements with private entities, albeit with such a participation that state-control is guaranteed, and for a limited duration only. The celebration of such agreement will require previous authorization by both chambers of Congress." Article 5 allowed for governmental associations with private companies as long as Congress gave prior approval. The addition of this article was politically controversial during the nationalization process, but its effects were not truly felt until the late 1980s, when marginal fields were opened to foreign investors. Essentially, the Apertura policy has its origin and justification in this article.

The 1998 Venezuelan presidential election, in which Chávez took power, focused on oil policy. Throughout his campaign, Chávez criticized PDVSA's policies and the government's use of oil revenues, believing that the relaxed royalty and tax structure benefited the foreign oil companies at Venezuela's expense. He also objected to PDVSA's increased control of oil policy formulation, calling the company "a state within the state." In the Apertura years, PDVSA changed its focus from fiscal revenues to maximizing volumes, and Chávez believed that the increased production that resulted from this change directly contributed to the collapse of oil prices in 1998. PDVSA not only ignored OPEC quotas, but also pressed for the country to leave the organization. When Chávez won the election, he appointed Alí Rodríguez as the minister of energy and mines and pledged they would work together to reverse the Apertura policies and reaffirm the country's role in OPEC.

Conflict between Chávez and PDVSA seemed inevitable as Chávez quickly moved to reestablish state control over the oil industry. In 1999 and 2000, he appointed three different presidents of PDVSA. Earlier we saw how this interference caused a 65-day strike that resulted in a severe drop in production and Chávez firing 18,000 PDVSA workers.

By 2000, Chávez had mandated oil production cuts and had hosted the second head-of-state meeting in OPEC history to promote understanding on quotas and prices. As a result of these new policies, Venezuela's revenues from hydrocarbon exports reached $27.3 billion in 2000, compared to the previous peak of $19.1 billion in 1981. In 1981, however, the export sales generated $13.9 billion in royalties and income taxes, but in 2000, the $27.3 billion of export revenues generated only $11.3 billion in royalties and income taxes. Between 1976 and 1992, royalties and income taxes accounted for 71 percent of export revenues on average. Between 1993 and 2000, this share averaged just 36 percent.[28]

The fall in fiscal revenues can be attributed to the country's adoption of the worldwide accounting method for reporting profits and losses and the contracts that PDVSA had negotiated for the foreign companies during the Apertura years. In 1989, Venezuela adopted a new accounting method that transferred costs incurred abroad to Venezuela, increasing the profits that accrued outside of the country. This move benefited PDVSA because it was subject to a 67.7 percent income tax in Venezuela compared to only a 34 percent income tax in the United States, for example. However, this also meant that a smaller proportion of PDVSA's revenues went to the government through taxes. Lastly, during the Apertura years, many companies paid only a 1 percent royalty rate instead of the customary 16.6 percent rate, further decreasing fiscal revenues.

As already stated, the hydrocarbon legislation of 2001 increased royalty payments from 1 percent (though some foreign companies were only paying 16.6 percent) to 20 to 30 percent. Simultaneously, the income tax on oil extraction was lowered from 67.7 to 50 percent. The reason for the increase in the royalty rate and the reduction of the income tax is that the royalty is paid up front, but income tax is applied only if profits are generated. Thus, the policy allowed the government to attempt to increase its revenue from the industry and especially from foreign companies.[29] The MEM has made it clear that royalties are the central revenue-producing device, since the worldwide accounting method makes effective higher income tax rates difficult to impose.

In the years after the 1976 nationalization of Venezuela's oil industry, the country's economy experienced a deep crisis, which eventually led to the reopening of the industry to private foreign investors. However, Chávez's renationalization of the industry seems more permanent than the initial nationalization. Not only has he renationalized the oil industry, but he has also nationalized the telecommunications, electricity, steel, and cement industries. In early 2008, Chávez dealt another blow to foreign oil companies and increased taxes on crude oil (net) exports. Companies must pay a per-barrel tax rate of 50 percent of the amount by which the monthly average price of Brent crude exceeds $70 per barrel, and this rate increases to 60 percent when the Brent price exceeds $100 per barrel.[30] This new tax policy could potentially generate up to $2 billion in additional government revenue.

CONCLUSION

Since commercial oil activity began in Venezuela, oil has been the focus of the country's economy. Soon after the major oil fields were discovered, oil replaced coffee as Venezuela's most important export. Today, Venezuela is one of the world's largest oil suppliers and potentially holds billions of barrels of heavy-oil reserves in the Orinoco Belt. Venezuela's oil policy has been characterized by "on and off" nationalization, with foreign oil companies dominating the industry until official nationalization in 1976, followed by the reopening of oil fields to foreign private investors in the late 1980s and early 1990s. When Hugo Chávez took office, he renationalized the industry, reversed the Apertura polices, and reaffirmed Venezuela's role in the global oil market.

Recently, President Chávez has used revenue from PDVSA's operations to fund various health, education, and discount food programs to redistribute the country's wealth to the poor. He has simultaneously reasserted Venezuela's sovereignty by regaining control of several oil fields that were opened to foreign oil companies during the Apertura years. While some of the social programs funded by oil revenues are working well, the country risks becoming even more dependent on oil exports than it already is. Nationalization allows the Venezuelan government to take advantage of its oil for other purposes, but it also exaggerates the cyclical nature of the economy. In the past, Venezuela's dependence on oil dollars has led to political, social, and economic turmoil, and it will be interesting to see whether Chávez's oil policies can avoid such problems in the future.

NOTES

1. Juan Carlos Boué, *Venezuela: The Political Economy of Oil* (Oxford: Oxford University Press, 1993).

2. United States Energy Information Administration, "Country Analysis Briefs: Venezuela," http://www.eia.doe.gov/emeu/cabs/Venezuela/pdf.pdf (2007).

3. Boué, *Venezuela: The Political Economy of Oil*.

4. Gustavo Coronel, *The Nationalization of the Venezuelan Oil Industry* (Lexington, MA: Lexington Books, 1983).

5. Coronel, *The Nationalization of the Venezuelan Oil Industry*.

6. Coronel, *The Nationalization of the Venezuelan Oil Industry.*

7. Boué, *Venezuela: The Political Economy of Oil.*

8. Coronel, *The Nationalization of the Venezuelan Oil Industry.*

9. Boué, *Venezuela: The Political Economy of Oil.*

10. United States Energy Information Administration, "Country Analysis Briefs: Venezuela."

11. Bernard Mommer, "Oxford Energy Comment: Venezuelan Oil Politics at the Crossroads," Oxford Institute for Energy Studies (March 2001).

12. Bernard Mommer, "Oxford Energy Comment: Changing Venezuelan Oil Policy," Oxford Institute for Energy Studies (April 1999).

13. United States Energy Information Administration, "Country Analysis Briefs: Venezuela."

14. Toyin Falola and Ann Genova, *The Politics of the Global Oil Industry* (Westport, CT: Praeger Publishers, 2005).

15. "Exxon Seeks Deal on Venezuela Oil," *BBC News* (September 13, 2007), http://news.bbc.co.uk/go/pr/fr/-/2/hi/business/6992487.stm

16. Coronel, *The Nationalization of the Venezuelan Oil Industry.*

17. Coronel, *The Nationalization of the Venezuelan Oil Industry.*

18. Coronel, *The Nationalization of the Venezuelan Oil Industry.*

19. Coronel, *The Nationalization of the Venezuelan Oil Industry.*

20. Coronel, *The Nationalization of the Venezuelan Oil Industry.*

21. United States Energy Information Administration, "Country Energy Profiles: Venezuela," http://tonto.eia.doe.gov/country/country_energy_data.cfm?fips=VE (August 2007).

22. Petroleos de Venezuela, S.A., http://www.pdvsa.com/ (accessed June 15, 2008).

23. United States Energy Information Administration, "Country Energy Profiles: Venezuela."

24. Información Estadística, Banco Central de Venezuela, http://www.bcv.org .ve/c2/indicadores.asp (accessed July 1, 2008).

25. United States Energy Information Administration, "Country Analysis Briefs: Venezuela."

26. United States Energy Information Administration, "Country Analysis Briefs: Venezuela."

27. United States Energy Information Administration, "Country Analysis Briefs: Venezuela."

28. Mommer, "Oxford Energy Comment: Changing Venezuelan Oil Policy."

29. Lus Giusti, "Venezuela's Energy Opportunities Rest on Political Climate, New Legislation," *Oil & Gas Journal* (January 2001).

30. "Venezuela Hits Exported Oil with New Tax," *Oil & Gas Journal* (April 28, 2008).

Chapter 6

Public Good or Inefficiency? Port Facilities in the United States and Canada

Throughout history, ports have played a significant role in the exchange of cultures, ideas, and economic factors. In this current era of accelerated globalization, they have become even more important centers of financial activity. The vast majority of international trade, which is essential to the economies of numerous countries, is carried out through maritime transport. Only a small amount of international trade is transported by air. Clearly, trade plays an important role in the growth and prosperity of the economy (see Table 6.1).

In addition to facilitating trade, ports stimulate local businesses and provide jobs for local residents. In the past, ports employed a large amount of labor because they needed people to load and unload cargo from the shipping vessels. The jobs created by ports fostered economic development were a boost for the local town. The development of large cargo containers, however, significantly reduced the need for human labor. In the past couple of decades, ports around the world have become more capital-intensive, resulting in an excess of labor.[1]

The prevalent use of containers has also led to an increase in the size of ships, which has created financial and environmental problems for the ports. Since vessel sizes are increasing at a rapid pace, the ports must accommodate by investing in new infrastructure. Furthermore, ports with relatively shallow harbors must dredge the harbor to make it deeper, which is expensive and damages the immediate ecosystem.

Despite the large costs, the port industry is still a profitable business. In fact, Dubai Ports World, a state-owned firm, offered $6.8 billion in 2006

Table 6.1   U.S. Imports and Exports $USD (in Billions)

Date	Imports	Exports
Jan 1990	629.8	552.1
Jan 1991	623.6	596.6
Jan 1992	667.8	635.0
Jan 1993	720.0	655.6
Jan 1994	813.5	720.7
Jan 1995	902.6	811.9
Jan 1996	964.0	867.7
Jan 1997	1,055.8	954.4
Jan 1998	1,115.7	953.9
Jan 1999	1,251.4	989.3
Jan 2000	1,475.3	1,093.2
Jan 2001	1,398.7	1,027.7
Jan 2002	1,430.2	1,003.0
Jan 2003	1,545.2	1,041.0
Jan 2004	1,798.9	1,180.2
Jan 2005	2,027.8	1,305.1
Jan 2006	2,240.4	1,471.1
Jan 2007	2,375.7	1,661.7
Jan 2008	2,553.8	1,843.4

Source: "A Guide to the National Income and Product Accounts of the United States"
(NIPA), (http://www.bea.gov/national/pdf/nipaguid.pdf).

to buy Peninsular & Oriental Steam Navigation, a British firm that operated various ports around the globe, including many in the United States. The U.S. Congress blocked the deal on the grounds that its completion would severely jeopardize national security, but this example illustrates the profitability of the industry.

U.S. PORTS

According to the American Association of Port Authorities, there are 183 commercial ports in the continental United States and its territories. Port authorities manage these institutions, and municipal or state governments establish the port authorities. The federal government does not control any aspect of these ports; indeed, "federal jurisdiction over harbors stops at the water's edge."[2]

Although they are state or local entities, U.S. port authorities have varying degrees of independence from government regulations. For example, the

Massachusetts Port Authority and the Port Authority of New York and New Jersey (the two states have a joint port authority) are autonomous and have less supervision from the state government than many other port authorities have. On the other hand, the port authorities in Hawaii, Maryland, and Virginia are considered to be part of the state government and are therefore more supervised.

The responsibilities and powers of the port authorities also vary by region. While most are required to operate and maintain the port, some also have permission to extend their control to "airports, bridges, tunnels, commuter rail systems, dredges, marinas, and other public recreational facilities." In addition, some port authorities can levy taxes and police their regions of influence.[3]

The sheer number of U.S. ports is important because it creates competition that port industries in other countries lack.[4] If a shipping company wishes to supply general goods to an area along the eastern coast of the United States, the company has a variety of choices: Massachusetts, New York, New Jersey, Baltimore, and so on. This competitive factor increases the efficiency of the industry but also increases the necessity for the ports to adapt quickly.

CANADIAN PORTS

In 1999, the Canadian Parliament drastically changed Canada's port management system with the passage of the Canada Marine Act. This piece of legislation targeted 18 of the most valued ports in the country and created an independent management entity for each of them. Titled Canada Port Authorities (CPAs), they operate the majority of Canada's "waterborne foreign commerce and virtually all of its breakbulk and containerized general cargo."[5] This deal also permitted the federal government to divest the ports that were not considered of strategic importance. Although 18 ports initially qualified for CPA status, the legislation allowed additional ports to apply to become a CPA. Currently, there are 20 ports designated as CPAs (see Table 6.2).

It is important to remember that CPAs are federal entities even though their management is independent. They pay an annual fee to the government but cannot borrow funds from it; all borrowed money must come from the private sector. Since the CPAs are self-sufficient and independent of each other, any profits are reinvested in the ports, for example, by buying more advanced equipment or creating new terminals.

Another difference between the U.S. port system and that of Canada is that the CPAs' activities do not go beyond those relating to the port. In other

Table 6.2   Canadian Port Authorities

1	Vancouver	11	Quebec
2	Montreal	12	Saguenay
3	Halifax	13	Saint John
4	Fraser	14	Sept-Iles
5	Hamilton	15	St. John's
6	Nanaimo	16	Thunder Bay
7	North Fraser	17	Toronto
8	Oshawa	18	Trois-Rivieres
9	Port Alberni	19	Windsor
10	Prince Rupert	20	Belledune

words, the CPAs cannot operate airports, bridges, and tunnels. Also, despite not having any shareholders, the CPAs must create annual financial statements and must observe high levels of transparency.[6]

THE PROBLEMS

The remainder of this chapter details the problems of the industry with a focus on the Canadian and U.S. port systems. It uses the model introduced in Chapter 2 to introduce the possibility of privatizing the industry and analyzes the effect of privatization on the stakeholders.

Technological Changes

The invention of containerized shipping has radically transformed the maritime transport industry. With containers, items can be stored for longer periods of time, allowing them to be transported to destinations that were previously considered economically unfeasible. This has improved efficiency and lowered shipping costs. Unfortunately, this development did not benefit the workers at the ports.

This significant shift to container shipping has made port operations more capital-intensive than before. The result is an inefficiency caused by an excess supply of labor. It also does not help that port workers belong to unions. As a result, this excess of labor is reflected in the costs to port operations and transferred to the customers (the shipping companies). The inability to eliminate this inefficiency hurts the port's competitiveness and causes it to lose current and potential customers.

Because of containerization, shipping firms can take advantage of economies of scale by constructing larger vessels and loading them with more cargo. These oversized transport vessels help the shipping companies but hurt the port authorities. Imagine that you are the manager of a port and your harbor is 30 feet deep, for example. One of your longtime clients comes to you and says that his company is going to start using these mega-vessels; however, this requires the harbor to be 40 feet deep. If you wish to keep this customer and the income stream, you have to dredge the harbor, but that requires a large amount of resources—time, money, and politicking. If you do not dredge the harbor, the customer will take his business to another port.

This technologically induced problem affects U.S. ports more than Canadian ports. Although CPAs are federal agents, they operate as private firms. That is, they are self-sufficient, borrow from the private sector in their own name, and even release annual financial statements. Their financial situation is not at the mercy of taxpayer money and how much their local or state government wishes to allocate to them. If they need to dredge the harbor to make it deeper, they can use their own money or borrow from a financial institution.

The situation in the U.S. ports differs because the local or state governments entirely own many of the ports. Thus, the port authorities in those regions must take into consideration government tax revenues before making any decisions. This problem is mitigated when the port is leased to a private firm or when the port generates enough income to cover its own costs. If the port is leased, the government acts as the landlord while the private firm covers all the costs for creating new infrastructure to support technological changes such as increases in vessel size.

Environmental Protection

Dredging creates an environmental problem in addition to its financial problem. Dredging, which is underwater digging, clears out the sediments and other materials that settle on the harbor's water floor. Periodic dredging maintains the depth of the harbor, and dredging is sometimes required to deepen the harbor to accommodate larger vessels. Unfortunately, this process destroys the natural habitat of certain creatures living in the aquatic ecosystem. This, in turn, creates larger problems because the organisms that depend on the affected groups suffer as well. This process can even affect humans because removing materials from the seabed can bring toxic chemicals to the surface. Thus, "environmental considerations are now among the most important constraints on port development."[7]

This environmental issue affects both Canadian and U.S. ports. Besides the necessary maintenance dredging, the prevalence of gargantuan shipping vessels will force the ports to dig deeper, both financially and physically. If the ports fail to deepen their harbors when requested, even though it hurts the environment, they stand to lose customers to rival ports.

National Security

Since the terrorist attacks of September 11, 2001, Americans have become very concerned about national security, and the government has acted accordingly. American ports are considered vulnerable targets because of their strategic locations and immediate surroundings. Ports are easily accessible because they are located on water and are surrounded by towns or cities. The neighborhoods of large commercial ports are occupied by millions of residents. Some fear that terrorists will transport a deadly weapon through a port. Therefore, many believe it is the ports' responsibility to install state-of-the-art technology that can detect radioactive materials and other dangerous weapons; however, this is costly.

Similar to the environmental problem caused by dredging, national security concerns affect both Canada and the United States. However, terrorism is not as location-specific as dredging because all ports in a region need to be secured in order for the region to be safe. For example, if a terrorist manages to sneak in a weapon through one unsuspecting port in Canada, that terrorist could then transport that weapon to the United States and throughout North America.

Public Budget

A clear implication of these problems is the requirement for additional resources. Ports need new equipment to deal with the larger ships and greater storage areas for the countless numbers of containers. They need money for dredging and developing more environmentally friendly ways of performing the process. As if those demands are not enough, the ports also need tighter security. Where will the money come from?

In Canada, the solution is already in place. The CPAs are self-sufficient and must borrow any necessary funding from the private sector. In addition, any ports that are not considered CPAs are divested from the federal government to municipal, provincial, or private entities. This not only increases the ports' efficiency, but also saves taxpayer money. Indeed, as of March 31, 2006, the Canadian government had saved taxpayers more than $210 million by using the CPA system and by transferring or terminating its interest "at 466 of the 549 sites identified at the outset of the program" (AAPA).

Since the control of U.S. ports is mixed between local or state governments and private firms, the capital comes from both the public and private sectors. Ports that are privately managed can borrow from the private sector and invest in new equipment and technology. Publicly owned ports, however, must rely on their respective local or state governments for funding unless the ports generate enough revenue to be self-sufficient. In recent years, local and state governments have spent much more than they have earned in tax revenues. This statistic does not bode well for publicly owned ports that need funding from the government for expansion projects and new equipment.

This inconsistent, and sometimes nonexistent, source of maintenance and investment resources begs the question, is there a better way of managing the port industry? Perhaps certain states and local governments can copy Canada's system and create APAs (American port authorities) to operate the ports. But that would require the ports to be in strategic locations where they could eventually generate enough revenues to become self-sufficient. However, the valuable waterways already have successfully established ports. Alternatively, the governments could look to the private sector for some assistance.

PRIVATIZATION

Using the model developed in the second chapter, the three questions pertaining to the game are (1) Is it voluntary? (2) Are there boundaries? and (3) Is the outcome uncertain? Privatization in the port industry is not a zero-sum (all-or-nothing) game. In other words, there are different levels of privatization, and each has its merits and its disadvantages. Some governments might decide that complete privatization will maximize economic benefits in their region, while other governments will only consider leasing the port for a certain amount of time.

The process itself is completely voluntary. A private firm only participates in the game if there is an opportunity to profit or increase market share. In Canada, opportunities for privatization exist, but they are not as lucrative as those in the United States. The Canadian ports that receive the lion's share of the commercial trade business have been designated as CPAs, and the government is in no hurry to get rid of them or to lease them because they serve as a source of revenue for the federal government and do not drain taxes. The ports that are for sale in Canada are the smaller ones. While they do not usually generate as much revenue as the CPAs, they might have niche markets that a private firm could exploit.

In the United States, however, there is no CPA program, so the state, city, or town decides the sale of its port. Although none of the ports are fully privatized, private firms do lease many of them. The firms keep the operating revenues but must pay the specified rent and can be regularly inspected. The opportunity to manage and operate a large commercial port is very enticing to both domestic and international firms.

A government cannot coerce a company to bid for one of its ports. However, a government can stop an offer from going through, which shows that there are rules for the player but not for the referee. In this case, the rules are the boundaries; the player is the firm; and the referee is the government. A good example of this scenario is the failed DP World deal.

In 2006, DP World purchased Peninsular & Oriental Steam Navigation (P&O), a foreign company, for $6.8 billion. P&O owned the leases to operate in several ports in the United States, including ports in New York, Baltimore, and Miami. Since P&O accepted the offer, the leases were to be transferred to DP World. When the media got hold of this news, the story spread like wildfire, and politicians from both parties started clamoring for the death of this deal. After being bombarded with a mountain of political pressure, DP World backed off and eventually sold the leases to an American firm. The audience was clearly in an uproar over the situation and successfully pressured the referee to bend the rules.

The main argument used by most critics of the transaction was that ports are vital strategic locations for the United States and should be owned and operated by American firms to ensure maximum safety. It is interesting to note that a foreign company, P&O, held the leases to those ports before the sale to DP World. The difference is that P&O is a British firm and DP World is an Arab, state-owned firm.

In this game of privatization, the private firms are allowed to compete against one another for the grand prize, which goes to the highest bidder. In fact, DP World outbid a Singaporean firm for P&O and its numerous port leases. However, just like referees in a sports game, the referees in a privatization game can also be biased. The outcome of a bidding war between a British firm and an Arab firm is no longer as uncertain as before. After the controversial DP World saga, it is quite clear that the British firm has the equivalent of a home field advantage. Even if the Arab firm offers greater financial compensation, it may lose. Sticking with the sports analogy, even if the away team executes a better overall performance, it may lose because of biased officiating (this scenario is not surprising to casual sports fans).

In light of the increased national security concerns of Americans, the process has become more unbalanced. This development might scare off potential players, which is disappointing for an industry that could benefit from an influx of new technology and management strategies.

THE STAKEHOLDERS

Improved efficiency and increased economic activity are attractive selling points in favor of privatization. However, there is more to the game than the boundaries, players, and referee. One must also consider the laborers at the port, the environmentalist groups, the citizens, the government, and the shipping companies.

Employees

In the general privatization case, the employees lead the fight against the process. They know that a privatized company would fire some employees to reduce costs and improve efficiency. As the port industry becomes more capital-intensive, the excess pool of labor is steadily expanding. Dockworkers are no longer required to bear the burden of loading and unloading cargo from shipping vessels. Nowadays, large cranes and other mechanical devices that are operated by a handful of workers load and unload the containers. This problem also affects the management group. If the port is owned and operated by the government, the managers do not have the incentive to work as hard as those working in a competitive firm.

An interesting point, briefly mentioned in the second chapter, is that labor stands to benefit in the long run if the port undergoes privatization, assuming that this leads to the growth of the industry. A more efficient and profitable private firm can invest more in the port, thereby increasing the port's capital stock and attracting more customers. As a higher level of maritime trade flows through the port, the surrounding economy grows, which ultimately leads to more jobs in the area.

Public Interest

Groups concerned with the environment and national security would prefer to keep ports under the control of the government. The reason is simple. The government answers to its citizens; the private firm answers to the customers and shareholders. In this industry, the private port operators cater mainly to the large shipping companies and not to the residents. Suppose that a public port is planning to carry out a massive dredging project that would drastically affect the harbor's ecosystem. An environmental group could gather enough support and tell the government officials to stop the project or else they will not be reelected. This is a very strong reason for the politician to act on behalf of the environmental group. The group would have much more difficulty convincing a private operator to stop the project.

The underlying problem with privatization in this scenario is the occurrence of externalities. A private firm has little or no incentive to consider the welfare of the residents living in the area. In this example, the externality is the damage caused to the environment by dredging the harbor. Some residents might be negatively affected because dredging can release toxic chemicals. The private firm cares about maximizing its profits or expanding its market share. The residents do not own the large, private conglomerate shipping companies and so do not wield much influence. Thus, citizens hope to keep the government in charge of the ports.

The firm only considers its own costs of operating the port. It cares solely about its marginal costs instead of the combined marginal and social costs. This occurs because the firm attempts to maximize economic profits, so it does not have the incentive to maximize the combined economic and social profits, which would be more expensive. The ideal outcome occurs when the supplier (port manager) considers the social implications in addition to the economic implications (i.e., operate on the social supply curve). That is, the owner does consider the surrounding environment, which dredging and expansion harm. Public interest groups prefer to have the government providing the service because the government accounts for social well-being in addition to economic well-being.

Government

The government's role in this process is unique because privatization is not an all-or-nothing game. If the state or local government wishes to privatize its port, it does not have to sell it completely. The state or city can reap the benefits of privatization by leasing the property to a firm. By doing so, the government receives regular rent payments from the company and experiences efficiency gains and economic growth.

Table 6.3 shows the top 10 U.S ports from 2006, ranked in order of total trade volume. Interestingly, none of the top ports are fully privatized. In fact, the majority of them are completely owned and operated by their respective

Table 6.3   U.S. Ports, Ranked by Trade Volume

Rank	Top 10 U.S. Ports	Total Trade Volume (tons)	Public	Private	Joint
1	South Louisiana, LA	225,489,499	•		
2	Houston, TX	222,146,750			•
3	New York/New Jersey	157,630,099	•		
4	Long Beach, CA	84,393,795			•
5	Beaumont, TX	79,485,704	•		
6	Corpus Christi, TX	77,557,478	•		
7	Huntington Tri-State, WV	77,157,809			•
8	New Orleans, LA	76,901,327	•		
9	Los Angeles, CA	65,978,238	•		
10	Mobile, AL	59,832,197	•		

local or state governments. These ports are also situated in advantageous geographic locations, which makes them prime destinations for shipping vessels. Because of the high volume of trade they receive, these ports are self-sufficient from the revenues they generate.

Since these 10 ports are self-sufficient, their respective state or local authorities have little incentive to sell or even lease the property and operations to private firms. This does not necessarily imply that the port authorities are operating as efficiently as possible, but they are doing a sufficiently good job. For the ports that do not receive as much trade, however, the privatization incentive increases because the port is more dependent on public funding. The incentive to privatize is especially significant given the large amount of debt that state and local governments have recently accumulated.

Efficiency

In certain cases, publicly owned seaports lack clear development plans and objectives, suffer from inexperienced or poor management, cannot obtain the necessary funds for development even if there are clear plans, and employ an excess amount of labor.[8] The introduction of competition into the market through privatization can solve or alleviate these issues.

The goal of all maritime ports is to operate at maximum efficiency. By doing so, they can cater to more shipping companies and increase their trade volume, leading to higher revenues. However, this leads to two main questions regarding the goal of efficiency. One, how does privatization increase efficiency? And two, how much does efficiency really matter in increasing trade?

First, private owners usually have specific goals and objectives in mind when they bid for the ports. These firms want to profit and expand their businesses, so the problem of not having clear plans does not exist. For instance, if the port is initially small and unequipped and has a low trade volume, then the new company will design and execute expansion plans. The short-term goal might be to expand land storage areas of cargo containers, then dredge the harbor to allow large vessels to dock, and finally aim to have a certain amount of trade volume flowing through the point by a certain date.

The firm has an advantage over the public port with its operations management. In general, firms in the shipping and port industry raise capital more efficiently and spend a substantial amount of resources on research and development. Consequently, they can develop more advanced technologies and better management strategies than the public port can.

The word "excess" in front of labor is the reason that employees usually do not favor privatization. A publicly owned port magnifies the problem of excess labor because the management has less incentive than a privately managed port to fire the excess portion of the labor force, so the dismissal process crawls along at a snail-like pace. In addition, these workers belong to unions and so can exert pressure on politicians to protect them. In return, the politicians are promised support and financial backing in their next election campaigns. A competitive firm, on the other hand, will fire the excess labor because high labor costs prevent the firm from gaining market share and maximizing profits.

In Canada and the United States, the problem of excess labor is not severe because there are great incentives to avoid unnecessary costs. In Canada, the self-sufficiency requirement of CPAs implies that management has to consider reducing labor costs. Although U.S. ports are not required by law to be self-sufficient, they still face competitive pressures from other state or local ports. Shipping companies can easily switch to a rival port, even if the port is further away from the destination, and receive a better value.

People often say, "There is no free lunch." Of course, these efficiency gains have a price. Groups concerned about the environment and national security might not want to sacrifice their concerns for increased economic activity at their ports. They would rather have more operating inefficiency than destruction of natural habitats. Also, a profit-maximizing firm might care about efficiency so much that it compromises safety, leading to national security problems.[9] For example, the greedy firm may unload and load the ships as quickly as possible without taking much time to check the cargo or ensure maximum safety for the workers and crew.

All of these privatization solutions are appealing, but is increased efficiency really necessary in lieu of the tradeoffs? The economic answer is "yes." International economics further elaborates on the importance of increasing efficiency. According to Peter Jones, "For most Latin American countries, transport costs are a greater barrier to U.S. markets than import tariffs."[10] This, by itself, is a very convincing argument for the local or state governments that manage struggling ports to consider leasing part of the operations to a private firm.

A prominent model in international trade theory is the gravity model, which states that bilateral trade between two countries is proportional to their size, in terms of GDP, and that the distance between countries reduces the volume of bilateral trade. The latter statement is relevant for this discussion because a 12 percent reduction in shipping costs through increased port efficiency is equivalent to reducing the distance between the two countries by 5,000 miles.[11] This astounding conclusion implies that a shipping company would rather go through a more efficient port that is much further away from its destination than through a relatively inefficient port that is closer to its destination. This is also rather intuitive. For example, a customer would rather shop at a distant grocery store if the customer received a better value, in terms of price and quality, at that store than at the closer store.

From this analysis, one can say that greater port efficiency does lead to a higher volume of trade and a faster-growing economy. But the story does not end here. One must also consider the issues of equality that are raised by privatization.

Equality

A major concern of critics is that privatization gives monopoly power to the firm, which allows it to charge more for its services. Assuming that the port's goal is to maximize profits, it will lower output and increase prices to accomplish that goal. Customers might receive a more efficient product, but they will pay more and perhaps disproportionately more than before according to this theory. While this is a legitimate concern, competition is so great in Canada and the United States that privatization would not likely give monopoly power to the firms.

Both countries boast superior inland transport systems, so if one port charged unfair, high prices, the shipping companies would not hesitate to use a port down the coast. However, this would not be a feasible option in a developing country or a relatively landlocked country where there are only a few operational maritime ports. Furthermore, several U.S. ports have competition within individual ports. If the port is large enough to house several terminals, the port authority can auction off leases for the individual terminals. There could be two or three different firms operating and competing within the same harbor. The pricing issue would all but disappear in this situation.

CONCLUSION

A vibrant trading port plays a significant role in increasing economic development in a region. It not only attracts more international trade but also boosts other industries such as tourism and finance. Unfortunately, not every city has a port, and even those with ports sometimes lack the means to make the ports successful and attractive to private investors. The problem(s) could include high labor costs, insufficient funding to modernize the ports, a dearth of incentives, or other forms of inefficiencies. Thus, other options are brought to the table.

One possibility is to lease parts of the port, or the daily operations of the port, to a private company. This strategy is adopted in some U.S. ports and has worked well because the local or state governments receive the rent payments and experience the efficiency gains created by the private companies, which have more resources to invest in the port and superior management strategies. Although the rules are straightforward, there could be unexpected disturbances such as government (referee) intervention on behalf of public interest groups or the audience. Such an example is DP World's failed attempt to acquire the leases to several key U.S. maritime ports after there was a public uproar over the fact that DP World is a state-owned, Arab company.

Privatization is not the only choice. Canada chose to create government agents to operate its ports. The Canadian Port Authorities are managed as if they were private firms, but they are federal entities and must pay annual fees to the government. In addition, this strategy avoids some of the drawbacks of privatization, such as having fewer social considerations, especially with regards to environmental issues and national security. Privatization is therefore not the answer for every port and should be decided on a case-by-case basis.

NOTES

1. Lourdes Trujillo and Gustavo Nombela, "Privatization and Regulation of the Seaport Industry," *World Bank Policy Research* Working Paper No. 2181 (November 1999), http://ssrn.com/abstract=623975.

2. Rexford B. Sherman, "Seaport Governance in the United States and Canada," American Association of Port Authorities, http://www.aapa-ports.org/files/PDFs/governance_uscan.pdf (accessed June 25, 2009).

3. American Association of Port Authorities, U.S. Port Industry, "America's Ports: Gateways to Global Trade," http://www.aapa-ports.org/industry/content.cfm?itemnumber=1022& navitemnumber=901.

4. Alga D. Foschi, "The Coast Port Industry in the U.S.A. A Key Factor in the Process of Economic Growth," Discussion Papers—Department of Economics No. 46 (December 2004), http://ssrn.com/abstract=720265.

5. American Association of Port Authorities, U.S. Port Industry.

6. American Association of Port Authorities, Canadian Port Industry (AAPA-Canada), "Public Seaport Governance in the United States and Canada," http://www.aapa-ports.org/Industry/content.cfm?ItemNumber=993& navItemNumber=902.

7. Brian Slack, "Globalisation in Maritime Transportation: Competition, Uncertainty and Implications for Port Development Strategy," FEEM Working Paper No. 8. (January 2001), http://ssrn.com/abstract=272131.

8. Trujillo and Nombela, "Privatization and Regulation of the Seaport Industry."

9. Trujillo and Nombela, "Privatization and Regulation of the Seaport Industry."

10. Peter W. Jones, "Maritime Transport Costs and Port Efficiency: A Historical Perspective" (November 10, 2005), http://ssrn.com/abstract=898468.

11. Peter W. Jones, "Maritime Transport Costs and Port Efficiency: A Historical Perspective" (November 10, 2005), http://ssrn.com/abstract=898468.

OTHER USEFUL WEB SITES

"A Guide to the National Income and Product Accounts of the United States" (NIPA), http://www.bea.gov/national/pdf/nipaguid.pdf.

American Association of Port Authorities. "Port Industry Statistics—2006 U.S. Port Cargo Tonnage Rankings." http://www.aapa-ports.org/Industry/content.cfm?ItemNumber=900& navItemNumber=551.

Association of Canadian Port Authorities. "CPA Facts." http://www.acpa-ports.net/industry/cpafacts.html.

Part Three

State-Operated Industries That Were Once Private Enterprises

Chapter 7

State-Controlled Liquor Stores I: Pennsylvania

Pennsylvania is one of 18 alcoholic beverage control states, commonly known as "ABC states." In an ABC state, the state government controls the sale and distribution of various alcoholic beverages, depending on state law. In Pennsylvania, wine and liquor are sold through state-owned stores; however, the stores do not sell beer. All wine and liquor in Pennsylvania are sold at a fixed price and quantity. This market power gives Pennsylvania a mandated monopoly over the wine and liquor industry.

Some states have privatized their ABC systems. Pennsylvania has attempted to privatize its system in the past but failed, and another privatization attempt is currently being discussed. Privatizing the system would consist of selling the state-owned entities to private entities and consequently replacing a "control system" with a "licensure system."

In theory, the privatization of a government-run business would disband the monopoly and its inefficiencies. This would drive price down to marginal cost with the establishment of a perfectly competitive market, and it would also maximize economic efficiency through sequential transactions. In addition, states can quickly increase funds through the liquidation of assets with privatization. State treasuries would be compensated from the sale with money to efficiently allocate for state needs.

Major beneficiaries of the privatization would include citizens in favor of decreased alcohol prices and citizens who are compensated from the allocation of increased Treasury funds. Employees of the state liquor system will lose from the privatization, since many will need to find other jobs. Citizens worried about potential negative externalities from price decreases will also lose from the privatization.

This chapter uses Pennsylvania liquor stores as a case study for the potential privatization of a government-run industry. The purpose is to present an analysis of the players involved with privatization of an ABC system. It will also juxtapose two privatization plans and how their proceeds can be used to better the community.

The first section of this chapter provides a brief history of the establishment of Pennsylvania's control system. This is followed by a discussion of the first major attempt at privatization in 1997 by Governor Tom Ridge. The third section presents the actions taken by Pennsylvania's control system board in the aftermath of the 1997 attempt at privatization. The details of the current privatization proposal by Republican state senator Robert Wonderling will then be analyzed. The fifth and sixth sections introduce opposition to privatization by social conservatives and unions and also analyze the financial proceeds from privatization and the economic implications of the current monopoly control system. Finally, a conclusion analyzes the privatization debate.

HISTORY OF PENNSYLVANIA WINE & SPIRITS STORES

The state-owned liquor stores of Pennsylvania are called Wine & Spirits stores. They are controlled by the Pennsylvania Liquor Control Board (PLCB), a state regulatory commission established after the repeal of Prohibition in 1933. "The second most populous state in 1933, Pennsylvania was home to many recent immigrants whose cultural practices included the consumption of alcohol as well as substantial numbers of fundamentalist Protestant prohibitionists."[1] At the time of Prohibition repeal, people were worried about the Great Depression and were not looking to completely allow the free sale of alcohol. Voters considered themselves to be either "wet" (permit alcohol consumption) or "dry" (no alcohol consumption) on the liquor control issue, much like Democrats and Republicans.[2] The Republican governor at that time, Gifford Pinchot, was a strong supporter of Prohibition but valued more strongly the will of the people during the national economic crisis:

> The central figure in this struggle was Pennsylvania's progressive Republican Governor, Gifford Pinchot, a lifelong believer in the wisdom of prohibition. Pinchot recognized that public opinion had turned against prohibition. Yet he believed it was his duty to protect

the people against the deleterious effects of beverage alcohol by pushing the state legislature to enact the most stringent control measure acceptable to the state's public and politicians. Pennsylvania was the largest and "wettest" state to adopt a state liquor monopoly due in no small part to Pinchot's efforts.[3]

Before Prohibition, Pennsylvania liberally allowed for the sale and distribution of liquor when compared to other states. "Pennsylvania had one of the most freewheeling saloon systems in the nation—by 1919 Pennsylvania would be one of only two states not to provide for prohibition by local option."[4] During the 1920s, Pinchot referred to Pennsylvania as the "Gibraltar of the Liquor Traffic."[5]

Pinchot was determined to not allow the open saloon to return to the state of Pennsylvania. However, he was willing to concede the sale of alcohol given certain restrictions and restraints on trade. Pinchot sought to decrease the profit from liquor sales and direct the sale of alcohol for off-site consumption.[6]

During the grave times of the Great Depression, Pinchot's first priority was to satisfy the will of the majority of the people, even if it meant discontinuing liquor prohibition. The majority of "wet" voters came from the urban parts of Pennsylvania, while "dry" supporters came from the central portion.[7] After the repeal of Prohibition, bills were quickly passed focusing on two aspects of liquor sales. The first group of bills pertained to the regulation of the sale of alcohol, while the second group involved the revenue from the liquor regulations. Together, they formed the Pennsylvania Liquor Control Act, or House Bill No. 10.[8]

The act originally called for the creation of the Pennsylvania Alcohol Permit Board, which would be composed of three members of Pinchot's cabinet. However, because of public disapproval, the Alcohol Permit Board provision was scratched in favor of the Pennsylvania Liquor Control Board (PLCB), an independent three-member organization that administered the sale of alcohol for the state.[9] The board would seek to cut down on bootlegging and retrieve any state and federal tax revenues. "No one, retailer or private citizen, was allowed to possess wine or liquor that had not been purchased from the state stores."[10] Profits from the sale of wine and liquor in the state store system were set low to deter consumers from purchasing through bootleggers.

Since the board was granted any necessary powers to carry out its primary duties, some feared that the legislature was setting a precedent for the commonwealth to be dominated by boards. State senator Henry L. Snyder said:

> If it is to be the continued policy of this State of Pennsylvania to create boards and commissions and bureaus; if we, as members of the bar, can no longer look to the pamphlet laws for the law, but must look beyond the law to rules and regulations the character and nature of which we leave entirely to the boards themselves . . .[11]

In late November of 1933, the Pennsylvania Senate approved the act 43–3, and the House voted 114–47.[12] By January 2, 1934, state stores in Pennsylvania were up and running. At the end of that same month, Pennsylvania operated 234 state stores.[13]

Reasons for establishing the control system rested on the public's interest and the examples provided by Canada, which had recently introduced state-controlled liquor systems. In other words, "proximity to Canada and the strength of anti-liquor voting sentiment in the state"[14] were the determining factors. Canadian provinces already had government-controlled stores, and these were used as a model for the Pennsylvania state store system. As has been noted, "State store systems, . . . had been established in all states that bordered Canada with the exception of New York, Wisconsin, and Minnesota."[15] Furthermore, when dry voters were given the choice between a monopoly control system and a license system, they overwhelmingly preferred the former system.[16]

Pinchot's liquor plan for Pennsylvania was characterized by three major parts. First, Pennsylvania would abandon complete prohibition in favor of control through liquor legislation. Second, smuggling and bootlegging would be combated through restrictions on profit to eliminate public incentives to buy outside of Pennsylvania. Third, educational systems would be established to inform the public, especially the youth, on the dangers of drinking.[17]

As a result, the PLCB controls the licensing, sale, transportation, importation, and manufacturing of wine, liquor, and brewed alcoholic beverages in Pennsylvania. The PLCB was to have power over and prohibit the manufacture and transactions of alcohol. The commonwealth's ultimate reasoning for this establishment was to care for the public welfare, health, and morals of its citizens.[18]

Today, The PLCB manages more than 600 Wine & Spirits stores, which are only involved in the sale of wine and liquor, not beer. All tax money and revenues from the state-controlled stores are submitted to the Pennsylvania State Treasury. The tax money includes all of the state and local liquor taxes. Therefore, a system for distribution and pricing controls was created with the establishment of the PLCB. "Despite continuing liberalization brought about by the pressures of competition from neighboring states, much of the system remains as Pinchot proposed it, in all of its progressive and provincial trappings."[19]

However, in the last 75 years, changes have been made to the control system. In 1959, liquor sales on Sundays were approved in Philadelphia and Pittsburgh. It was not until 2003 that the PLCB allowed for 10 percent of its stores to operate on Sundays. Pennsylvanians were allowed to shop in "self-service stores" in 1969. In 1987, credit cards were finally accepted at the Wine & Spirits stores.[20]

THE 1997 ATTEMPT AT PRIVATIZATION

Republican governor Tom Ridge held office in Pennsylvania from 1995 to 2001. Throughout his campaign, he proposed the sale of the Wine & Spirits stores. In 1997, he made the first attempt to privatize the state liquor store system since Governor Dick Thornburgh had tried in the 1980s.[21] It was reported that "Governor Ridge unveiled a responsible plan to close Pennsylvania's government-run liquor stores, replacing them with a private system that will be more consumer friendly, while generating hundreds of millions of dollars to invest in an endowment."[22] He also planned to increase penalties on sales to minors to maintain a conservative hold on the sale of alcohol. Ridge said, "The government is here to serve the people, not to serve them alcohol."[23]

Ridge gave detailed financial breakdowns for the proceeds from the privatization of the Pennsylvania liquor stores. He estimated that the sale would generate $605 million over 10 years. To appease PLCB employees, Ridge set aside $20 million to state-store employees and offered future employers a $2,000 state tax credit for hiring a former PLCB employee. Ridge also allocated $57.5 million for alcohol education and enforcement. He aimed to establish a Better Communities Fund that would "build local projects approved by the General Assembly" and would receive $388 million. Ridge wanted to use the remaining $129 million to award at least 4,000 four-year scholarships each year to graduating Pennsylvania high school seniors, paying $1,000 annually for each student.[24]

Ridge proposed to close all of the Wine & Spirits stores in Pennsylvania and to auction off the 757 franchises. The state would maintain control of the wholesale distribution system. Purchasers of the 10-year franchises would pay both an initial fee and annual fees. They could not buy more than 10 percent of the franchises or have a 40 percent share in a region.

Ridge also planned to push down the wholesale price of liquor and wine for consumers. This proposal would therefore completely abolish the monopoly system previously used by the PLCB in favor of private competition. In addition, stores would not be able to operate near schools or churches, and Pennsylvania state police would still enforce previous liquor laws. The PLCB would still distribute alcoholic beverage licenses to businesses.[25]

Ridge made sure to appease his opposition with his plan. He argued that even though the government was exiting the alcohol sale business, it was improving its regulation, enforcement, and education practices. However, because he was met with the predicted strong opposing views, Ridge did not succeed in his attempt to sell the Wine & Spirits stores. The major opposition came from social conservatives, those who wanted to maintain the revenue from state profits on liquor and wine sales, and unions, which wanted to protect jobs.[26]

Social conservatives feared increased alcohol consumption with the sale of the stores. If the government sold the stores, then the price of alcohol would decrease and it would become more readily available for individuals, especially minors. This would lead to increased driving accidents, underage drinking, and family breakdowns. The Pennsylvania Council of Churches opposed Ridge's privatization plan on the basis that alcoholism is a treatable disease. The council favored the control system and opposed the increase in alcohol advertising associated with privatization.[27]

In regards to increased drinking and driving accidents, the *Pittsburgh Business Times* published an article on privatization's effects on alcohol-related accidents for Iowa, West Virginia, and Ohio. Iowa privatized its state store system in 1987, West Virginia in 1990, and Ohio in 1991. The article noted, "The number of alcohol-related driving fatalities, already in decline prior to privatization, has continued to decrease since privatization—by 30 percent in Iowa, 32 percent in Ohio, and 23 percent in West Virginia." The article also stated that, according to the National Highway Traffic Safety Administration, control states do not have fewer alcohol-related driving fatalities than those states with a private system. "Pennsylvania, despite having the strictest liquor control system in the country, fell right at the national average in 1995 with 41 percent of all driving fatalities being alcohol-related."[28]

Social conservatives still held the strong religious views of "dry" voters back in 1933. Alcohol in the free saloon days was pervasive, and conservatives maintained that privatization would be detrimental to public safety and protection. They believed that it was appropriate for the state to continue its control of alcohol distribution and sale, rather than have a private licensing system. According to another *Pittsburgh Business Times* article, "Pennsylvania would be awash in drunken madness after privatization."[29]

The second opposition was related to economics. The alcoholic beverage control system used by the state of Pennsylvania ensured a constant source of income for the state Treasury. All profits from the sale of alcohol in Wine & Spirits stores and tax revenues were given to the commonwealth to pay for public goods and services. The state currently collected a 6 percent sales tax and an 18 percent liquor tax on all sales of alcohol. The state would still collect this money in a private system. However, the profits from the Wine & Spirits stores ranged from $50 million to $155 million in the seven years prior to Ridge's proposal.[30]

In 1997, legislators were skeptic about the potential loss of this constant stream of income for the state. Ridge tried to assure people that the proceeds from the privatization would be used to fund public projects such as museums, libraries, convention centers, zoos, aquariums, and new sports arenas through the Better Communities Fund. The main draw for the Better Communities Fund was that the fund would last forever. Therefore, the state would not have to borrow money and increase debt for new projects.

However, legislators still opposed the idea of selling the state stores. Ridge went so far as temporarily refusing to fund capital projects so that the General Assembly would even consider his privatization plan for ending the state's monopoly of retail liquor stores. In a *Bond Buyer* article, according to Rep. Mark Cohen, a Democrat from Philadelphia, "[Ridge is] trying to build up a constituency for selling the liquor stores, but I don't think it's going to work. It's a very unpopular issue; it's going nowhere."[31]

Another important aspect of the alcoholic beverage control system debate is that all employees of the PLCB are state employees and unionized workers. Three unions represent different groups of PLCB employees. "The stores' assistant managers and clerks are represented by four locals of the United Food and Commercial Workers Union; the managers by the Independent State Store Union; and Liquor Control Board office workers in Harrisburg by the American Federation of State, County and Municipal Employees (Union)." Consequently, unions had significant power in the privatization dispute. They argued that the privatization of the stores was a tactic to break up unions within the commonwealth. "The [United Electrical, Radio & Machine Workers of America] denounced Ridge's proposal as 'union busting,' and argued that Ridge was attempting to pay off his 'political cronies.'"[32]

In addition, the potential breakdown of unions translated into the loss of jobs with benefits high enough to support a family. If the Wine & Spirits stores were sold, the union jobs would be replaced with minimum-wage salaries. Unions asserted that with private stores, there would be less accountability for the store owners. Minors would more easily be able to access alcohol, and drunken driving accidents would increase. The unions also supported maintaining the revenue provided by the state stores. They argued that if the store system were privatized, state taxpayers would be expected to make up the loss in the government revenue.[33] This is directly contrary to Ridge's claims that the sale to the highest bidder of the individual franchise stores would compensate the commonwealth for lost revenue.

By September of 1997, Ridge had abandoned the battle to privatize the Wine & Spirits store system. Despite advocating a free-market economy and funding for public capital projects, Ridge was defeated by the social conservatives and unions.[34] "Good jobs at good wages is a Pennsylvania mantra, and the unions representing state store workers successfully used it to kill the necessary legislative support for reform, even if their good wages came with good jobs that the state has no business providing."[35] In the end, social conservatism over the regulation of alcohol and the persistence of state store revenues defeated any plan Ridge had for privatization.

THE PLCB AFTER THE 1997 PRIVATIZATION ATTEMPT

Since the privatization attempt in 1997, the PLCB has made numerous changes to reform its monopoly system. The public clarified that it wanted socially conservative policies during the 1997 privatization proposal period, and these changes reflected those ideas.

However, the shopping patterns of residents near bordering states demonstrated that they favored a free-market economy for wine and liquor sales. A 1998 *New York Times* article chronicled the habits of Pennsylvanians buying from neighboring states and crossing state lines, even though it is illegal in the state of Pennsylvania to purchase wine or liquor from another state and transport it into Pennsylvania. The PLCB used to have liquor control agents who enforced the liquor laws for the commonwealth, but the article noted that the liquor control agents and their "out-of-state stakeouts" ended in 1994.[36]

Pennsylvanians frequently travel to Delaware, Maryland, New Jersey, New York, Ohio, and West Virginia to save money on alcohol purchases.

As the same article noted, "In New Jersey, they save roughly 10 to 15 percent on wine and liquor." Therefore, the PLCB lost money on potential purchases. Instead, Pennsylvanians sent their money to neighboring states through the neighboring states' alcohol taxes. "The PLCB estimates that 5 to 7 percent of Pennsylvanians' liquor and wine purchases are made in other states," but this may be a conservative estimate. "Critics say the losses are much higher, and point out that total sales of wine and liquor are 40 percent higher in New Jersey than in Pennsylvania even though Pennsylvania's population is 50 percent larger."[37]

Pennsylvanians have also traveled to other states to experience better service. Because New Jersey has a private system, store owners need to be informed about their products, as opposed to the state employees at Wine & Spirits stores. "In Pennsylvania, you may be dealing with a clerk who doesn't know the difference between a case of fine wine and a case of tomatoes."[38]

In 2003, five years later, the PLCB responded to this problem by encouraging Pennsylvanians to purchase alcohol within the state through Wine & Spirits outlet stores instead of traveling to the neighboring states for cheaper prices. The PLCB had converted four Wine & Spirits stores along state borders into outlet stores. To bypass the law that all Wine & Spirits stores have to sell alcohol at the same price, these stores sold alcohol in larger bottles or in two-bottle packages at a lower price. All of the stores are located in highway traffic areas near state borders in an attempt to regain some of the out-of-state purchases by Pennsylvania citizens. Also in 2003, the PLCB allowed 10 percent of its stores to sell alcohol on Sundays.[39]

The PLCB lost its case in 2005 to maintain a ban on Internet and mail-order shipments of wine. The result of the case allowed for wineries to directly ship their products to residents and not have to sell through the state stores. Essentially, the monopoly ban on wine sales that had been in place since Governor Pinchot's establishment of the PLCB was lifted. The Pennsylvania consumer, who could now purchase wine from any state and transport it legally to Pennsylvania, was the big winner. The decision also benefited Pennsylvania wineries. "The ban may have cost Chaddsford 25 percent of its business, or almost 7,000 cases," according to Lee Miller, co-owner of Chaddsford Winery, the state's largest winery, in a Bloomberg article. "Selling through the state store system adds the 18 percent liquor tax and a $4.50 handling fee for each order, on top of the state's 6 percent sales tax."[40] Removing the ban clearly increased the sales for this Pennsylvania winery.

In December 2006, Democratic governor Ed Rendell, the former mayor of Philadelphia, appointed former Republican state senator Joe Conti to a CEO position for the PLCB. The chairman of the board, Jonathan Newman, did not have any influence in appointing Conti, despite his protests. "Newman voted against the appointment, saying he learned of the decision Tuesday and would have preferred to have a detailed study conducted to see if the board even needs a CEO."[41] However, the PLCB's chairman, Patrick Stapleton, welcomed the addition to help deal with increasing costs for the liquor system. The board voted 2–1 in favor of Rendell's nomination of Conti for CEO. Conti opposes privatization. According to Conti, "Public interest in selling the system to private ownership appears to have waned."[42]

A year later, Newman resigned from his chairman position because of Conti's appointment. Now, Newman has started his own company, Newman Wine & Spirits, in the private sector. While he was chairman, Newman had "Chairman's Selection specials" for wine lovers. He now sells his famous discounted wines in Pennsylvania's bordering states. "Begun in 2004, the Chairman's Selections leveraged Pennsylvania's clout as one of the world's largest buyers to obtain steep discounts on premium wines." Newman's departure left the PLCB without premium wines for its customers, allowing the board to revert to a monopoly with overpriced alcohol.[43]

SENATOR WONDERLING'S PRIVATIZATION PLAN

Early in 2007, 10 years after Ridge's privatization proposal, the issue of selling state stores was revisited. According to a *Pittsburgh Post-Gazette* article, the 1997 proposal projected benefits of $605 million for the state, while a current sale could earn over $1 billion. In addition, Newman's politically motivated resignation from the PLCB left the public in disapproval of joining a monopoly on wine and liquor with politics. However, the traditional opponents, social conservatives and labor-protecting liberals, still opposed privatization. According to the article, "Rendell, when campaigning for governor in 2002, said he thought liquor-store privatization is 'basically a good idea,' but thought the prospects were poor since he was to be pitted against a GOP legislature."[44]

State senator Robert Wonderling, a Republican from Montgomery County, spoke that summer about his plans for selling the state store system. Wonderling's ideas differed greatly from Ridge's of 10 years prior. In Wonderling's plan, the state would sell 51 percent of the liquor monopoly to a private equity group. Wonderling wanted a private equity firm to help eliminate "inefficiencies before selling it off completely." Pennsylvania is one of 18 "control" states left in the United States but is "typically grouped with Utah as being the most restrictive." Wonderling immediately faced opposition regarding underage drinking, drunk driving, and intoxication. Rebecca Shaver, regional executive director of Mothers Against Drunk Driving (MADD), met with Wonderling shortly after his announcement. "One of the biggest concerns, she said, is underage drinking. She is skeptical that a network of private retailers can match the stores' training program for spotting underage or intoxicated customers."[45] Wonderling obviously disagreed with this reasoning.

Despite the privatization rumors, the PLCB continued to plan for the future and announced a renovation plan for its stores using 2006 profits. According to Stapleton, the renovation would help to change public perception that the stores offered limited alcohol selection at high prices, despite Pennsylvania being one of the largest alcohol purchasers in the country.[46]

On February 4, 2008, Wonderling formally introduced legislation, Senate Bill 1273, to privatize the state liquor stores. According to Wonderling, the government is not in the business to sell alcohol.[47] Private entities would allow more convenient stores and selection for consumers, removing the imposed choices made by the PLCB. In Wonderling's recent proposal, two-thirds of the state's 623 Wine & Spirits stores would be sold by auction, while the remaining third would be sold to a private equity firm. However, Pennsylvania would maintain a 49 percent share, and the private equity firm would have a 51 percent share. Wonderling estimates that the state could earn over $1 billion from the sale of the Wine & Spirits stores. Unlike Ridge's plan, where the majority of the money was placed into a perpetuity fund for capital projects, Wondering proposes to use the proceeds to "expand existing state resources for Medicare and the adult basic health insurance program as proposed in Governor Rendell's Cover All Pennsylvanians proposal." The plan would require all licensed vendors to participate in mandatory training sessions to prevent the sale of alcohol to minors, addressing one of the main concerns with privatization. The bill would also change distance regulations on liquor stores from 300 feet to 500 feet away from churches and schools. Furthermore, hospitals, playgrounds, and charitable organizations would be added to this category.[48]

Wonderling called his bill a "hybrid approach" to the privatization of the state stores. The private equity firm would eliminate inefficiency within the system, such as underperforming stores, and then sell the stores to the highest bidder. In addition, whereas Ridge advocated 10-year franchises for the sale of the stores, Wonderling proposed 30-year franchises for the sale of the first two-thirds of the stores.[49]

Weeks after Wonderling's proposal, former governor Dick Thornburgh, who tried to privatize the state store system in the 1980s, offered Wonderling and his supporters some advice: "Keep plugging." Stapleton reacted to the proposed bill by saying that it will not withstand public scrutiny because there are too many social, financial, and economic arguments against it. People are reluctant to change a system that generated $1.6 billion in sales revenue last year. Wonderling will also have to face unions, who lead the opposition that defeated Ridge's proposal. "Any plans to privatize the system will have to get past the Independent State Store Union, which represents workers in the more than 600 state-run liquor stores."[50] President W. David Wanamaker said, "Historically, we've been opposed to efforts at privatization. We also believe in the control philosophy, that it works."[51]

Since his bill's announcement, Wonderling has made additions and changes to his proposal. Apparently, he told MADD to "find the toughest alcohol-related enforcement measures in the nation and he would include those features in the bill." Additionally, Wonderling plans to place an estimated $800 million of the sale into an interest-bearing account for health care.[52]

PUBLIC REACTIONS

Wonderling will face the same oppositions that Ridge faced roughly 10 years ago in his privatization efforts. A *Pittsburgh Post-Gazette* article quoted Stapleton as saying, "I think the arguments against [privatization] are even stronger than they were 10 years ago."[53] Stapleton referred to issues of social costs, underage drinking, and financial implications.

John Basial, council to Wonderling, said in a Pennsylvania State University's *Daily Collegian* interview that the bill would decrease liquor costs and increase selection in stores. Furthermore, Basial said that underage drinking would decrease due to restriction and a "whole host of safeguards" and that states make more money after privatization. According to Hillary Lewis, University Park Undergraduate Association president, "People are going to buy liquor . . . regardless of the price." Yet, Elizabeth Goreham, State College Borough Council president, had a different opinion: "The possibility of increased liquor sales may not necessarily be a positive influence on the borough. I understand the need to come up with funds. We ought to think it through."[54]

A February 8, 2008, editorial from *The Morning Call* cited reasons to approve Wonderling's bill. The private equity group would sell the remaining stores at a "premium price." Additionally, the first $350 million would directly benefit the state's Medicaid plan. The state would also allocate some of the proceeds to the Pennsylvania State Police and Mothers Against Drunk Driving. Eighty percent of the second round of sales would be deposited into the state's General Fund. "And, there is no reason to believe that private stores won't be able to prevent sales to minors." The bill calls for restrictions on future operating hours and mandated training for workers on sighting underage or intoxicated customers.[55]

A February 6, 2008, editorial from the *Pittsburgh Post-Gazette* called the Pennsylvania Liquor Control Board a "mock tribute to government monopoly, inefficiency, and paternalism." The article mentioned that 68 percent of the $482.7 million profit that the PLCB gave to the Treasury came from taxes. Stores that lose money also continue to remain open because of the political power of representatives in their areas. The PLCB allows only Pennsylvania wineries to sell directly to the consumer. However, despite the U.S. Supreme Court ruling three years ago, which determined that in-state and out-of-state wineries must have equal opportunity, the legislature has yet to pass a law allowing for sales by out-of-state wineries. In short, the PLCB is in a "state of antiquity."[56]

A week later, the *Pittsburgh Post-Gazette* published an editorial with a differing opinion. The editorial stated that proponents of privatization offered no proposals for replacing the money besides raising taxes on alcoholic beverages that the PLCB generates for the state. The benefits return to the taxpayers in the form of an increased value in Treasury money. It argued that "privatization would flood many of our communities with small, poorly stocked and poorly maintained stores that would be a blight on our neighborhoods." The editorial also said that privatization would mean that rural Pennsylvanians would not have access to a store within a reasonable distance, and it pointed out that the current system has growing sales with a proven success rate in preventing sales to minors. In short, the state store system is "efficient and effective."[57]

ECONOMIC IMPLICATIONS OF THE PRIVATIZATION

The Allegheny Institute for Public Policy prepared a policy brief in the spring of 2007 regarding the sale of Pennsylvania liquor stores. The brief declared that since alcohol is not a core function of the state government, privatizing the system would make sense in order to generate immediate funds for the state. Privatization would convert Pennsylvania from a "liquor control state" to a "licensure state." Pennsylvania is currently one of only 18 states that control the retail and distribution of alcohol, along with bordering states Ohio and West Virginia. Other bordering states—Delaware, Maryland, New York, and New Jersey—are licensure states.[58]

The brief also argued that the privatization of the stores would provide immediate funds for the state. In 2006, the PLCB transferred $80 million in profits to the state Treasury. The writer stated, "If the Commonwealth can sell the state store system for an amount that is more than the present value of $80 million per year, then they should do so. Using a six percent discount rate can put the sale price at $1.2 billion or higher."[59]

Second, employees of the PLCB would be removed from the state's payroll. Although the employees' salaries are paid with revenues prior to the transfer of funds to the Treasury, employees are still eligible for benefits. In 2005, $24.7 million was given for compensated absences. In the same year, $15.89 million was distributed for disability compensation. All employees are eligible for the state retirement plan. In 2005, the PLCB contributed $2.1 million to the State Employees Retirement System.[60]

Third, privatization would lower the alcohol prices for consumers. Control states charge a markup on prices even beyond the taxes. However, these high prices cause consumers to shop elsewhere, as shown through articles on Pennsylvanians buying out-of-state alcohol. "If consumers don't buy alcohol from Pennsylvania State stores, then the Commonwealth loses the markup as well as the considerable liquor taxes."[61] For this reason, Pennsylvania opened the seven previously mentioned outlet stores near its borders to regain lost sales to neighboring states. Sales from the seven stores alone reached $55.2 million in 2005. The brief argued, "With outlet stores so successful, why not let all Pennsylvanians benefit from competitive pricing?"[62] Currently, residents who do not live near the border are at a disadvantage because they cannot take part in competitive pricing. Competition would result in lower prices for everyone and would also bring more consumer-friendly stores and more variety in selection.

In the same season, Wonderling wrote a brief article for the Commonwealth Foundation for Public Policy Alternatives in which he acknowledged other areas where the government has searched for assistance in the private sector.

The reason we should privatize the state stores is because government should not be in the business of selling alcohol. The role of state government should be to regulate the sale of alcohol, not profit from it.

Currently, the Commonwealth allows private beer distributors to sell beer. There is no reason why wine and liquor stores can't be run the same way.[63]

Wonderling also accused Rendell of not following campaign promises to privatize the system, but instead driving out Newman. He said that the PLCB was an "antiquated bureaucracy" that stood in the way of progress and change.[64]

Geoffrey Segal of the Reason Foundation said that privatization would not result in the loss of tax revenue. Instead, "Taxpayers and commuters would benefit as untapped value is extracted to invest in our infrastructure without raising taxes."[65] Privatization would bring lower prices and create more choices. With privatization, inefficient and unprofitable stores would cease to exist because stores would only exist where there was demand.

Critics of privatization contend that sales of alcohol would increase with any loss of state control. Segal countered that the state has little ability to affect alcohol problems through its distribution system. However, the state should focus its attention on education, regulation, and enforcement to curb societal problems involving alcohol.[66]

Without question, the PLCB holds a monopoly over the wine and liquor industry in Pennsylvania. "From inventory, to distribution, to pricing, to the number of outlets and hours of doing business, Pennsylvania maintains one of the tightest, most restrictive liquor-control systems in America."[67] Proponents of the system, usually union workers and social conservatives, acknowledge the benefits of the system through purchasing power, regulation, and constant income for the state. Quality selection is available for reasonable prices, which include the state markup and state alcohol tax, also known as the Johnstown Flood Tax. Revenue from the system funds alcohol education programs for underage citizens. There are over 4,000 employees of the PLCB, who are all union workers. The average store clerk salary is $30,000 with health benefits and state pension. "Whatever inefficiencies and inconveniences exist, though, one thing seems certain— the PLCB continues to be a money machine, with its control over which wine and spirits come into the state, in what quantity and at what price."[68]

Opponents of the system target the inefficiencies within the PLCB. Nonprofitable stores, high salaries, high prices, and low selection are the major reasons for abolishing the monopoly system. In addition, according to Mark Squires, a Philadelphia lawyer and wine enthusiast, "The government should not be in the business of selling wine, and the idea that they could do a good job of it is illusory." Other professionals point to the employee payroll system as a major problem. "I'm not saying they are undeserving, but the main beneficiaries of the current system are probably the employees who work for the liquor stores. If you look at the wages and benefits and compare them with employees in unregulated states, you will find significantly better salaries," said Holger Sieg, a professor of economics at Carnegie Mellon.[69]

The PLCB has adapted over the years by shifting toward a private system. Originally, state stores did not allow customers to browse the aisles for their purchases. Instead, there was a ticket order system where the clerks went to gather the requested alcohol. Aisles were eventually opened, and the selection was widened for customers. However, Newman, a chairman who focused on expanding selection, left his position after Conti's appointment. If the monopoly system continues to shift toward a private system, why not just privatize the state stores?

Last year, the PLCB earned $1.7 billion in revenue, which covered its $1.2 billion in expenses, including inefficiencies. For instance, all wine delivered to the state of Pennsylvania must be transported to three factory locations: Philadelphia, Pittsburgh, and Scranton. Therefore, if alcohol is being imported from a neighboring state far away from one of these locations, it must first travel to a warehouse before it is shipped back toward a Pennsylvania region located near the original supplier. Many unprofitable stores remain open as well. "In some cases, these stores have connections to, or sit within the district of, influential state politicians."[70]

CONCLUSION

The Wine & Spirits stores system is mired in controversy. The liquor stores are based on the liquor code enacted by Governor Pinchot after the repeal of Prohibition. The original intent of the liquor code was "to prohibit forever the open saloon."

Pennsylvania citizens near bordering states leave the commonwealth to purchase alcohol in other states at lower prices and with a wider selection. As a result, Pennsylvania loses money from the markup on its goods and the alcohol tax that it would gain by keeping those sales in Pennsylvania. This tax money would be recovered if there were no incentive for citizens to leave the state. Therefore, a private system, with lower prices without the markup, would provide incentive to stay in Pennsylvania for alcohol purchases. According to Squires, "The reality is that if you live somewhere near New York, New Jersey, or Delaware, you have many better choices."[71]

Yet, the system remains in place. The legislature faces the question of whether the inefficiencies and higher prices associated with the system are worth better control of underage drinking, drunk driving, and intoxication, or whether privatizing the system is the better way to go.

NOTES

1. David A. Schell, "Keeping Control: Gifford Pinchot and the Establishment of the Pennsylvania Liquor Control Board," PhD dissertation, Temple University, Pennsylvania, 2006. Retrieved February 13, 2008, from ProQuest Digital Dissertations database. (Publication No. AAT 3211904).
2. Schell, "Keeping Control."
3. Schell, "Keeping Control."
4. Schell, "Keeping Control."
5. Schell, "Keeping Control."
6. Schell, "Keeping Control."
7. Schell, "Keeping Control."
8. Schell, "Keeping Control."
9. Schell, "Keeping Control."
10. Schell, "Keeping Control."
11. Schell, "Keeping Control."
12. Schell, "Keeping Control."
13. Schell, "Keeping Control."
14. Schell, "Keeping Control."
15. Schell, "Keeping Control."
16. Schell, "Keeping Control."
17. Schell, "Keeping Control."
18. Schell, "Keeping Control."
19. Schell, "Keeping Control."
20. Schell, "Keeping Control."
21. Schell, "Keeping Control."
22. Commonwealth Competition Council, "Pennsylvania's Plan to Privatize State Stores," *Competition Watch* 2 (June 1997).
23. Commonwealth Competition Council, "Pennsylvania's Plan to Privatize State Stores."
24. Commonwealth Competition Council, "Pennsylvania's Plan to Privatize State Stores."
25. Commonwealth Competition Council, "Pennsylvania's Plan to Privatize State Stores."
26. Schell, "Keeping Control."
27. Schell, "Keeping Control."
28. Rebecca Rees, "Privatization of Liquor Stores: No Public Safety Threat," *Pittsburgh Business Times* (September 5, 1997).

29. "Hung Over Again: Pennsylvania's Liquor Anachronism Survives a Challenge," *Pittsburgh Business Times* (September 26, 1997).

30. Schell, "Keeping Control."

31. Michael Demenchuk, "Pennsylvania Capital Projects May Suffer Because of Liquor Bill," *Bond Buyer* 321 (August 11, 1997): 3.

32. UE News, "District 6 Opposes State Store Sell Off," http://www.ranknfile-ue.org/uen_0897_d6.htm (accessed June 25, 2009).

33. UE News, "District 6 Opposes State Store Sell Off."

34. Schell, "Keeping Control."

35. "Hung Over Again."

36. Laura Mansnerus, "Buying Power: Joining Pennsylvania Drinkers in Interstate Bargain Hunt," *The New York Times* (February 8, 1998), sec. 14NJ, 6.

37. Mansnerus, "Buying Power."

38. Mansnerus, "Buying Power."

39. Mark Hoffman, "Pennsylvania Liquor Stores Get More Competitive" (July 14, 2003), http://www.stateline.org/live/ViewPage.action?siteNodeId=136& languageId=1& contentId=15316 (accessed March 12, 2008).

40. Sophia Pearson, "Pennsylvania's Prohibition-Era Monopoly on Wine Sales to End" (November 11, 2005), http://www.bloomberg.com/apps/news?pid=10000103& sid=aSADeilKbzkI& refer=us (accessed March 12, 2008).

41. Mark Scolforo, "Former State Senator Hired to Head Pa. Liquor Board," *The Pittsburgh Post-Gazette* (December 13, 2006).

42. Scolforo, "Former State Senator Hired."

43. Craig LaBan, "Not All Are Toasting Changes Uncorked by LCB," *Philadelphia Inquirer* (February 3, 2008).

44. Bill Toland, "Spirits of Privatization Are Likely to Stay Bottled Up," *The Pittsburgh Post-Gazette* (February 16, 2007).

45. Steve Twedt, "Is Time Right to Sell State Stores?" *The Pittsburgh Post-Gazette* (June 12, 2007).

46. Marcia Moore, "LCB Seeks Renovations; Foes Seek Privatization," *The Daily Item* (December 15, 2007).

47. Steve Twedt, "Bill Would Privatize State Retail Liquor Sales," *The Pittsburgh Post-Gazette* (June 5, 2008).

48. Robert Wonderling, "Senator Wonderling Introduces Legislation to Privatize Wine and Spirits Stores," news release (February 7, 2008), http://www.senatorwonderling.com/newsreleases/default.asp?NewsReleaseID=1696& SubjectID= (accessed March 12, 2008).

49. Twedt, "Bill Would Privatize State Retail Liquor Sales."

50. Reggie Sheffield, "Pennsylvania Liquor Reform Bill Likely to Face Stiff Opposition," *Patriot-News*, Harrisburg (February 21, 2008).

51. Sheffield, "Pennsylvania Liquor Reform Bill Likely to Face Stiff Opposition."

52. Brad Bumsted, "Lawmaker Adds Incentives for State Store Selloff," *The Pittsburgh Tribune-Review* (February 25, 2008).

53. Steve Twedt, "Legislators Plan Hearings on Privatizing Liquor Stores," *The Pittsburgh Post-Gazette* (February 20, 2008).

54. Mandy Hofmockel, "Bill Could Privatize Liquor Sale," *The Daily Collegian* (February 8, 2008).

55. Editorial, "Wonderling Bill Is a Reasonable Plan to Get State out of Retail Business," *The Morning Call* (February 8, 2008).

56. Editorial, "State of Antiquity," *The Pittsburgh Post-Gazette* (February 6, 2008).

57. Editorial, "Don't Sell the State Stores; Pennsylvania's Liquor Distribution System Is Efficient and Effective; Leave It Alone," *The Pittsburgh Post-Gazette* (February 13, 2008).

58. Frank Gamrat and Jake Haulk, "Selling Pennsylvania's Liquor Stores," *The Allegheny Institute for Public Policy* 7 (April 19, 2007).

59. Gamrat and Haulk, "Selling Pennsylvania's Liquor Stores."

60. Gamrat and Haulk, "Selling Pennsylvania's Liquor Stores."

61. Gamrat and Haulk, "Selling Pennsylvania's Liquor Stores."

62. Gamrat and Haulk, "Selling Pennsylvania's Liquor Stores."

63. Robert Wonderling, "Privatize Pennsylvania's Wine and Spirits Stores," The Commonwealth Foundation for Public Policy Alternatives (April 25, 2007).

64. Wonderling, "Privatize Pennsylvania's Wine and Spirits Stores."

65. Geoffrey Segal, "Liberate the Liquor Business; What's Not to Like about the Privatization of State ABC Stores?" The Reason Foundation (April 30, 2007).

66. Segal, "Liberate the Liquor Business."

67. Steve Twedt, "Pa.'s Liquor Control System Lets State Keep a Tight Grip on the Bottle," *The Pittsburgh Post-Gazette* (January 27, 2008).

68. Twedt, "Pa.'s Liquor Control System."

69. Twedt, "Pa.'s Liquor Control System."

70. Twedt, "Pa.'s Liquor Control System."

71. Twedt, "Pa.'s Liquor Control System."

OTHER USEFUL WEB SITES

Buck, Andrew J., and Simon Hakim. "Privatization of Alcohol Beverage Distribution in Pennsylvania." http://isc.temple.edu/economics/wkpapers/alcohol/COMMON.html (accessed April 28, 2008).

Federal Tax Administrators. "State Liquor Excise Taxes." 2008. http://www.taxadmin.org/fta/rate/liquor.html.

Substance Abuse and Mental Health Services. "2005–2006 National Surveys on Drug Use and Health." http://www.oas.samhsa.gov/2k6State/AppB.htm#TabB-12.

Twedt, Steve. "State Store in Near Empty Mall Is No.1." *The Pittsburgh Post-Gazette* (January 28, 2008).

Chapter 8

State-Controlled Liquor Stores II: New Hampshire

New Hampshire motor vehicles' license plates display the state motto "Live Free or Die." This motto is evident throughout the state, exemplified by such freedoms as its lack of gun regulations and its nonexistent sales and income tax. Economically, this motto implies a favorable view of free-market competition.[1] Yet in 2007, the New Hampshire State Liquor Commission (SLC), a state-run monopoly, contributed $106 million to the state of New Hampshire.[2] How can New Hampshire swear by its famed motto with an entity of its government directly contradicting it?

This chapter will examine the background and economic impact of the SLC, along with analyzing attempts to privatize the system. It begins with the history of the SLC since Prohibition. Next, it investigates several proposals of privatization bills, submitted for various reasons: newfound budget deficits, ideology, and boosting revenues. The chapter then analyzes proposals to change the distributional system, spurred by entrepreneurial efforts and the increasing popularity of wine. From there, the chapter examines the consequences of privatization for several of the players: consumers, unions, and society. Finally, the financial and economic perspectives are considered.

BACKGROUND OF THE SLC

When the 18th Amendment passed the National Prohibition Act on January 16, 1920, many expected a decrease in American alcohol consumption. President Hoover's "great social and economic experiment" failed, however, as consumption levels certainly did not decrease. Moonshiners distilled alcohol, rum-runners imported it, and bootleggers sold it. Gangsters across the United States took over the alcohol industry, and the government lost substantial tax dollars. A mere 13 years later, the 21st Amendment voided the 18th, ending Prohibition in December 1933.[3]

With the regulation of alcohol returned to state control, New Hampshire instated the SLC under the New Hampshire Laws of 1933 to manage the "manufacture, possession, sale, consumption, importation, use, storage, transportation, and delivery of wine, spirits, and malt or brewed beverages."[4] Governor John Winant, a prohibitionist, spearheaded the push for monopoly control. By allowing New Hampshire to be a "wet" state, Gov. Winant intended to use proceeds from liquor sales to reduce the state's debt.[5] New Hampshire became an "alcoholic beverage control state," like the example of Pennsylvania in the last chapter. As a result, it not only regulated the wholesale of alcohol to retail liquor stores, but also operated these retail stores.[6] By the 1960s, liquor contributed more revenue to New Hampshire's operating budget than any other item.[7]

The SLC is headed by three commissioners, each serving six-year terms and appointed by the governor. To keep agendas at bay, no more than two of the three may belong to the same political party. The Laws of 1996 separated the SLC into the Bureau of Enforcement, Licensing, and Education; the Bureau of Marketing and Sales; and the Bureau of Administrative Services. Having autonomous agencies with different goals allows the SLC to properly balance its three main objectives: maintaining proper controls and regulations, generating revenues, and providing efficient means for consumers to purchase alcohol.[8]

The SLC generates revenue in multiple ways. First, it sells spirits, wines, and any other beverage with an alcohol content greater than 6 percent in state-operated "Liquor and Wine Outlets." There were 77 of these superstores operating in 2007, all with set prices and generating revenues of $443.7 million at fiscal year end. With this monopoly control, the SLC also has access to "bailment revenues," fees that vendors must pay in exchange for storing their alcohol in state-owned inventory warehouses. This source generated $1.1 million in revenues for fiscal year 2007. Other sources of revenue derive from a beer tax equivalent to $.30 per gallon sold, licensing fees, and the joint venture between SLC and the NH Lottery Commission for selling sweepstakes. All of these accumulate in the Liquor Fund, which is transferred daily into the state's General Fund. The net contribution of transfers for fiscal year 2007 equaled $106 million.[9]

1991 BUDGET DEFICITS

With the state budget exceeding $2 billion for 1990 and 1991, Gov. Judd Gregg began considering several methods to raise much-needed funds. Discussion circulated regarding privatizing several agencies. Allowing a private hospital to take over portions of the Department of Mental Health or turning over a state park to a local community would raise an immediate windfall for the state to fund its overall operations. With the SLC closing eight stores due to lower profit margins, privatizing its operations began to be considered as well.[10]

An idea proposed by Rep. Edward Densmore consisted of issuing revenue bonds to receive an immediate $25 million boost and then using the revenues generated from the sale of liquor stores to repay the issuance. Furthermore, Densmore claimed, "The state can equal, if not better, our revenues without softening border sales, by putting a straight tax on booze and getting out of the business." SLC chair Joseph Acorace swiftly rebutted, explaining that New Hampshire would "lose the identity" it has in the liquor industry. Competitive stores could raise prices, and New Hampshire would lose its out-of-state customers, who generated the majority of SLC total revenues.[11]

Later that year, Rep. Thomas Christie entered an official bill to the New Hampshire General Court to end the SLC's monopoly on retail liquor stores. It stated, "This bill privatizes the sale of liquor in New Hampshire on June 30, 1992. The liquor stores and warehouses shall be closed and the inventory and buildings and leases sold by the department of administrative services. All employees in the liquor purchase, sale, and promotional aspects of the commission shall be terminated as of June 30, 1992."[12] The SLC would still exist if the bill passed, but only to regulate the licensing of vendors and enforce the laws. To maintain revenues, New Hampshire would institute a liquor tax on a per-gallon purchase basis, in the same manner as the state taxed beer.[13]

When this proposal was ruled "inexpedient to legislate" by the Regulated Revenues Committee, Rep. Janet Pelley submitted a less extreme bill. With her plan, the state would sell some of its less profitable Liquor and Wine Outlets and convert them to private retail stores. Former SLC chair Jean Wallin supported this bill, pointing out that in recent years, the SLC net profits had not increased nearly as much as gross sales had, implying increased costs. She also noted that the much-bragged-about profit contribution to the state was distorted because it included license fees, liquor sales to licensees, and wine revenues from grocery and convenience stores, all of which could continue under a privatization plan.[14]

A hearing for the privatization discussion was held on September 25, 1991, before the Regulated Revenues Committee with testimony from Acorace to defend the accusations that the SLC was facing a steady decline in profits. Maintaining state control, he argued, allowed for the most effective combination of maximum revenue and regulation.[15]

First, in terms of sales, the SLC developed a strategy of "maximizing total net revenue by maximizing the number of units sold." The SLC's Liquor and Wine Outlets service the residents of New Hampshire, but 60 percent of their sales are to out-of-state customers. Residents of Massachusetts, Vermont, Maine, and Canada purchase their liquor from the SLC largely because its monopoly status generates lower costs of goods, and thus a lower sales price. Since it manages all of its retail outlets, the SLC can purchase immense quantities of alcohol from suppliers at a lower price. Additionally, the SLC bypasses a layer of middlemen because it serves as the wholesaler, supplying to its own retail stores. With separate entities maintaining these, the wholesaler would have to charge a premium, but since the SLC controls both, no extra layer is necessary. New Hampshire can therefore charge a lower price on a standard bottle than other states, but make the same profit margin. In fact, the SLC generated a profit margin of 21.08 percent in fiscal 1991. To put this in perspective, Acorace compared this level to that of *Business Week*'s top 1,000 companies in market value, noting that only 6 of the top 150 companies achieved a greater percentage profit margin.[16]

How would this change under a privatized system? Acorace feared losing cross-border sales because of the inevitable price increase. The economies of scale would end, with stores competing against each other rather than cooperating with each other. The SLC would either need to charge a premium as wholesaler to retail stores or, using the example of regulating 600 stores, "charge a ridiculous license fee of $41,000 to remain revenue neutral." Losing these sales could lead to negative economic externalities, such as the loss of sweepstakes sales and the need for sales and income taxes to support state budgets, thus only exacerbating the current deficits.[17]

Delving into the SLC's other function, Acorace claimed that privatization would make regulating both more difficult and more expensive. The SLC would lose its control on the retail end, and the liquor sales industry would transition into a profit-maximizing market. With societal costs taking a backseat to revenue generation, incentives to sell to minors and the inebriated would increase. More stores would also spread enforcement forces thin, so to maintain the same level of safety, enforcement would have to increase its costs. This does not even consider the far-reaching future consequences, with damages to New Hampshire ranging from increased DUIs to welfare costs.[18]

Acorace's rationales were convincing enough that debates favoring liquor privatization to reduce expenditures and eliminate the budget deficits were halted. The SLC continued forward with no change in its monopoly control, as the state realized that any attempt at privatization could destroy the entire system.[19]

A GOVERNOR'S DUTY AND POLITICAL CORRUPTIONS REVEALED

In 1993, Stephen Merrill was elected governor of New Hampshire. When asked of the possibility of privatizing some industries, Gov. Merrill responded, "If we haven't discussed the possibility of privatization, if we haven't looked into how much money we can save and can the job be done better, we will have failed the citizens of our state."[20] With this mindset, Gov. Merrill nominated Miriam Luce, his Libertarian opponent, to be a commissioner of the SLC, asking her to entertain the notion of privatization. This was an issue she championed in her campaign, labeling the state government a "vice lord," as the SLC had the conflict in interest of both approving liquor licenses and encouraging sales.[21]

Luce's appointment to the SLC severely lessened much of the political influence that the SLC historically wielded. Its influence began in the 1960s under commissioners William Loeb, Constas Tentas, and Nathan Battles. Loeb was publisher of *The Union Leader* newspaper and regularly criticized sales and income tax on his front-page editorials. Liquor revenues were crucial in preventing the state from enacting these taxes. Battles was a senator, turned SLC commissioner, turned liquor broker—a position that made him extremely wealthy.[22] Tentas continued the SLC's "impenetrable power structure," serving for 28 years on the commission. He was even labeled a man "with more staying power than any elected state official in our history" by Gov. Hugh Gallen.[23]

The system that these commissioners created developed the SLC into the $100 million industry it became, but not without corruption. Liquor brokers negotiated with liquor distillers to purchase products for the SLC. The commissioners took advantage of this, creating large business opportunities for brokers by recommending their names to the distillers. They also prominently displayed these brokers' brands in the Liquor and Wine Outlets. In exchange, the brokers were expected to contribute to political campaigns in the interests of the SLC. When it became illegal in

1991 to manipulate their selection, "brokers . . . began giving commissioners holiday gifts or picking up the tab for vacations," to stay unnoticed. Charges were never filed and investigations always failed, as brokers would never testify.[24] Additionally, with the SLC generating such successful revenues, it was assumed it was operating well, and no questions were ever asked.[25]

On August 3, 1991, Richard Colbath, New Hampshire's top liquor broker, was arrested for driving under the influence. Richard Boisvert, a commissioner at the time, called the arresting officer, asking "Is there something you can do for him?" The DUI was replaced with a speeding violation, proving that special treatment due to the relationships of commissioners and liquor brokers had never ended.[26] A few weeks later, Boisvert resigned from the SLC and Colbath's charges returned to driving under the influence. Further investigation revealed that Acorace, then chair, had met earlier that evening with Colbath along with Richard McEvoy of Carillon Importers.[27]

With Luce replacing Boisvert, liquor privatization seemed like a strong possibility, especially with the follies of the SLC becoming publicized. Her plan consisted of leasing the SLC's highway superstores, which accounted for 50 percent of all sales, and selling the rest of its assets. Furthermore, the SLC could tax the new noncontrolled retail stores. Overall, this would lead to a liquidation amount of approximately $500 million, along with annual lease and tax revenues. By placing this money in a "trust fund" and investing it "conservatively," Luce believed that the SLC could remain revenue-neutral. After she sent these ideas in a proposal to Gov. Merrill, he responded, "I am unpersuaded." Unsurprisingly, Luce asked not to be considered for another term after this unsuccessful attempt.[28]

ADDITIONAL UNSUCCESSFUL SUBMISSIONS OF PRIVATIZATION BILLS

In 1994, Reps. Hall, Gorman, and Riley submitted a bill to the Regulated Revenues Committee proposing to privatize the retail aspect of the SLC. Their plan suggested the creation of "market zones" across the state based on "economic, transportation, and demographic factors." Additionally, each market zone would be appointed a "Class A" or "Class B" zone. Class A zones would have one licensed franchise that could open a specific number of stores as decided by the SLC. Class B zones would have multiple licensees, but each licensee would be permitted to operate only one store. Also, one person would not be allowed to control more than 10 percent of licenses or operate stores in adjacent market zones.[29]

To generate revenue, the proposal called for bidding on these licenses. After due diligence checks on potential candidates, a bid would be submitted for a particular class of license in a zone. This bid would entail (1) a yearly payment to the SLC, and (2) a monthly percentage of sales due to the SLC. Additionally, the SLC could deny a license in a market zone if the highest bid would generate less revenue for the state than an SLC-run Liquor and Wine Outlet. In this instance, the SLC would retain control of its retail operation for that zone. If the SLC granted a bid, the license would be eligible for six years, and at the conclusion, the process would begin again.[30]

The SLC would still maintain significant control over liquor in New Hampshire. As stated above, it would determine who would operate retail stores. Furthermore, these retail stores would still be required to purchase liquor from the SLC's wholesale operation, so the SLC would also continue to determine the quantity and type of alcohol that each store sold. Finally, it would enforce advertising standards and issue civil penalties to violators, brandishing the power to revoke licenses. Even with these checks in places and a seeming guarantee of revenue neutrality, the proposal was ruled inexpedient to legislate.[31]

Rep. George Rubin introduced another liquor privatization bill in 1999. Budgetary concerns once again plagued New Hampshire; a 1997 decision known as *Claremont II* demanded that the state must sufficiently fund public education through a "proportional and reasonable" tax system. Wealthier communities could achieve this through property taxes, but in poorer communities, this was not feasible. Gov. Jeanne Shaheen estimated a desired need of $57 million, even after increasing the cigarette tax an additional $.23. One plan that was under consideration was the installation of video gambling machines. With negative externalities such as increased crime and social disintegration, this was not a popular solution.[32]

Rubin proposed to privatize the SLC and sell all of its assets, including its inventory and real estate. This would immediately solve the newly created budget deficit. Additionally, the SLC would impose a liquor tax of $.60 for every gallon of liquor sold, similar to the preexisting $.30 beer tax. In this way, New Hampshire could "tax the store and tax the sale." He also gave the SLC the responsibility during the transition period of constructing additional measures to obtain revenues based on sales. As with previous plans, the SLC would still exist, but it would serve to license and enforce, rather than sell.[33]

Upon analysis of the proposal and using previous financial numbers, the SLC determined that the New Hampshire General Fund would decrease by $72,333,697. Factoring in the new liquor fee (8,561,357 gallons × $.60) and reduction of operating expenses ($16,000,000), the net loss per year would still be $51,196,883. To remain revenue-neutral, the SLC would have to charge an absurd license fee. Furthermore, these numbers did not consider the potential increase in enforcement and regulation costs from the necessary increase in retail stores. Also, this assumed that sales would stay true to their trend. Testimony from SLC chair John Byrne alerted the Executive Departments and Administration Committee that privatization would lower sales because the price would necessarily increase due to the decrease in volume purchasing. Adding on the liquor tax, New Hampshire would run the risk of losing its competitive advantage in the New England liquor market. With 60 percent of sales from out-of-state residents, contributions to the General Fund would decrease drastically.[34]

As information from the 1991 hearing was also used, Acorace's previous arguments further stabilized Byrne's. This bill was also ruled "inexpedient to legislate," with the Executive Departments and Administration Committee citing, "To tinker with the system would be disruptive to the budget." Attempts to privatize, once again, had been stifled.[35]

THE WINE EXPERIENCE AND DISTRIBUTION CHANGES

The previously illustrated brokerage system cemented New Hampshire's control on alcohol. The SLC could choose its products through the liquor brokers and would supply its outlet stores accordingly. The increasing demand for wine led to alterations in this system, however.

In 1989, the SLC changed its regulations to allow approved wine and liquor importers to directly deliver to retail outlets instead of going through SLC-owned warehouses. This occurred after the success of a trial program with specialty wine importer Atlantic Trade Group. Though bypassing the warehouses, the SLC would still regulate importers with audits and credit checks, and by requiring approval for all orders. This new process increased efficiency for the importers by cutting costs, and it increased selection for consumers.[36] Liquor brokers feared this would end the SLC's monopoly control on distribution, but Atlantic Trade Group proved to be the only exception to the warehousing system, for the time being.[37]

In September 1998, New Hampshire instituted a new direct shipping policy whereby consumers would be able to have their choice of wines and spirits shipped to them from other states. This required out-of-state suppliers to obtain a license from the SLC.[38] Additionally, the SLC required shippers to use a licensed carrier, clearly marking the parcel as containing alcohol. This guaranteed that they paid taxes, allowing the SLC to generate revenue.[39] The SLC tracks these orders, and as popularity levels of specific types achieve a certain standard, it begins to stock them in the Liquor and Wine Outlets. To further stimulate this increasing demand for wine, the SLC introduced numerous programs for further education. One example is its "Wine & Food," a free newsletter to New Hampshire residents that provides basic distinctions between types of wine and pairs different wines with corresponding meals. Also, the SLC hosts wine-tasting events for consumers to experiment with unique flavors, offering tips throughout the free sessions.[40] Currently, 35 states allow direct shipment, along with 12 of 18 control states.[41]

With greater options and less reliance on the SLC for wine products, the wine market in New Hampshire has shifted away from the monopoly format toward a more competitive market in both distribution and retail.

CONSUMERS' OPINION

Unlike most monopolies, the SLC is able to maintain lower prices on liquor than a competitive market would. This is due to its immense Liquor and Wine Outlets, allowing it to achieve economies of scale by ordering from suppliers in bulk. Additionally, since it operates as both the wholesaler and retailer, with no middleman, it does not need to charge a premium. Finally, the SLC does not place a tax on liquor, as it believes that a tax increasing the price of liquor would lead to the loss of the prized out-of-state consumers.

Consumers from all over New England and even Canada take advantage of these low prices and therefore do not favor privatization movements.[42] The monopoly also offers an incredible selection of 6,000 brands at its 77 superstores. Not only is this considerably more than a retail store is capable of holding, but the SLC tracks orders in the aggregate and supplies information on its Web site about what type and in what quantity each store holds. This allows for extreme convenience to the consumer and puts the most popular products on the shelves throughout the state.[43] The SLC's Store No. 38, located at the Portsmouth traffic circle, has been called "the largest retail volume outlet for wine and liquor in the world." It is strategically positioned at the junction of Interstate 95 and Routes 4 and 16, so that tourists must come through here going north to Maine. A randomly selected afternoon in May yielded consumers from more than a dozen states and Canada, reinforcing Acorace's estimate, at the time, that 85 percent of Store No. 38's customers were from out of state.[44] Privatization would end the SLC's price advantage, displacing both New Hampshire citizens and out-of-state customers. Maine and Vermont, both control states, experimented with the concept of an agency store by allowing the opening of a few private retail stores. These stores engulfed the preexisting state stores, destroying their previous systems and price structure. As a result, residents of Maine and Vermont flocked to New Hampshire to buy liquor.[45]

So for the consumer, are there any benefits to privatizing the system? In October 1990, Acorace, then chairman, tasted New Hampshire Winery's Lakes Region white and red wine, and professed them to be "garbage" and tasting "like vinegar." As a result, he pulled them from the shelves of all Liquor and Wine Outlets.[46] Should one man's opinion determine if a type of wine is to be stocked in every liquor store in New Hampshire? No matter how putrid this wine may have tasted, under a privatized system, it would probably still be available somewhere. To not be able to even experiment with it is a detriment to the consumer. Another such example occurred in 1995 under SLC chairman John Byrne when he removed all 190-proof grain alcohol from the retail shelves, remarking, "It can be kept in a back room for those who have a legitimate need for it."[47] Finally, under the current system, it is extremely difficult to enter the liquor market because of the impenetrable barriers to entry. A private system would allow for equity in that sense.

UNION OPPOSITION

In fiscal year 2006, the SLC employed 297 full-time and approximately 400 part-time employees.[48] Official privatization bills call for "all employees in the liquor purchase, sales, and promotion aspect of the commission" to be terminated.[49] Why is this? Employees of the SLC are represented by the State Employees Association, a union that demands higher wages. In turn, this leads to a higher cost to the SLC of delivering its product, as a competitive retail market surely would drop a sales clerk to close to minimum wage. Sen. Gordon Humphrey remarked, "You'd have better employees in the private sector," defining "better" as those who "work for less and for longer hours," because their employment is dependent on the profitability of the store.[50]

The State Employees Association does not support a privatization of the New Hampshire liquor market; those they represent in the retail aspect of the industry would lose their jobs. Additionally, they would lose all the benefits that accrue from being part of the SLC. Select employees are trained in management by the University of New Hampshire's Whittemore

School of Business. With this training, the commissioners allow employees greater decision-making responsibility, even allowing store managers to construct internal budgets.[51] These skill sets are invaluable, educating liquor managers for future employment. SLC full-time employees are also eligible for retirement pensions and postemployment health care benefits.[52] As Denis Parker, former executive director of the State Employees Association, queried, "What's wrong with workers getting a fair wage and decent benefits?"[53]

THE SOCIETAL CONSEQUENCES OF THE SLC

As a control state, New Hampshire balances making a profit against protecting its citizens from the dangers associated with alcohol consumption. The primary fear with privatization is that transitioning to competitive retail stores would lead to a hardened quest solely for profits. The market would become set against the protectors, the SLC, rather than working concurrently for an appropriate equilibrium. Acorace also highlighted the fact that, with privatization, the sheer quantity of stores would multiply, and available hours would increase. The SLC's Enforcement Division at its current budget would not be able to regulate the industry as effectively, so "sales to minors, sales to intoxicateds, and the hazards of pilferage" would rise. Furthermore, studies from the National Alcohol Beverage Control Association show that annual consumption of liquor is 16 percent less in control than in license states, whereas the difference in beer consumption, not strictly controlled in either type, is negligible.[54]

This is a double-edged sword, though, because there is a conflict of interest with a government entity profiting from alcohol. Higher sales lead to more money in the General Fund. If the budget needs a quick boost in a certain year, why not ease up on regulating a bit, and increase store hours? Or increase advertising? A large amount of trust is placed in the hands of the three commissioners to balance this vital responsibility. The case of Maine exemplifies this problem. Upon losing sales to New Hampshire's lower prices, Maine's liquor commission dropped prices in an attempt to generate revenue. At the same time, Maine's "alcohol abuse" was leading to the price tag of "$1 billion and 400 lives annually."[55] How does the state decide which issue is more pressing? Furthermore, New Hampshire "pioneered the building of supermarket-style state liquor stores" and as of 1993 was the only state that constructed stores on highways.[56] Commissioner Luce referred to them as the "crown jewels of our revenue stream," as these highway stores accounted for approximately 50 percent of all sales.[57]

Although in most cases, the consumer probably does not open the bottle in the parking lot and drive home, this placement can send the wrong message.

FINANCIAL PROCEEDS

Under the monopoly system, the SLC generates revenues from the following: liquor sales, bailment costs, licensing, and the beer tax. Fiscal year 2007 had revenues of $443.7 million.[58] All profits are transferred to New Hampshire's General Fund and serve to support the state's budget. With a system that has been in place since the end of Prohibition, these contributions have stability and have become necessary to New Hampshire.

How would privatization change this cash flow? No longer would the bulk of the SLC's revenues be from the profit margin between the selling price of liquor and its cost of goods sold. Essentially, all aforementioned plans called for a tax to be instated upon liquor similar to the $.30 per gallon beer tax, along with additional, unique ways to make up this revenue. These ranged from increasing retail license fees, to selling revenue bonds and investing the proceeds, to being allocated a percentage of monthly sales. Nearly all of the changes in the proposal claimed to be revenue-neutral, but none were accepted.

One reason why the changes were rejected is that a majority of the SLC's sales come from out-of-state residents, as the SLC is able to offer an incredible selection at convenient locations. Additionally, its prices are among the lowest in the country, for the most part, undercutting adjacent states. It can do this because there is no liquor tax, there is no middleman premium because the SLC acts as wholesaler and retailer, it achieves economies of scale by ordering from suppliers in vast quantities, and it profits by holding suppliers' inventories.[59] Eight of the top 10 stores in terms of gross sales are on the borders of New Hampshire (see Table 8.1). The remaining two, the Hooksett stores, are right on Interstate 93, a high-traffic area for both commuters and tourists.

Privatizing runs the risk of jeopardizing this way of generating revenue.[60] In addition, lottery sweepstake tickets, sold at Liquor and Wine Outlets, could no longer be fully contributed to the fund.[61] Retail stores could either choose to not sell them or demand a portion of the revenues from the sales. This is certainly a large risk to take, as these annual revenues are a large reason why New Hampshire is the only state that has never had a sales or income tax.[62] Both supporters and opponents of privatization

Table 8.1   Top 10 Store Locations, by Gross Sales

	Location	Annual Gross Sales (millions of dollars)
1	Hampton-North	25.3
2	Hampton-South	22.8
3	Portsmouth Traffic Circle	20.3
4	Salem	17.4
5	Hooksett-North	14.7
6	Nashua-Coliseum Avenue	12.7
7	Nashua-DW Highway	11.9
8	Hooksett-South	11.6
9	West Lebanon	9.7
10	Keene	8.6
	Total:	**154.9**

Source: SLC 2007 Annual Report.

concur that as soon as the industry is privatized, it would be extremely difficult if not impossible to immediately reverse it.[63] One could also look to the aforementioned example of Maine and Vermont, which experimented with a few private stores and ended up losing some monopoly control on their distribution.[64] Thus, in addition to the potential loss of sales to out-of-state residents, New Hampshire could lose sales from its own residents, who may choose to shop in other states if prices are competitive.

ECONOMIC IMPLICATIONS OF THE SLC

Theoretically, privatizing a monopoly allows competition to drive down the price of a product. Since the liquor market would no longer be controlled by the state, nonunion workers could be hired and paid a lower wage. The market would set the price of alcohol, and firms would compete, driving down the price. But as examined before, the SLC is unique in that prices probably would not be lowered because a privatization would increase the cost of the good on the market, thus offsetting the benefits of competition on pricing. Though the privatization proposals suggested revenue-neutrality, this is not guaranteed, as it is impossible to determine exactly how much the price would increase, and this would affect both in-state and out-of-state consumers.

CONCLUSION

Though revenue has been the primary concern in most privatization attempts, one must also consider the many negative externalities of a privatization. No longer having economies of scale due to shelf space and the cost of inventory, the selection in retail stores would become more homogenous. As Tentas related, "Agency stores are only going to carry those items which are nationally known and the best of sellers," compared to the "20 different codes of blended whiskies" Liquor and Wine Outlets are known to carry.[65] Also, with more stores to regulate that are maximizing profit as their only goal, sales to minors and those already intoxicated will increase. Along with this, some allege that there will be an increase in driving under the influence. If this is the case, the state will have to choose between the dilemma of hiring more regulators or dealing with the inevitable societal consequences.

Though the state will be released from its obligations to sell alcohol, allowing competition to drive the market and fulfilling its motto, the potentially detrimental consequences seem to outweigh the benefits. New Hampshire is dependent on alcohol revenues, and it runs the risk of losing them with privatization attempts. It could lose its valuable competitive advantage of being able to offer lower prices, casting away its out-of-state consumers and potentially even consumers who live in New Hampshire. Finally, society would have to pick up the costs, be it through taxes, a lower standard of living, or even lives lost. In conclusion, it appears that the SLC should not be privatized, unlike its Pennsylvania cousin. So the question remains: Why is privatization preferable in one state and not in another state?

NOTES

1. Jack Kenny, "Lawmakers to Take Long Look at Privatizing Liquor Sales," *New Hampshire Business Review* (May 3, 1991).

2. New Hampshire State Liquor Commission, "Annual Report and Statistical Section, Fiscal Year June 30, 2007," http://www.nh.gov/liquor/2007annualreport.pdf.

3. James M. Goldberg, "The American Experience with Alcohol," National Alcohol Beverage Control Association, http://liq.wa.gov/3ttf-site/NABCA.pdf (accessed June 4, 2008).

4. New Hampshire State Liquor Commission, "Annual Report and Statistical Section, Fiscal Year June 30, 2007."

5. John Milne, "N.H. Liquor Stores: Lifeline or Liability? After Years of Controversy, Another Debate on Privatization Looms," *The Boston Globe* (September 1, 1993).

6. New Hampshire State Liquor Commission, "Liquor Commission," http:// www.nh.gov/liquor/.

7. Milne, "N.H. Liquor Stores: Lifeline or Liability?"

8. New Hampshire State Liquor Commission, "Annual Report and Statistical Section, Fiscal Year June 30, 2007."

9. New Hampshire State Liquor Commission, "Annual Report and Statistical Section, Fiscal Year June 30, 2007."

10. John Milne, "Move to Go Private a Hot Issue," *The Boston Globe* (December 16, 1990).

11. Milne, "Move to Go Private a Hot Issue."

12. Thomas Christie, "HB 370," Regulated Revenues Committee (1991).

13. Kenny, "Lawmakers to Take Long Look at Privatizing Liquor Sales."

14. Kenny, "Lawmakers to Take Long Look at Privatizing Liquor Sales."

15. Regulated Revenues Committee, "Hearing on HB 747—Privatization" (September 25, 1991).

16. Regulated Revenues Committee, "Hearing on HB 747—Privatization" (September 25, 1991).

17. Regulated Revenues Committee, "Hearing on HB 747—Privatization" (September 25, 1991).

18. Regulated Revenues Committee, "Hearing on HB 747—Privatization" (September 25, 1991).

19. Regulated Revenues Committee, "Hearing on HB 747—Privatization" (September 25, 1991).

20. John Milne, "Merrill on Taxes, Politics, Liquor, Education," *The Boston Globe* (January 3, 1993).

21. John Milne, "N.H. Governor Tells Pick for Liquor Panel to Eye Privatization," *The Boston Globe* (August 26, 1993).

22. Milne, "N.H. Liquor Stores: Lifeline or Liability?"

23. Lisa Prevost, "Liquor Chief Tentas Reflects as His 28-Year Era Ends," *New Hampshire Business Review* (June 16, 1989).

24. Milne, "N.H. Liquor Stores: Lifeline or Liability?"

25. Milne, "Merrill on Taxes, Politics, Liquor, Education."

26. John Milne, "Nominee to Liquor Panel Knows Ropes: Luce Points to Experience in Paper Business, Politics," *The Boston Globe* (August 29, 1993).

27. Milne, "N.H. Governor Tells Pick for Liquor Panel to Eye Privatization."

28. "Mass Competition Closing in on N.H. Liquor Stores," *New Hampshire Business Review* (July 30, 1999).

29. Hall, Gorman, and Riley, "HB 1547," Regulated Revenues Committee (1994).

30. Hall, Gorman, and Riley, "HB 1547."

31. Hall, Gorman, and Riley, "HB 1547."

32. Jack Kenny, "Will Video Gambling at Tracks Be Funding Schools?" *New Hampshire Business Review* (March 13, 1998).

33. George Rubin, "House Bill 348-FN," New Hampshire Executive Departments and Administration (1999).

34. Rubin, "House Bill 348-FN."

35. Rubin, "House Bill 348-FN."

36. Lisa Prevost, "Days of Wine and Warehouses," *New Hampshire Business Review* (July 14, 1989).

37. Gary Ghioto and Matt Bai, "N.H. Split on Liquor Changes, Governor Denies Trying to Aid Friend," *The Boston Globe* (August 13, 1995).

38. "News Briefs: New Hampshire Implements Direct Shipping," *Food & Drink Weekly* (July 20, 1998).

39. "Pa. Wine Lovers Fight Control of Shipped Purchases," *The Boston Globe* (August 17, 2008).

40. New Hampshire State Liquor Commission, "Annual Report and Statistical Section, Fiscal Year June 30, 1998."

41. "Pa. Wine Lovers Fight Control of Shipped Purchases."

42. Bob Hohler, "N.H. Bargain Hunters Find a Proof of Low Price," *The Boston Globe* (May 26, 1992).

43. New Hampshire State Liquor Commission, http://www.nh.gov/liquor/.

44. Hohler, "N.H. Bargain Hunters Find a Proof of Low Price."

45. "N.H. Liquor Store Privatization Plan Criticized by Some," *Bangor Daily News* (April 30, 1994).

46. Joseph Pereira, "In a Decision Involving Bad Taste, It Might Have Been Sour Grapes," *The Wall Street Journal* (October 25, 1990).

47. "High-Proof Liquor off Shelves in N.H.," *The Boston Globe* (September 9, 1995).

48. New Hampshire State Liquor Commission, "Annual Report and Statistical Section, Fiscal Year June 30, 2006." http://www.nh.gov/liquor/2006annualreport.pdf.

49. Rubin, "House Bill 348-FN."

50. Kenny, "Lawmakers to Take Long Look at Privatizing Liquor Sales."

51. Rod Paul, "Computer-Aided Liquor Sales Rebound," *New Hampshire Business Review* (May 22, 1987).

52. New Hampshire State Liquor Commission, "Annual Report and Statistical Section, Fiscal Year June 30, 2006."

53. Kenny, "Lawmakers to Take Long Look at Privatizing Liquor Sales."

54. National Alcohol Beverage Control Association, "The Control State Systems," http://www.nabca.org/States/States.aspx (accessed June 25, 2009).

55. "What Is Maine Doing in the Booze Business? A Dispute over Pricing Shows How Inappropriate It Is for the State to Sell Alcohol," *Portland Press Herald* (December 8, 1997).

56. Milne, "Nominee to Liquor Panel."

57. "Mass Competition Closing in on N.H. Liquor Stores."

58. New Hampshire State Liquor Commission, "Annual Report and Statistical Section, Fiscal Year June 30, 2007."

59. Regulated Revenues Committee, "Hearing on HB 747—Privatization."
60. Kenny, "Lawmakers to Take Long Look at Privatizing Liquor Sales."
61. Regulated Revenues Committee, "Hearing on HB 747—Privatization."
62. Milne, "N.H. Liquor Stores: Lifeline or Liability?"
63. Milne, "Move to Go Private a Hot Issue."
64. "N.H. Liquor Store Privatization Plan Criticized by Some."
65. Prevost, "Days of Wine and Warehouses."

Chapter 9

Public Transportation Regional Authorities: Should the Boston, Philadelphia, and New York City Systems Be Privatized?

Although thousands of individuals have recently increased their use of urban mass transportation in the wake of rising gas prices, many mass transit authorities still face growing deficits and efficiency problems. The shift away from automobiles in search of a cheaper alternative for commuting has amplified the importance of the methods for ownership and operation of mass transportation. Boston's MBTA, for example, increased ridership by 6.1 percent in the 2008 fiscal year,[1] yet its deficit will likely still increase because of higher gas and electricity prices. As people stop driving and look for other modes of transportation, many urban mass transportation systems face a serious problem: the inherent unprofitability of public mass transportation.

Public mass transportation authorities face high construction, operating, and maintenance costs but receive only a small amount of revenue from the low fares.[2] As with any other public service, mass urban transportation authorities must work in the best interest of the public while coping with immense government regulation and negotiating with unions, often running unprofitable routes as a result. In order to supposedly help society, the public mass transportation authorities lose money while running inefficiently. However, government control of mass transportation systems certainly gives the poor access to transportation that private control could eliminate, and in discussing a possible change in the ownership and operation of mass transportation, this issue must be considered. Moving away from government control and operation, however, would likely increase efficiency and decrease costs. So, would it make sense to shift back to private control, or is there some way to balance the efficiency and equity concerns? At this critical junction in the history of mass transportation—a history that has evolved for hundreds of years—the industry must weigh the pros and cons of both private and public mass transportation and determine which method of ownership and operation will most benefit the public today while continuing to build toward a successful future.

HISTORY

Before determining whether mass transportation systems can shift toward privatization in the future, it is necessary to examine the evolution of these systems and discuss their successes and failures. As a general trend in the United States, ownership and operation shifted from private to public control in the early 1960s.[3] Private firms tended to have financial difficulties at this time because they lost demand from the growing suburban populations that used automobiles.[4] The Boston, Philadelphia, and New York mass transit systems, for example, experienced similar transitions from private ownership and operation to the current public structures. It is in this struggle to balance private and public that the origins of the privatization problem began.

Boston

The growing city of Boston experimented with multiple types of public transportation in its earliest years, beginning with the ferry and progressing through the omnibus, horse cars, and cable cars.[5] These different methods of transportation all shared one commonality, however: each operated under private ownership.

A rapidly expanding population led to the incorporation of the privately owned Boston Elevated Railway Company in 1894, the first of its kind to reach Boston. It soon absorbed the largest Boston streetcar company, which had experienced financial difficulties.[6] The El expanded throughout the next half-century but ultimately faced financial problems itself and consequently transitioned to "temporary public trusteeship"[7] as an attempted solution. The incorporation of the automobile into the American life decreased the reliance on mass public transportation, however, and the El suffered.[8]

In 1947, Massachusetts created the Metropolitan Transit Authority (MTA), which served as a political subdivision of Massachusetts. The MTA bought out the Boston Elevated Railway Company, and a new era of public control of mass transit began. The government subsidized the MTA to encourage it to remain in the mass transit business.[9] In contrast, the previous private transit companies, many of whom eventually ran into financial problems, did not receive financial assistance.

The final major change in Boston urban mass transportation occurred in 1964 with the creation of the Massachusetts Bay Transportation Authority (MBTA). The MBTA, like its predecessor the MTA, served as a political subdivision of Massachusetts.[10] The MBTA quickly expanded to increase ridership, attempting to solve a problem that had plagued mass transit systems since the rise of the automobile. Also in 1964, the Urban Mass Transportation Administration (UMTA) began funding capital improvements for public mass transit agencies. The MBTA used this to its advantage; it immediately modernized 10 of its mass transit stations and continues to use UMTA funds to this day.[11] These UMTA funds helped the MBTA purchase a network of commuter rail lines that helped start the commuter rail network that is still in place.[12] The state helped the MBTA with its financial deficit, "contributing up to 90 percent of the capital cost of the new transit extensions and a portion of the commuter rail subsidy."[13] This public funding has allowed the MBTA to maintain its status as one of the five largest public transit systems in the United States.[14]

Philadelphia

Philadelphia also experienced a growth of private subway and streetcar lines in the first half of the 20th century.[15] Five different private companies developed during the World War II years, with high ridership leading to high profitability. After World War II, the suburbs of Philadelphia grew, as they did in Boston, and automobile use increased rapidly as well. Ridership decreased, and consequently, so did profits.

The private companies simply could not survive in this environment, at least not by providing passenger service. Many companies considered making a transition to other types of railroad service,[16] where they could make larger profits. This forced the government to intervene to ensure that Philadelphia kept at least some passenger service. In 1963, the Southeastern Pennsylvania Transit Authority (SEPTA) held its first meeting[17] to "coordinate government subsidies to the railroads and transit companies."[18] During the next few years, SEPTA absorbed multiple railroad companies,[19] and two commuter rail companies operated under its authority. By 1983, SEPTA had bought the commuter lines and consolidated the local Philadelphia transit system. Like Boston's MBTA, SEPTA runs one of the five largest mass transit systems in the United States today.

New York

Like Boston and Philadelphia, New York City began with privately operated public transportation. It did so in the form of stagecoaches, omnibuses, trolley cars, and finally the subway, in 1904. Individual companies operated individual lines throughout different sections of the city. By 1915, service—originally limited to Manhattan—had expanded to include the Bronx, Brooklyn, and Queens.[20]

In 1932, the New York City government created a city-run subway line that became the only owner and operator of New York City subway and elevated train lines. In 1953, the state government of New York took this development one step further by creating the New York City Transit Authority "as a separate public corporation" that managed and operated all public transportation in the city.[21] The Metropolitan Transit Authority (MTA), which the state created in 1968 to oversee the New York City Transit Authority, remains the publicly owned and operated system used in New York today. The MTA currently has the largest subway car fleet in the world. Its subway system is much larger than any other subway system,[22] and the MTA has a much larger operating budget than either MBTA or SEPTA.

In addition to the large city subway network, the MTA has a commuter rail network. It is slightly different from the MBTA and SEPTA commuter rail networks, however, because of the multiple states that it crosses and the different providers of the service. The MBTA only briefly enters Rhode Island to bring service to Providence. SEPTA does the same, crossing the river into New Jersey to bring service to Trenton. SEPTA's service is also supplemented with PATCO, a separate commuter rail system that brings passengers into Philadelphia from the rest of New Jersey. The MTA provides commuter service to the New York and Connecticut communities through its subsidiaries, the Long Island Rail Road and the Metro-North Railroad, but the MTA does not provide service to the New Jersey communities directly across the river. The New Jersey Transit Authority, NJ Transit, has control over the New Jersey commuter rail lines outside of New York City, providing a large amount of service.[23]

THE PUBLIC PROBLEM

These publicly owned and operated mass transportation authorities face an increasingly difficult problem to solve, as declining ridership creates an increasing deficit. The industry shifted to public control because of these losses, since private companies could not handle the increasing debt. Federal capital grants were not available to the El in Boston, for example, but are available to the publicly owned and operated MBTA.[24] In fact, the MBTA only had to pay for one-fourth of its capital improvements from 1965 to 1990, while the federal government paid for the rest.[25] Expansions and improvements using government funding helped to stabilize the declining ridership, but did so at a high expense, increasing the deficit that continues to grow larger each year.

The problem arises because controlling the deficit comes at the cost of losing political support.[26] It is certainly possible to control the deficit, and many simple methods could dramatically reduce it; however, most of the methods have extremely visible costs. Tolling autos, for example, would encourage commuters to take the available mass transportation and would increase ridership; controlling labor costs would decrease expenses and decrease the deficit; and cutting less productive services or raising fares would decrease the deficit. But each of these changes would have visible outcomes that would lose politicians votes in their next elections; consequently, the costs for politicians to pass legislation outweigh the benefits for them of decreasing the deficit. The gains for cutting the deficit are far less visible and far less concentrated.[27]

Since cutting the deficit by the aforementioned methods would likely face much opposition and lack political support, transportation authorities would have to look elsewhere. One possibility would involve reducing service to the least profitable areas. A private company could certainly do this, but an authority such as the MBTA cannot cut service because it is a public company.[28] The least profitable areas of mass transit systems usually extend to the poorer sections of the cities, where "low-income travelers [are] much more dependent on mass transit than other groups."[29] Reducing or eliminating this service would severely hinder the ability of these citizens to work and improve their lives. Subsidization occurs here because the value of public transportation to society exceeds what riders will pay for the service. In the poorer areas of a city, subsidies allow service to continue where riders cannot afford the higher fare otherwise needed to cover costs. Because the transit authorities cannot increase fares in these areas and are reluctant to do so elsewhere, the government must subsidize the systems and the transportation deficit increases even further.

Political forces also prevent the transit authorities from decreasing service and considerably increasing fares. Politics generally inhibits change that would improve efficiency.[30] In order to improve the efficiency of the system, it is therefore necessary to shield it from politics because policy makers tend to respond more to political forces than market forces.[31] With public control over the transportation systems, political forces will always influence decisions and prevent the systems from operating at peak efficiency.

This low efficiency under public ownership and operation is the real problem for transportation systems in the United States. Publicly owned and operated systems have low managerial autonomy, have little interaction between decision makers and users, and face long governmental lags.[32] Furthermore, they lack profitable goals because the government can increase its subsidies or the deficit, giving the systems little motivation to make a profit.[33] Public systems are often poorly managed as well; for example, SEPTA had adequate funds but excessive spending for many years.[34] As soon as SEPTA brought in outside evaluators as advisers, it cut 1,200 positions and thus saved as much as $60 million per year. The outside evaluators determined that SEPTA could save at least $150 million per year with more efficient management.[35] SEPTA took initiatives to improve efficiency and benefited greatly; however, this case exemplifies how poor the management of many public transportation authorities can be. Finally, many of the publicly owned and operated transportation systems have a monopoly on mass transit for their cities, so the lack of competition removes another incentive to improve operations. This monopoly status and lack of innovation further decreases efficiency and hurts the publicly operated transportation systems.[36]

The Public Experience

Throughout its existence, the MBTA has used many methods to survive while confronting the financial problems of public transportation. Faced with the possibility of losing the commuter rail system around the Boston metropolitan area because of the decline in ridership during off-peak hours, in 1976, the MBTA bought much of the commuter rail system that serviced the Boston area and Maine.[37] This kept suburban commuters satisfied even though the MBTA could not solve the off-peak problem. Instead, the MBTA has used government subsidies to keep the commuter rail operating to the present day.

Also in the 1970s, the MBTA considered allowing subdistricts to decide how much service they wanted and then requiring that each subdistrict pay a fee relative to the amount of service provided;[38] each subdistrict would pay for the service that it received. This idea failed because of the interdistrict and intercommunity nature of the MBTA routes. The Boston communities would have had trouble splitting the costs fairly because of the difficulties of splitting the routes by district or community. Even if the cost-splitting scheme had succeeded, the MBTA would still have faced the problem of providing service where high costs make efficiency impossible. In that situation, poorer areas could not pay for service, yet may need it the most. As the situation stands today, the MBTA must still balance equity and efficiency. Rising deficits suggest that the MBTA should cut costs[39] to improve efficiency, yet reducing service to do so would create a political problem and an issue regarding social equity.

More recently, the MBTA has had trouble dealing with the strong labor unions in the area. Negotiations have led to results such as "lifetime pensions after 23 years of service, no matter their age."[40] An individual who began working at the age of 18 could retire with a lifetime pension at the age of only 41 years old. Philadelphia has also had somewhat recent problems with the labor unions,[41] and labor costs have risen dramatically while ridership has declined.[42] Privatization could streamline the company, decrease the amount of labor needed, and negotiate better deals without the extreme government regulations by which public companies must abide. SEPTA's spending problem discussed earlier in this chapter exemplified that these large public agencies should work harder to improve efficiency and decrease the deficit. Since labor is such a large operating expense,[43] privatizing the industry and changing concessions to labor would logically improve efficiency and decrease the deficit.

Unlike the MBTA, SEPTA has some competition in the commuter rail service. The Port Authority Transit Corporation (PATCO), which provides service between Philadelphia and New Jersey, is cheaper and runs more frequently than SEPTA commuter rail lines.[44] SEPTA communities tend to have higher incomes than PATCO communities,[45] which corresponds to the higher PATCO ridership. New Jersey motorists must also pay tolls for a bridge that Pennsylvania commuters do not cross. This added fee further encourages commuters to take PATCO. This example shows that alternative solutions, such as increasing tolls, can increase ridership and help the public transit authorities maintain profits.

New York City Transit, which is very different from the Boston and Philadelphia transportation systems because of its size, still faces similar public problems. The MTA, like the MBTA and SEPTA, purchased commuter rail services to keep them running, even though the services lose money.[46] The New York City Transit Authority also keeps the city subway in poor condition, probably because public control has deteriorated the system.[47] Yet the MTA has no reason to improve quality because it has a monopoly of fixed-rail rapid transit in the area;[48] this lack of direct competition allows the system to decline without losing all of its customers.

New York City does not face the off-peak problem as much as cities like Boston and Philadelphia because the New York City system has a steady flow of passengers, yet a problem arises with the flat fares because of the distance passengers can travel in the system. The flat fare discourages short trips that would help the system make money, while it encourages long trips that cause the system to lose money.[49] This choice of equity over efficiency costs the subway system and makes it difficult to expand because expansion would only result in an increase in the longer trips that cost the system money.[50] Politicians encourage a low fixed fare to keep public support, but this costs the government through subsidization. Increasing the fare would have a lower cost to society than the cost of these subsidies, yet the public willingly sacrifices this efficiency for the additional tax cost of subsidization. This clear choice of equity over efficiency again illustrates the lack of balance in the two when maintaining a public transit system such as the MTA.

THE PRIVATE POSSIBILITY

Clearly, having public ownership and public operation of a mass transit system can lower efficiency and create financial problems. But would a private system remove these problems or create new ones? The history of mass transit demonstrates that a private system has its own flaws; that is why most American systems are now public. Cities tried the private approach, and it failed. But if the private systems had had the subsidization and government assistance that current public systems receive, would they have failed? It is certainly possible to think about privatizing the mass transit industry on the theoretical level, but the feasibility of doing so in the real world remains an issue.

The Game

For a fair privatization process to occur, firms would need the ability to bid for rights to the entire system, part of the system, or service that they wanted to control. This cannot happen using the current format because the state governments do not want to introduce competition to their monopolies, which lose money even without it. Privatizing any part of the industry would simply create competition with the government's share of the industry and put extra pressure on the government monopoly, so this approach is unlikely. Furthermore, the law should encourage private firms to enter the industry in some form, instead of subsidizing the large monopolies already in place. The government could give tax breaks, subsidization, or some other form of assistance to encourage competition instead of driving it away.

A private service would face a substantial challenge competing against firms with prior monopoly status. The government's large subsidies keep fares superficially low for existing transportation systems and would thus make it difficult for private firms entering the industry to compete. Removing these subsidies, however, would force the systems to increase fares and abandon the poorer markets that could not afford the higher fares. Shifting to complete privatization without any subsidization would force the private firms to abandon these markets. They would need to favor efficiency over equity simply to stay in business, and the poorer areas would suffer from the loss of equity.

A simple solution to this loss of equity would be to subsidize the areas that could not survive without subsidization while simultaneously privatizing any parts of the system that could survive without subsidization. This would promote equity while also improving efficiency for the system as a whole. A balance between efficiency and equity, this simple solution seems great at the theoretical level, but labor protections of the Urban Mass Transportation Act make it difficult for local transit agencies to contract with private firms.[51] Multiple levels of privatization exist, including leasing, competitive contracting, and complete privatization, and it is necessary to examine each one to determine the best and most feasible option.

The mass transit authorities should consider leasing parts of their systems as the first step toward privatization.[52] For example, the MTA could lease some of its New York City subway lines to private firms but continue to control other lines. The MTA could continue to operate some of the lines and use government subsidies to maintain the lines that would operate unprofitably in the private sector. This would improve the efficiency of the system through partial privatization. At the same time, the MTA would meet equity concerns by using subsidization to operate lines that private companies would otherwise remove.

The mass transit authorities could then give incentives to their lessees.[53] For example, the MTA could lease one line to each of several different companies and then give the more successful and efficient companies extra lines to operate as a reward. This competition would certainly improve the efficiency of the system. On a more basic level, the public transit authority could offer incentives if the private company outperformed the public one.[54] This would force the private company to cooperate while the public company would need to improve its efficiency to match the private sector.[55] Consequently, the entire system would become more efficient while continuing to address the main equity concerns.

The private sector does face significant barriers to entry under this scenario, however, including the huge cost of access to capital and the regulatory environment involved. The government could pass legislation to decrease the regulatory environment and give the private companies substantial freedom in their operations. The private firms would receive the capital at market price or a fair, reduced price to encourage them to join the sector. Leasing would allow firms to overcome the barriers to entry and begin privatization. If leasing proved successful, then it could serve as the ultimate solution; however, if it failed, urban mass transportation could always return to public operation or authorities could try a different form of privatization.

The mass transportation industry could also choose to privatize through competitive contracting.[56] In this scenario, if the transit agency can purchase any of its services from a private firm at a lower cost than it provides those services itself, it must do so.[57] For example, if four different private companies can provide subway car maintenance services more cheaply than the transit agency can provide those services, then the transit agency must choose from one of those four private firms to provide the service using a reasonable selection process such as bidding. Giving these competitive incentives to the industry would lead to reduced costs and better, increased services.

The monopolies that exist today have increasing costs and decreasing output, and competitive contracting would reverse this. This method would only give private control to the operation of the mass transit system, but would not give private ownership to the industry. By making only the operation of the mass transit system private, the transit authority could improve efficiency by hiring private contractors while maintaining the public decision-making process. Because the system would still have public ownership, any risk of losing equity would disappear. Public control of the system would remain, so nobody would have to worry about the private problems such as closing down unprofitable lines. The mass transit system would still run as a public service, but would do so more efficiently. It would strike an important balance between equity and efficiency, a balance that does not exist as most systems currently operate. Competitive contracting would increase efficiency while allowing the public to balance the tradeoff between cost and service.

Alternatively, the public mass transportation systems could fully restructure the organization through complete privatization. This would eliminate any public control whatsoever and return closer to the model that failed in the first half of the 20th century. Obviously, the systems would have to make some basic changes to avoid a repeat of that failure, but this option still has far more risk involved than the other possibilities. But does it also have more potential reward?

With complete privatization, the public transit systems could sell off each line as a separate company.[58] For example, the New York City MTA could sell each of its numerous lines to different companies and entirely relinquish control over those lines. The private companies could then raise fares to offset cost increases based on the costs of each individual line, further encouraging them to control costs.[59] The private companies could also hire nonunion labor to lower costs.[60] Even if they chose not to do so, the mere threat of hiring nonunion labor would take away the ability of workers to strike because of the other options available;[61] consequently, labor costs would decrease and the system would increase its efficiency.

In addition, a competitive subway system would better match supply and demand to maximize its profit.[62] The proximity of lines would also lead to good competition, especially in the New York City example. Because of the profit incentive created from complete privatization, the subway system would greatly increase its efficiency. It would improve equity by increasing service variety and price variety because each company would try to find a niche in the market for its line to increase ridership and profitability.[63] Profit-sharing could make complete privatization somewhat feasible, as it would decrease the advantages that some companies would have over others due to the different profitabilities of lines, but this is still a very unlikely situation. It did not succeed in the past, forcing a transition away from private ownership and operation; it is also unlikely to succeed in the present, since the same profitability concerns without enormous subsidies make private ownership unlikely.

The Players

Clearly, a shift toward any form of privatization would greatly impact numerous "players," which would affect the possibility of completing that shift. Employees of the mass transit industry would certainly react strongly toward a shift because a private company would try to increase efficiency and streamline its operations by laying off employees, as the SEPTA example of cutting costs showed earlier in this chapter. The shift to privatization would also significantly affect the employees in the industry. Because private systems can easily find cheap labor without unionization, the shift toward privatization would lead to pay cuts and overall lower worker compensation. The employees would face the alternative of losing their jobs to people willing to take lower wages, different hours, or reduced benefits. The systems would only retain the same number of employees if they expanded their services; however, firms would encounter financial difficulties if they chose to expand. Since the private companies would probably not expand and might not even be able to do so, employees would almost certainly lose their jobs. Employees lose the most in the privatization process, as the emphasis on efficiency results in private companies streamlining the labor force. Thus, employees would definitely prefer to keep the public transportation as it currently exists.

Public interest groups would also oppose privatization, especially complete privatization. With complete privatization, many people could lose their transit service simply because the private company might find it unprofitable. For example, if the company that bought the MBTA's blue line in Boston found that the last few stops had extremely low ridership and decreased profits, the company could simply cut those stops out of the route. Groups of people who did use those stops would likely organize into a public interest group with the goal of keeping service to their stations. People would understand that complete privatization would likely result in a number of similar changes, such as removing stations or reducing service to cut costs. Faced with the possibility of losing political support if privatization succeeded and these groups organized, politicians would oppose privatization in the interests of their constituencies. Decreases or losses in service in their areas would reflect poorly on politicians, as would increases in fares to pay for the cost of service. Politicians are also much more removed from private firms than they are from publicly owned ones and may be able to influence decisions regarding a public mass transit system in ways that private mass transit systems simply would not allow. Therefore, politicians would join the efforts of public interest groups to oppose complete privatization.

Firms and industries would give their full support to a privatization process. Currently, the public nature of the mass transportation industry leaves little room for other firms to enter the market and compete with the publicly owned system. A privatization process would allow firms to compete with each other for control of services or for leases to different lines.

For example, multiple firms would have the opportunity to provide services for the mass transportation agency using competitive contracting. If the firm could inspect the subway cars at a cheaper cost than the public agency could, then it would have the opportunity to do the inspections. Firms could even operate some of the lines using leasing, so they would definitely support the leasing process because success could lead to increased control and profits. Finally, a complete privatization process would enable firms to take complete control over a part of the system and allow them to enter the urban mass transportation industry. Firms would love this opportunity, even under the conditions of competition. The government would essentially break up its monopoly to create competition through fair methods. It would allow bidding for services that would enable each firm to determine a fair and profitable price to run each part of the system on which it bids.

In general, most customers would support privatization, although some might oppose it. Customers would oppose privatization mostly because of the effects it would have on their fares. Although the total cost of publicly owned transit is high, the government bears much of the costs through subsidies. The $1.70 fare from downtown Boston out to a suburb does not capture the true cost of that trip to the system. The costs of running the public transportation systems are much higher than the revenue that the fares generate, and the government pays much of that excess cost. With privatization, commuters would certainly bear an increased portion of the cost. The government would no longer pay large subsidies, and the companies would not willingly keep the fares low and lose money. They would not have to increase every fare, however. They could increase the fare at peak hours, or charge different fares based on the length of the trip. This would serve the purposes of equity, as a person traveling two stops on the subway would not have to pay a higher fare so that a person using the transit system to commute in from the suburbs would get the same cheap rate. Charging differently based on the time of day—charging higher fares for peak-hour service and lower fares for off-peak service—could also increase ridership during off-peak hours. Peak-hour travelers and long-distance commuters would oppose these changes, however, so may oppose a privatization process. They could lose access or have increasingly expensive access, so while privatization may be more efficient on the whole, it could cost some individuals more than others.

Many customers would support privatization, however, because the increased efficiency and resulting decrease in subsidies would allow the government to spend tax dollars in other areas. It might make the users pay more for their service, but nonusers would not care about the increased fares.

The majority of people do not rely on mass transportation systems and so would support increased costs for the individuals who use it most. The overall cost to society would decrease due to increased competition and improved efficiency, and the mass transportation systems would be more equitable in the sense that nonusers would not have to pay for a service that they did not use.

Finally, the government would likely support some kind of privatization. By privatizing and improving the efficiency of the system, the government could decrease subsidies substantially and decrease the deficit. Furthermore, it could invest in other parts of the economy with the funds previously used for subsidies. The government would likely want to retain some control, instead of going back to an industry filled with pure profit-seeking firms. Assuming the government wanted to retain some control, the mass transportation industry could not shift to complete privatization, which would eliminate all aspects of government control. Complete privatization could give the government relief from subsidization and improve the government's finances, but the lack of government control would allow firms to eliminate service throughout much of the metropolitan area, which the public would not want.

The government could instead experiment with the other types of privatization. Leasing lines to private firms would satisfy the government, the public, and firms while retaining public control over the system. Competitive contracting could work as well, as it would alleviate some of the government's responsibilities while lowering the costs and increasing efficiency through privatization. In addition to leasing or competitive contracting, the government could continue to run or support lines that need government control or assistance. For example, private companies would likely avoid bidding on lines that run into poorer areas. If private companies kept the current fares, then the lines would continue to lose money, but the government could continue to operate these lines or offer subsidization to private companies to lease the lines so that they could profit while still improving the efficiency. The government could also simply contract out some services while maintaining responsibility for the line. The line would lose money, but individual contractors would profit while improving the efficiency and maintaining equity by continuing to service the areas that could not profit without government assistance.

CONCLUSION

Is it possible to return to privately owned or operated urban mass transportation? It did not succeed the first time, so there is definitely no guarantee that it would succeed if tried again. In the past decades, ridership has decreased substantially, so the old system of complete private ownership and operation will not work. Given the rising gasoline prices and the very recent increase in ridership, however, improvements in mass transportation should definitely receive more public support. It is clear that the current system of public mass transportation has problems and will continue to operate at great financial expense to the public. Something about mass transportation must change, and finding a middle ground between public and private ownership and operation would serve as a first step to increase efficiency and improve urban mass transportation.

The leasing and competitive contracting models would improve the efficiency of urban mass transportation systems while addressing the problem of maintaining equity. By avoiding complete privatization with these models, the systems could retain service for the poorer areas that would otherwise lose that service. Maintaining some public control would ensure that the fares remain reasonable; it would also allow the government to give subsidies where needed to keep service. These models would thus enable the public to require some degree of equity while simultaneously improving efficiency and cutting costs through incentives for good performance and efficiency. The industry could target efficiency objectives through these incentives. As public ownership and operation continue to increase the deficit, mass transportation authorities call for larger and larger subsidies. The industry must begin the shift toward privatization while it can still use the currently high ridership to build a good foundation for the future.

NOTES

1. Noah Bierman, "T Warns of Fare Hike If Agency Is Not Rescued," *The Boston Globe* (August 5, 2008), A1.

2. Sock-Yong Phang, "Urban Rail Transit PPPs: Survey and Risk Assessment of Recent Strategies," *Transport Policy* 14 (2007): 214–231.

3. Matthew Karlaftis and Patrick McCarthy, "The Effect of Privatization on Public Transit Costs," *Journal of Regulatory Economics* 16 (1999): 27–43.

4. Karlaftis and McCarthy, "The Effect of Privatization on Public Transit Costs."

5. Massachusetts Bay Transportation Authority, "History," http://www.mbta.com/about_the_mbta/history/ (accessed June 24, 2009).

6. Massachusetts Bay Transportation Authority, "History."

7. Jose A. Gomez-Ibanez, "Big-City Transit Ridership, Deficits, and Politics," *Journal of the American Planning Association* 62 (1996): 30.

8. Massachusetts Bay Transportation Authority, "History."

9. Massachusetts Bay Transportation Authority, "History."

10. Massachusetts Bay Transportation Authority, "History."

11. Massachusetts Bay Transportation Authority, "History."

12. Alan Black, *Urban Mass Transportation Planning* (New York: McGraw-Hill, 1995).

13. Gomez-Ibanez, "Big-City Transit Ridership, Deficits, and Politics."

14. Massachusetts Bay Transportation Authority, "History."

15. The Philadelphia Chapter of the National Railway Historical Society, "SEPTA History," http://www.trainweb.org/phillynrhs/septa.html (accessed June 25, 2009).

16. The Philadelphia Chapter of the National Railway Historical Society, "SEPTA History."

17. SEPTA, "History of SEPTA," http://home.comcast.net/~trolleydriver/history_of_septa.htm (accessed June 25, 2009).

18. The Philadelphia Chapter of the National Railway Historical Society, "SEPTA History."

19. SEPTA, "History of SEPTA."

20. MTA New York City Transit, "New York City Transit—History and Chronology," http://mta.info/nyct/facts/ffhist.htm (accessed June 23, 2009).

21. MTA New York City Transit, "New York City Transit—History and Chronology."

22. Charles A. M. de Bartolome and James B. Ramsey, "Privatizing the New York City Subway," in *Privatizing Transportation Systems,* ed. Simon Hakim, Paul Seidenstat, and Gary W. Bowman (Westport, CT: Praeger Publishers, 1996), 285–315.

23. NJ Transit, "Rail System Map," http://www.njtransit.com/pdf/rail/Rail_System_Map.pdf (accessed June 25, 2009).

24. Gomez-Ibanez, "Big-City Transit Ridership, Deficits, and Politics."

25. Gomez-Ibanez, "Big-City Transit Ridership, Deficits, and Politics."

26. Gomez-Ibanez, "Big-City Transit Ridership, Deficits, and Politics."

27. Gomez-Ibanez, "Big-City Transit Ridership, Deficits, and Politics."

28. Gomez-Ibanez, "Big-City Transit Ridership, Deficits, and Politics."

29. Alan Altshuler, James P. Womack, and John R. Pucher, *The Urban Transportation System: Politics and Policy Innovation* (Cambridge, MA: The MIT Press, 1979).

30. Clifford Winston, "Government Failure in Urban Transportation," *Fiscal Studies* 21 (2000): 403–425.

31. Winston, "Government Failure in Urban Transportation."

32. Priyanka Jain, Sharon Cullinane, and Kevin Cullinane, "The Impact of Governance Development Models on Urban Rail Efficiency," in *Transportation Research Part A: Policy and Practice* (in press).

33. Jain, Cullinane, and Cullinane, "The Impact of Governance Development Models on Urban Rail Efficiency."

34. Wally Nunn, "When the Public Trust Runs off the Rails," *Policy Review* 91 (1998): 9.

35. Nunn, "When the Public Trust Runs off the Rails."

36. George M. Smerk, "Urban Mass Transportation: From Private to Public to Privatization," *Transportation Journal* 26 (1986): 83–91.

37. Massachusetts Bay Transportation Authority, "History"; Donald V. Harper, *Transportation in America: Users, Carriers, Government*, 2nd ed. (Englewood Cliffs, NJ: Prentice Hall, 1982).

38. Gomez-Ibanez, "Big-City Transit Ridership, Deficits, and Politics"; Robert G. Smith, "Reorganization of Regional Transportation Authorities to Maintain Urban/Suburban Constituency Balance," *Public Administration Review* 47 (1987): 171.

39. Gomez-Ibanez, "Big-City Transit Ridership, Deficits, and Politics."

40. Yvonne Abraham, "Big Mess at the T," *The Boston Globe* (August 6, 2008), B1.

41. Michael H. Cimini and Charles J. Muhl, "Transit Settlements," *Monthly Labor Review* 118 (1995): 74.

42. Nunn, "When the Public Trust Runs off the Rails."

43. Daniel Kruger and Arleen Jacobius, "Philadelphia's SEPTA Talks Seen as Indicative of Big-City Transit Problems," *Bond Buyer* 323 (1998): 3.

44. Richard Voith, "Public Transit: Realizing Its Potential," *Business Review* (Federal Reserve Bank of Philadelphia) (1994): 15.

45. Voith, "Public Transit: Realizing Its Potential."

46. Harper, *Transportation in America: Users, Carriers, Government.*

47. John Hibbs, "Sell the Tubes," *Journal of Economic Affairs* 3 (1983): 173.

48. De Bartolome and Ramsey, "Privatizing the New York City Subway."

49. De Bartolome and Ramsey, "Privatizing the New York City Subway."

50. De Bartolome and Ramsey, "Privatizing the New York City Subway."

51. Michael I. Luger and Harvey A. Goldstein, "Federal Labor Protections and the Privatization of Public Transit," *Journal of Policy Analysis & Management* 8 (1989): 229–250.

52. David Osmon, "The Future of the Tube," *New Economy* 7 (2000): 59.

53. Osmon, "The Future of the Tube."

54. Osmon, "The Future of the Tube."

55. Osmon, "The Future of the Tube."

56. Wendell Cox and Jean Love, "Applying Competitive Incentives to Public Transit," in *Privatizing Transportation Systems,* ed. Simon Hakim, Paul Seidenstat, and Gary W. Bowman (Westport, CT: Praeger Publishers, 1996), 257–267.

57. Cox and Love, "Applying Competitive Incentives to Public Transit."

58. De Bartolome and Ramsey, "Privatizing the New York City Subway."

59. De Bartolome and Ramsey, "Privatizing the New York City Subway."

60. Black, *Urban Mass Transportation Planning.*

61. De Bartolome and Ramsey, "Privatizing the New York City Subway."

62. De Bartolome and Ramsey, "Privatizing the New York City Subway."

63. Charles A. Lave, "The Private Challenge to Public Transportation—an Overview," in *Urban Transit: The Private Challenge to Public Transportation,* ed. Charles A. Lave and John Meyer (San Francisco: Pacific Institute for Public Policy Research, 1985), 1–29.

Part Four

Proposed and Newly Privatized Industries

Chapter 10

The Evolution and Scope of the Privatized Prison Industry

President Ronald Reagan launched the Grace Commission in 1982 to investigate waste and inefficiency in the federal government. Although Congress ultimately decided not to act on the panel's recommendations in 1984, its findings made it clear that the U.S. government would need some radical changes. Federal and state governments had long been the sole provider of many social services, including public transportation, housing assistance, and correctional facilities. As a result, federal and state budgets had expanded dramatically and in some cases created a budgetary crisis. Many of these services were deemed essential, so governments looked to alternatives beyond simply cutting programs or raising taxes. A growing number of people began to believe that the same services could be provided either cheaper or more efficiently (or both) by the private sector instead of the government. Thus, the privatization of many social services became more common across the United States, especially in the operation of correctional facilities.

In 1983, the Corrections Corporation of America (CCA) was incorporated in Tennessee, becoming the first for-profit private corrections company in the United States. One year later, it opened its first detention center outside Houston under a contract with the Department of Justice to house detainees for the Immigration National Services (INS). In 1984, it also earned the first contract to manage a public facility from Hamilton County in Tennessee. The U.S. Corrections Corporation, another upstart, earned the first state-level correctional management contract in 1985.[1] Wackenhut Corrections Corporation (now known as the Geo Group) was also formed, and the private correctional management industry began to take off. Since then, a number of other competitors have entered the market, including the Cornell Corrections Corp. and the Management and Training Corporation, as the demand for prison beds has far exceeded the government's ability to provide them.

Today, 34 states and a myriad of federal and local agencies have contracts with private correctional management firms. As of the middle of 2007, private correctional facilities of varying degrees of security housed 7.4 percent of the estimated 1.59 million prisoners in the United States.[2] The CCA alone owns and operates 46 of its own facilities and operates 20 more under leases from government agencies.[3] It houses more prisoners than any entity except the Federal Bureau of Prisons (FBOP) and the state correctional systems of California, Florida, Texas, and New York.[4] Both the Geo Group and the CCA earn over $1 billion annually. Many signs point to continued growth in the industry, as crime enforcement laws grow tougher and correctional expenditures increase, creating budgetary pressures to reduce costs. Since private prison operators and their proponents claim that they can provide correctional services both cheaper and more efficiently than the government can, privatization of correctional facilities continues to look like an attractive alternative to government-run facilities.

However, do private prisons actually deliver on their promises of lower costs and more efficient service? Is privatization attractive in all situations? While some evidence suggests that privately operated facilities do deliver on their promise, other evidence suggests that contracting for private correctional services can have unintended and unforeseen costs that could push the total cost of contracting out services above the original expenditures of running a publicly administered prison. Critics also cite a number of opportunity costs that are often overlooked in the contracting decision process. Furthermore, opponents of corrections privatization raise a number of social and ethical issues. Many critics argue that private prison facilities do not provide a greater level of service than public facilities, and several lawsuits have been filed against the industry in the past few years. Although at a first glance, privatization appears to solve a number of issues plaguing the provision of correctional services, it raises a number of new issues and is highly controversial on many levels.

This chapter seeks to provide greater insight as to whether privatizing correctional facilities is a viable alternative to publicly administrating the facilities. It begins by reviewing the driving forces behind the privatization of all government services. It examines the different ways of organizing privatization efforts and begins to illustrate how these apply to privatizing correctional services. It also looks into the arguments in favor of privatizing prisons, giving special consideration to the specific factors that influence the decision to privatize and examining how private correctional companies claim to benefit the agencies they contract with. Finally, this chapter examines data on public prison expenditures and assesses whether private correctional services can actually deliver on their claim to reduce corrections expenditures.

A REVIEW OF PRIVATIZATION IN THE UNITED STATES AND THE PRIVATE PRISON INDUSTRY

As mentioned previously, the privatization of government activities has primarily been a phenomenon of the last 30 years. It began largely under Reagan with the sale of many government-operated enterprises at the federal level and continued under Bill Clinton. Some notable examples include Conrail and the U.S. Enrichment Corporation. However, privatization has arguably been most useful at the state and municipal levels. Since states and municipalities face the prospect of bankruptcy, they cannot run the same kinds of deficits as the federal government. Thus, in providing services, there is a greater need to do more with less. Additionally, the demand for accountability for how taxes are used is higher at the state level because it is closer to and thus more directly affects constituents.[5] For these reasons, while consideration will be given to privatized corrections at the federal level, the primary focus will be on privatization of corrections at the state level.

A number of forces support the growing popularity of privatization. None of them can independently explain the rise of privatization, but each gives insight into the rationale for promoting privatization as a viable alternative to government-administered services. According to E. S. Savas, the four predominant forces behind privatization are as follows:[6]

- Pragmatism
- Commerce
- Ideology
- Populism

In many cases, two or more of these forces can drive the decision to privatize a public service, but it is unlikely that all four would simultaneously occur in a single case. The desire for better government is generally at the root of pragmatic approaches to privatization. The core belief is that competition to provide public services, both between competing private agencies and between any public agencies, will yield either the same level of service at a lower cost or a higher level of service at the existing cost. This theory uses the idea that privatization introduces market pressures that didn't exist before and thus creates incentives for public agencies to improve their levels of service or face elimination in favor of private firms. If public agencies improve, then the service delivery will likely remain a mix between public and private, but if they do not improve, then the service will likely become entirely privatized. The pragmatic approach is especially relevant at the state and municipal levels of government, although it also works for the federal government.

The commercial approach follows a similar line of reasoning as the pragmatic, but it is mainly directed at creating more opportunities for private business. Since government spending is such a large part of the overall economy, some believe that it would be better to give the money to private firms instead of government agencies. This implicitly suggests that private firms would make better use of government money and assets than the government itself. This idea can be reflected in the divestiture of government-sponsored enterprises at the federal level, and it can also explain some of the support for private correctional facilities. Economic pressures for privatization follow the idea that growing affluence makes people less dependent on government to provide their needs. Thus, as people rely on the government less, the provision of services should return to the private sector for private citizens to engage in when needed. As a result, this view often leads to approaches to reduce the size of the "welfare" state.

The ideological argument for privatization often yields a similar result as the economic arguments, but the reasoning differs slightly. The ideology is most directly tied to a desire for less government involvement and views government as too big and too intrusive into people's lives. Privatization reduces the size of the government and helps stop this problem. Similarly, the populist belief is that people should better be able to voluntarily assess their communitarian needs and devise a way to best serve those needs instead of the government dictating what needs to satisfy. Essentially, this view states that the people, not the government, know how to best create a suitable society. However, it is worth noting that these two approaches also have opposing arguments against privatization, with some people favoring a larger government and less privatization, and others believing that government can best direct the needs of the people.

For the purposes of examining the private prison industry and its interaction with state correctional agencies, the pragmatic and commercial approaches appear to be the driving forces behind ongoing privatization. While the ideological approach could possibly qualify as the original impetus for the creation of the industry, budget realities and capacity shortages have created a need for pragmatic solutions to the problems. There are a variety of reasons for growth in government expenditures, and to understand how the forces behind privatization have been able to get a foothold, it is important to examine the pressures on government budgets.

Total spending by all levels of government has increased steadily over the 20th century and as of 2006 accounted for 36.1 percent of GDP, up from 23.1 percent of GDP in 1960.[7] There are three primary reasons why expenditures have increased at such a rate: increased demand for government service, increased supply of services, and increasing inefficiency. Increasing demand causes a rise in expenditures because the people begin to expect the government to provide more and more necessary services. On the other hand, some phenomena within government also increase the supply of services. Furthermore, the government creates inefficiencies when it overstaffs and overpays its employees, often increasing the amount of money spent while receiving diminishing marginal benefits. Since all three are increasing simultaneously, there is no impetus to decrease spending. Thus, each of these reasons plays a distinct role in pushing governments toward privatizing correctional facilities.

A variety of factors drive the increasing demand for public services. Demographic changes lead to a propensity for privatizing the incarceration of criminals. Savas notes that the demographic shift of increasing urbanization increases demand for public services because new government action is needed to regulate and ameliorate the potential harm of individual actions.[8] As a direct result of urbanization, crime rates are likely to increase, leading to a need for higher police presences, expanded court systems, and increased prison capacity to accommodate the increases in the number of convicted criminals.

Additionally, the urbanization effect can be compounded by socioeconomic changes; wealthier people are more likely to favor harsher criminal penalties to keep criminals off the streets, while poorer people are more likely to turn to crime if living in unsavory conditions. Thus, a population shift in either direction could potentially lead to increased demand for law enforcement and security from the government. Fred Becker notes that people are "reluctant to rely on private organizations for any service delivery functions which are critical for the safety and security of society."[9] While he cites both police patrols and the incarceration of criminals under this observation, one must realize that people are much more open to prison privatization than police privatization, given that private prisons are widespread and private police forces are not. When state and local law enforcement and criminal justice budgets are hemorrhaging, it is more palatable to try to reduce costs by privatizing prisons than by privatizing local and state police forces.

As demand for public services rises, there are no shortages of groups and individuals willing to provide a subsequent increase in supply to meet the demand. Savas notes a variety of reasons, including enlarging bureaucracies, government monopolies, and overproduction,[10] but perhaps none have as much of a direct effect on prison privatization as "gaining votes" does. This is essentially another way of saying that political pressures lead to an increase in the supply of government services. Politicians usually respond to their constituency's desires (increased demand for something) by providing remedies to the desires (increasing the supply). This can take a number of different avenues, such as pressure for better schools leading to increased funding or pressure for city beautification leading to an increase in public works projects. In response to the desire for prison privatization, politicians can enact stricter laws and provide more tools to enforce those laws.

In order to gain votes, politicians appease those seeking remedies to increasing crime rates by instituting law-and-order policies, which increase the incarceration rates and create a demand for more prisons. Judith Greene notes: "Draconian sentencing and get-tough correctional policies led to an unprecedented increase in jail and prison populations, driving the United States' rate of incarceration head and shoulders above that of other developed nations."[11] Obviously, any increase in the number of people incarcerated is a potential boon for the private prison industry. The CCA's 2008 Form 10-K even states the following: "As a result of demand for prison beds from both our federal and state customers and the utilization of a significant portion of our existing available beds, we intensified our efforts to deliver new capacity to address the lack of available beds that our existing and potential customers are experiencing."[12] For reasons that will later be explained in greater detail, private prisons provide a rapid solution to increasing the supply. As politicians willfully enact tougher laws, the end result pushes state and local governments to privatize correctional facilities in order to meet the rising costs of providing more prison beds and preventing overcrowding, both of which result from longer sentences and increases in the number of convicts.

Some studies do show statistically significant relationships between increasing supply and demand for government services and increasing state expenditures on correctional facilities. A study by John W. Ellwood and Joshua Guetzkow found that overall state spending on corrections grew in both current and constant dollars between 1977 and 1998. In addition, corrections spending has also grown as a percentage of a state's total budget.[13] Incarceration rates, a function of crime rates, have mostly driven the overall trend. However, it should be noted that these rates do vary from state to state. A state's personal income level significantly explains the variety in total spending on corrections. Growth in the rate at which correctional expenditures increase is positively attributed to increases in the price index and growth in the incarceration rate. The study also found growth in expenditures to be negatively related to overall growth in personal income levels.[14] Since incarceration rates are a function of rising crime rates, as well as some other socioeconomic factors, growth in the crime rate triggers demand for more incarceration to cope with the problem. Since increases in correctional expenditures are in part driven by increased incarceration rates, increased demand for government services such as incarceration clearly contributes to the rise in state correctional expenditures.

The Ellwood and Guetzkow study also sought to see if a relationship existed between increased correctional expenditures and a relative reduction in expenditures in other areas. They concluded that there was no statistically significant relationship; all expenditures experienced growth over the period.[15] However, that does not necessarily mean that there is no effect at all. Anything spent on corrections is still one less dollar available to spend on something else. It seems that the majority of spending increases come from the availability of new funds. Even though correctional spending as a percentage of budgets has increased, it doesn't necessarily mean that the increase has come at the expense of other budgetary items, although this study does have some flaws. It was unable to take into account that some budgetary items are constrained by laws and therefore cannot be offset with cuts in other areas. Also, the state budgets were simplified into six major categories; consequently, the information may not have been complete enough to draw any real conclusions. Lastly, the models did not consider that states' revenues may not match expenses. In reality, the availability of revenues is what will most likely drive spending cuts, rather than increases in specific areas of the budget. However, when expenditures exceed revenues, privatizing correctional facilities to cut spending could be a viable alternative given the relative growth of correctional spending as percentages of state expenditures.

The last factor driving the increases in government expenditures is inefficiency. Two of the major drivers of inefficiency are overstaffing and overpaying. At lower levels, public sector employees are compensated at much higher rates than private sector employees who perform similar functions, although it should be noted that employees at higher levels in the private sector are paid better than comparable public sector employees.[16] On average, health and retirement benefits are also much more generous in the public sector, leading to an increase in the cost for government to provide the same level of service as a private company.[17] Therefore, it should be no surprise that reduced labor costs are often one of the arguments offered in favor of privatization programs. Overstaffing generally arises as bureaucracies grow; more people are needed to handle the size increases, and some inevitably wind up duplicating tasks. At lower pay levels, expenditure increases can be compounded by government employees being comparatively overpaid. Additionally, overstaffing can in some cases be a function of regulatory requirements that dictate the number of people that must be staffed at a given time.[18]

In the face of strained budgets, the cost problems associated with overstaffing and overpaying are much more difficult to control than the decision to privatize an entire department. Many government employees belong to unions, which makes reducing pay and eliminating certain positions very difficult. Thus, in some cases, privatization may be the only way to control or reduce the expenditure. The ability to reduce labor costs is a crucial part of this argument. While the effect of lower labor costs will be explored in depth later, it's worth noting that even private prison objector Michael A. Hallett notes that "hiring fewer staff with lower benefits"[19] is one of the few places that private prisons can demonstrate a cost savings over publicly administered correctional facilities.

ARGUMENTS AND APPROACHES

Rising expenditures are a compelling reason for the pressure to privatize prisons, but what about corrections makes privatization attractive? Specifically, why is privatization in this area a viable alternative to privatizing tax collection or public works departments? Savas outlines two major principles by which to examine goods and services. One principle is exclusion, or the feasibility of the supplier being able to deny a good or service to a potential user if the user does not meet the supplier's required criteria to engage in a transaction. The other principle is consumption, or the degree that a good or service is shared by one or more individuals.

Along these two dimensions, goods and services can be classified into four major categories:[20]

- Individual goods and services: feasible to exclude, consumed individually (e.g., market purchases)
- Toll goods and services: feasible to exclude, consumed jointly (e.g., utilities)
- Common-pool goods and services: not feasible to exclude, consumed individually (e.g., rivers and lakes)
- Collective goods and services: not feasible to exclude, consumed jointly (e.g., national defense)

Of these four categories, incarcerating criminals falls under collective goods and services. All citizens benefit from the services provided by correctional facilities, but correctional facilities, whether public or private, cannot exclude any citizens from receiving these benefits. Thus, collective goods and services will be examined in greater detail than the other three categories.

The scope of collective goods and services has increased over time, and more often than not, the provision of collective goods and services has fallen under the control of the government. Some collective goods and services, such as national police and fire departments, cannot feasibly be provided solely by private organizations; thus, government certainly has a role to play. Yet, private actors with profit motives can partially provide these goods or services even if government also plays a significant role in their provision. For example, police departments are responsible for providing security and safety to the general populace; however, most major office buildings retain private security forces to ensure that safety is provided to the building. Therefore, it is possible for government and private actors to provide the same collective good simultaneously. Moreover, any competition between private actors and government to provide goods and services may actually improve the overall quality of the good or service in question.

The problem with solely providing collective goods and services through the government is that decisions are made by political appropriations processes and not by market choices.[21] Individuals compete for resources and are therefore likely to choose the best alternative to provide a good or service. While that concept doesn't entirely apply to a collective good or service by nature, the lack of any competition for the resources allows the government to inefficiently provide them because of a lack of available substitutes. Without substitutes, there is no incentive to allocate resources to the best alternatives. However, the private sector can adequately provide for correctional facilities. If private firms could not do so, there would not be equity investors ready to receive the residual claims of providing this service. Thus, their mere presence shows that it is possible for the private sector to provide for correctional facilities.[22] Their presence should also, in theory, force the government to attempt to provide this good at least as well as private firms can. It is unlikely that state governments would ever improve without the existence of market alternatives to help find the most efficient way to house inmates. However, the key to actually deriving any potential benefit from the existence of a private sector is rooted in the structure of the relationship between government and the private sector.

Collective goods can effectively be arranged in one of four ways: government provision, intergovernment agreements, contracting, and voluntarily.[23] Of these, contracting is the only acceptable alternative for providing private correctional services. Government provision and intergovernment agreements are both public sector functions, and the need for some authority to use coercive force to imprison an individual makes any voluntary arrangements infeasible. As a result, a large majority of privatized correctional facilities are operating on the basis of contracts with state and local governments. Contracts introduce competition into the operation of correctional facilities, but only if multiple firms bid for the same contract. While private firms do foster some competition with any government providers of a collective good or service, the overall effect of introducing competition can be diminished without substantial competition between firms. Thus, if there are only one or two dominant players, the effect of competition is significantly lower. Additionally, if no-bid contracts are a common practice, contracting will not foster the same level of competition as the free market.

Beyond introducing competition to a previous government monopoly, privatization through contracting can yield several other advantages over the government provision of goods and services. Governments can still rapidly respond to changing needs when using contracting. This flexibility allows them to adjust the size and scope of a program relative to changes in demand for the good or service or a change in fund availability. With the exception of a possible principal-agent problem for corporations, contracts put cost-benefit decisions into the hands of those with a direct stake in running an efficient operation, and these decisions factor into the pricing of the contract bids. Thus, the true costs of providing a good or service can possibly become more transparent than they would be under a government monopoly, and this also provides the government with a mechanism to compare its own costs.[24] Additionally, private firms often don't face the same constraints and thus can foster innovations that won't occur under government monopoly.[25]

Proponents of private correctional facilities cite many of the preceding advantages of contracting as conditions that make it an ideal arrangement. It is easy to specify and measure the benefits of the services, and firms can use part-time labor in some situations to cut costs, an advantage that the government does not have. Moreover, private firms can also retain any in-house expertise on prison administration while still trying newer, more innovative methods. Correctional facilities also have many costs that do not directly affect operating budgets. In publicly administered prisons, the costs of building and maintaining the infrastructure, fringe benefits for employees, overhead, and liability insurance may be part of other budgets, thus obscuring the true total cost of operating a prison. Since these costs are still borne by the government regardless of the budget they're attributed to, the potential for overall expenditures to rise increases. Private prison operators have an incentive to price all of these indirect costs into their contract bids in order to adequately provide the service and still make a profit. However, it should be noted that many of these indirect costs, especially fringe benefits, tend to be much lower for private sector firms than the government, thus yielding some cost advantages to the private sector.

Prisons contracts are usually structured based on the facility. If an existing facility is publicly owned and operated, two contracting arrangements are generally used that still maintain public ownership. The most common is a contract to operate and maintain (O&M), under which the state pays the private firm to operate and maintain the existing facility. The public doesn't have to relinquish ownership of an existing capital asset, but it still gets the benefits of lower costs through this type of privatization. Another arrangement uses lease-build-operate (LBO) contracts, in which the private corrections provider gets a long-term lease to make improvements and to operate a facility.[26] This arrangement is less common because the government simultaneously takes money for the lease and gives it right back through the contract fees; it is only seen when the facility needs many significant upgrades.

One of the most distinct reasons that prison privatization has gained popularity is that private facilities can be built more quickly and cheaply than publicly owned and operated ones. Cost savings on private corrective systems are estimated to be anywhere from 15 to 25 percent over government projects. Time savings are even more dramatic, as private firms can complete the entire construction process in half the time it would take the government to build a similar facility.[27] There are several reasons for these savings. First, since private capital is at risk, construction would not begin unless the firm deemed it economically feasible, whereas government might undertake the project for less prudent reasons. Also, private capital providers hope to recoup their investment as soon as possible, thus ensuring that they complete construction quickly and economically to allow the facility to generate profits as soon as it can. For the government, the risks are more spread out and the incentives to develop the facilities efficiently and expediently are not in place. Finally, government procurement regulations slow development and reduce flexibility, thus increasing costs and time over a comparable private sector project.[28] Furthermore, the constraints of public finance, such as arranging the sale of municipal bonds or financing through general revenues, are not shared by private firms, who have easy access to both debt and equity capital markets to finance their construction needs.

The rise in prison privatization can be directly attributed to the ability of private companies to cheaply and quickly finish construction. While operational cost efficiencies do arise and are a large consideration, a major impetus in favor of privatization comes from this distinct advantage over government construction. It can even be observed in state prison spending budgets; the Bureau of Justice reports that public spending on prison capital expenditures fell nearly 25 percent from 1996 to 2001.[29] The increase in private prison capital expenditures can at least partly explain that drop. Most of the original opportunities for private prisons resulted directly from prison overcrowding. Michael A. Hallett writes:

> Although cost savings is perhaps the most frequent label used to justify prison privatization to the public, overcrowded prisons created . . . a market opportunity: high demand and low supply. In a classic supply and demand business proposal, entrepreneurs sought to meet what they knew would be a steady and increasing demand; incarceration rates and sentence durations were up, whereas supply of prison bed space was limited.[30]

This problem was compounded by increasing operating costs due to overcrowding, declining tax revenues, and other budgetary constraints that left little money available to increase capacity through new construction.[31] Entrepreneurs could therefore take advantage of the considerable cost and time advantages that privatization afforded them to solve a serious problem for many states. Additionally, the states received the added advantage of lowering their own operating costs by contracting with private firms to operate the new facilities. As capacity increases, the overall operating costs should be lower, assuming demand stays relatively stable.[32]

Using private firms, this capacity could be increased in various ways: (1) renting a facility; (2) contracting to build and operate with a state prior to the start of construction; or (3) building speculative prisons. As with facilities that remain under government ownership, several different contract arrangements can be established to construct a new facility. A build-transfer-operate (BTO) arrangement is more common. The private firm builds the facility and transfers ownership to the government when it completes the construction; the firm then operates the facility on a contracting basis, recouping its investment costs as it is paid for operating. This gives the government the private sector's construction advantages while allowing government ownership of the facility. A build-operate-transfer (BOT) arrangement is similar to a BTO arrangement, but the transfer occurs after the private firm has operated the prison for a term; since the ownership transfer occurs in the distant future, the facility is effectively owned by the private company for some period of time.

With existing facilities that need some new construction done, the ideal privatization contract is a buy-build-operate (BBO) arrangement. Under a BBO, the existing facility is sold to the private firm, renovated to take advantage of private construction efficiencies, and then operated under a contract by the private corrections company.

However, the contract seen most often is a build-own-operate (BOO) contract. The private firm develops and constructs the prison under this contract, then maintains its ownership and continues to operate the facility under a contract, generally in perpetuity, for the prison authority.[33] This is the most common arrangement for prison privatization when a new facility is constructed, and it is generally the best method for rapidly increasing prison capacity.

Speculative prisons are controversial, but the rationale behind the practice has merit. Instead of contracting prior to starting the construction, the firm builds a prison without knowing if it will fill its capacity. After finishing construction, the private firm solicits contracts with prison authorities to provide them with inmates. This is the most pure form of prison privatization, as the prison authorities have no input in the design of the facility. Since demand for prison capacity continues to increase, speculative prisons afford the government what it seeks in most states.

By now, it is clear that prison privatization has several advantages, but it would be naive to assume that contracting realizes all of these advantages. The costs of operation and construction are clearly lower with privatization, but critics claim that this does not mean that privatizing prisons will automatically save prison authorities a significant amount of money, if any at all. Thus, in the following sections, several tests have been conducted to see what potential benefits are realized through prison privatization.

TESTING THE IDEA OF PRIVATIZATION

Data

The data used to conduct the test comes from three sources: the 2001 report on state prison expenditures issued by the Bureau of Justice Statistics, the 2006 report of inmates under state authorities, and the 2006 10-K for the Corrections Corporation of America. For the purposes of the test, the CCA's 2006 performance will be used as a proxy for the private prison industry, as the CCA has a market share of nearly 50 percent. According to the 10-K, average revenues and operating expenses per inmate per day in owned and managed facilities were $61.03 and $41.47, respectively.[34] This translates to annual per inmate revenues of $22,276 and annual per inmate expenses of $15,137. In leased and managed facilities, average revenues and operating expenses per inmate per day were $38.39 and $32.86, respectively,[35] and this corresponds to annual revenues of $14,102 and annual operating expenses of $11,994 per inmate.

Since state prison expenditures were not available for 2006, the total expenditures by state in 2001 were increased by a compounded annual inflation rate of 2 percent to give an estimate for 2006. The estimated total expenditures were then divided by each state's 2006 inmate population to estimate the expenditures per inmate.

Results

Clearly, the "issue" of the privatization game for prisons is whether or not they can provide a cheaper method to house immates. If we can examine Tables 10.1 and Tables 10.2, it does appear that private prisons enjoy a vastly reduced cost structure when compared to operating expenditures of state correctional authorities. This confirms that the private sector is better able to take advantage of cheaper labor costs and save from relaxed material procurement regulations, two of the most-often cited reasons in favor of privatization. In both cases, the results are statistically significant.

Table 10.1   Comparison between Operating Expenses of State versus Private Prisons

Mean State Expenditure (in $000s)	23.155
Private Prison Expenditures Standard Error of the Mean	15.137

Table 10.2   Comparison between Operating Expenses of State versus Leased or Managed Prisons

Mean State Expenditure (in $000s)	23.155
Private Prison Expenditures Standard Error of the Mean	11.994

However, whether or not private prisons cost less for state prison authorities present a less clear picture. Table 10.3 shows the payments from state correctional authorities for inmate incarceration are essentially the revenues earned by private corrections companies. Therefore, any demonstrable cost advantage in contracting out to private prisons should be noticeable if revenues are significantly less than state expenditures. In the case of owned and managed private facilities, there are not statistically significant cost savings for state correctional authorities. If owned and managed revenues per inmate decreased to $21,331 per year, then a statistically significant cost savings for states would emerge.

On the other hand, there is a statistically significant difference between the revenues paid to leased and managed facilities and state correctional expenditure as shown in Table 10.4 is considerably less than the test statistic, indicating that there is a high level of significance attached to this finding. This makes sense intuitively, as the revenues earned in leased facilities are less than the operating expenses per inmate of an owned and managed facility.

It should be noted that there could be discrepancies in the data that may have swayed some findings in different ways. The state operating expenditures are clearly broken into wages/salaries/benefits and other expenses, which includes health care, food, and utilities, among others. However, what constitutes the operating expenses for the CCA is even less transparent. It is possible that the two groups could have some discrepancies between them; if possible, certain costs would have been isolated to ensure congruence in comparison. Additionally, it remains unclear what causes the difference for private firms in operating a leased or an owned facility. If it could control for those differences, the study would be strengthened further.

Table 10.3   Comparison between Operating Costs of State versus Private Prisons

Mean State Expenditure (in $000s)	23.155
Private Prison Expenditures Standard Error of the Mean	22.276

Table 10.4   Comparison between Operating Costs of State versus Leased and Managed Prisons

Mean State Expenditure (in $000s)	23.155
Private Prison Expenditures Standard Error of the Mean	14.012

For those interested, at the end of the chapter, Table 10.5 contains the actually data used in assembling Tables 10.1, 10.2, 10.3, and 10.4.

CONCLUSION

Overall, it appears that private prisons are more cost-effective than government-run prisons. Private prison cost structures are much lower than state correctional cost structures; however, this can change depending on how much private firms charge for their services. The operating margins on facilities that are owned and managed by the private firms are much higher than those on facilities that are leased and managed. It is possible that these operating margins could be decreased slightly in order to make private ownership and management of prisons a more attractive option for states, at least on a cost basis, since there are other considerations in the decision process.

At any rate, there is a lot of variance in the differences between per-inmate operating expenditures for each state. It may not be possible to definitively say that privatizing prisons will save money, but at the very least, states should explore the privatization option on a case-by-case basis when they make decisions about their correctional system. It may be viable in some cases and not in others.

There are still greater insights that can be gathered from this study. Overcrowding will likely continue to persist in the future. Thus, prison privatization will likely play a role in the future of the correctional system, if only to take advantage of the private sector's construction advantage, allowing a rapid increase in capacity. This study's findings imply, however, that states may want to institute more BTO contracts if the primary reason for privatization is overcrowding. This would allow states to take

Table 10.5 State Prisons

			Operating Expenditures				
			2006 Operating Expenditures (in thousands)				
	2006 Inmates	Total	per Inmate	Wages	per Inmate	Other	per Inmate
AL	28,241	244,856	8.7	169,009	6.0	75,847	2.7
AK	5,069	170,201	33.6	89,991	17.8	80,209	15.8
AZ	35,892	673,390	18.8	451,081	12.6	222,309	6.2
AR	13,729	212,658	15.5	120,301	8.8	92,357	6.7
CA	175,512	4,535,392	25.8	3,172,096	18.1	1,363,295	7.8
CO	22,481	480,316	21.4	303,727	13.5	176,589	7.9
CT	20,566	559,664	27.2	349,438	17.0	210,226	10.2
DE	7,206	179,299	24.9	122,278	17.0	57,021	7.9
FL	92,969	1,605,112	17.3	1,055,270	11.4	549,841	5.9
GA	52,792	994,686	18.8	749,631	14.2	245,055	4.6
HI	5,967	129,289	21.7	71,559	12.0	57,730	9.7
ID	7,124	102,482	14.4	57,855	8.1	44,627	6.3
IL	45,106	1,100,479	24.4	787,584	17.5	312,895	6.9
IN	26,091	496,181	19.0	335,983	12.9	160,198	6.1
IA	8,875	205,688	23.2	164,551	18.5	41,138	4.6
KS	8,816	201,666	22.9	118,933	13.5	82,733	9.4
KY	20,000	302,964	15.1	137,775	6.9	165,189	8.3
LA	37,012	507,530	13.7	216,486	5.8	291,046	7.9
ME	2,120	82,953	39.1	56,470	26.6	26,482	12.5
MD	22,945	698,606	30.4	388,493	16.9	310,113	13.5

(*Continued*)

Table 10.5 *(Continued)*

	Operating Expenditures					
		2006 Operating Expenditures (in thousands)				
	2006 Inmates	Total	per Inmate	Wages	per Inmate	Other	per Inmate
---	---	---	---	---	---	---	---
MS	21,068	292,033	13.9	138,060	6.6	153,973	7.3
MO	30,167	400,151	13.3	243,770	8.1	156,381	5.2
MT	3,572	78,576	22.0	39,390	11.0	39,186	11.0
NE	4,407	110,259	25.0	71,022	16.1	39,237	8.9
NV	12,901	199,655	15.5	135,843	10.5	63,814	4.9
NH	2,805	66,553	23.7	46,897	16.7	19,656	7.0
NJ	27,371	848,664	31.0	489,367	17.9	359,297	13.1
NM	6,639	163,679	24.7	83,388	12.6	80,292	12.1
NY	63,315	2,812,593	44.4	2,174,763	34.3	637,830	10.1
NC	37,460	927,811	24.8	666,790	17.8	261,021	7.0
ND	1,363	26,740	19.6	15,163	11.1	11,576	8.5
OH	49,166	1,326,298	27.0	839,839	17.1	486,459	9.9
OK	26,243	416,656	15.9	209,148	8.0	207,508	7.9

OR	13,707	441,010	32.2	217,796	15.9	223,213	16.3
PA	44,397	1,306,865	29.4	844,664	19.0	462,200	10.4
RI	3,996	133,778	33.5	112,615	28.2	21,163	5.3
SC	23,616	412,097	17.4	294,257	12.5	117,841	5.0
SD	3,359	40,884	12.2	22,033	6.6	18,851	5.6
TN	25,745	465,709	18.1	185,811	7.2	279,897	10.9
TX	172,116	2,507,322	14.6	1,483,287	8.6	1,024,035	5.9
UT	6,430	147,597	23.0	90,702	14.1	56,894	8.8
VT	2,215	49,537	22.4	29,416	13.3	20,121	9.1
VA	36,688	771,867	21.0	595,751	16.2	176,116	4.8
WA	17,561	507,672	28.9	330,552	18.8	177,120	10.1
WV	5,733	67,563	11.8	40,908	7.1	26,655	4.6
WI	23,431	661,433	28.2	364,374	15.6	297,058	12.7
WY	2,114	53,472	25.3	25,754	12.2	27,718	13.1

Source: Corrections Corporation of America. Form 10-K for the fiscal year ended on December 31, 2008. Filed with the United States Securities and Exchange Commission, Washington, DC.

advantage of the ease of construction in the private sector while also taking advantage of the lower cost to the state of leasing facilities to private firms. Although the private sector may prefer other types of contracts due to the lower margins of BTO contracts, the correctional authorities do have some leverage to structure contracts in whatever fashion they please, as private prison operators are entirely dependent on them for revenues.

It is also important to consider the problems with prison privatization that go beyond cost and capacity. First, private prisons have been accused of "cherry-picking," or only accepting inmates that cost the least (non-violent offenders, prisoners without severe health issues). This could wind up increasing costs for the states if they are left with the most expensive prisoners.[36] The issue of monitoring private prisons is another potential pitfall for states, as those costs can quickly escalate if the prison is not within close proximity. Also, labor turnover is much higher because of the lower wages and salaries, which increases risk due to inexperienced workers. Finally, there are tax implications. Lower wages to employees reduces revenues from income taxes, and private prisons often use real estate investment trusts (REITs) to help avoid paying taxes.[37] Many of these hidden costs can quickly diminish the benefits of private prisons.

In addition, as a matter of social policy, do Americans want to live in a society where punishing crime is a market opportunity? Is there a point where social disorganization should be about something other than cutting costs? These issues are some of the reasons why Becker (cited near the beginning of this chapter) typically reserves services requiring coercive force as candidates that are not ideal for privatization. This doesn't even take into account the possibility of creating a "prison-industrial" complex. If private firms create too much excess capacity, there could be major issues with pressure to fill prisons down the road. First, closing facilities could be difficult for a number of reasons, including the multiple legal hurdles[38] and the likelihood that livelihoods would become dependent on the jobs that prisons provide. Thus, even if incarceration is not the most effective way to rehabilitate offenders and prevent recidivism, it could be increasingly seen as a solution just because prisons need to be filled.

Although these issues certainly do deserve some deliberation before jumping into the debate about prison privatization, there is still something to be gained from debate over privatizing prisons. It is unlikely that all correctional facilities in the United States will be privately held in the future, but a mix of private and public prisons could foster a level of competition that would make state and other government correctional authorities more efficient. Private facilities are also an ideal place to pursue newer techniques that improve incarceration, which would then allow the public authorities to replicate those techniques. Either way, prison overcrowding and pressure on budgets will likely continue, and prison privatization should therefore continue to grow. It may not be possible to make any definitive conclusions on its overall viability, but in some circumstances, privatizing correctional facilities certainly has some merit.

NOTES

1. Charles W. Thomas, "Correctional Privatization in America: An Assessment of Its Historical Origins, Present Status, and Future Prospects," in *Changing the Guard: Private Prisons and the Control of Crime,* ed. Alexander Taborrak (Oakland, CA: The Independent Institute, 2003), 57–124.

2. Stephanie Chen, "Larger Inmate Population Is Boon to Private Prisons," *The Wall Street Journal* (November 19, 2008).

3. Corrections Corporation of America, Form 10-K for the fiscal year ended on December 31, 2008, filed with the United States Securities and Exchange Commission, Washington, DC.

4. Thomas, "Correctional Privatization in America."

5. Fred W. Becker, *Problems in Privatization Theory and Practice in State and Local Governments* (Lewiston, NY: The Edwin Mellon Press, 2001).

6. E. S. Savas, *Privatization and Public-Private Partnerships* (New York: Chatham House Publishers, 2000).

7. Savas, *Privatization and Public-Private Partnerships.*

8. Savas, *Privatization and Public-Private Partnerships.*

9. Becker, *Problems in Privatization Theory and Practice in State and Local Governments.*

10. Savas, *Privatization and Public-Private Partnerships.*

11. Judith Greene, "Banking on the Prison Boom," in *Prison Profiteers,* ed. Tara Herivel and Paul Wright (New York: W.W. Norton and Company, 2007), 3–26.

12. Corrections Corporation of America, 2008 Form 10-K.

13. John W. Ellwood and Joshua Guetzkow, "Causes and Budgetary Consequences of State Spending on Corrections," in *Do Prisons Make Us Safer?* ed. Stephen Raphael and Michael A. Stoll (New York: Russell Sage Foundation, 2009).

14. Ellwood and Guetzkow, "Causes and Budgetary Consequences of State Spending on Corrections."

15. Ellwood and Guetzkow, "Causes and Budgetary Consequences of State Spending on Corrections."

16. Savas, *Privatization and Public-Private Partnerships.*

17. Becker, *Problems in Privatization Theory and Practice in State and Local Governments.*

18. Savas, *Privatization and Public-Private Partnerships.*

19. Michael A. Hallett, *Private Prisons in America: A Critical Race Perspective* (Chicago: University of Illinois Press, 2006).

20. Savas, *Privatization and Public-Private Partnerships.*

21. Savas, *Privatization and Public-Private Partnerships.*

22. Bruce L. Benson, "Do We Want the Production of Prison Services to Be More Efficient?" in *Changing the Guard: Private Prisons and the Control of Crime,* ed. Alexander Taborrak (Oakland, CA: The Independent Institute, 2003), 163–216.

23. Savas, *Privatization and Public-Private Partnerships.*

24. Savas, *Privatization and Public-Private Partnerships.*

25. Becker, *Problems in Privatization Theory and Practice in State and Local Governments.*

26. Savas, *Privatization and Public-Private Partnerships.*

27. Thomas, "Correctional Privatization in America."

28. Savas, *Privatization and Public-Private Partnerships.*

29. United States Department of Justice, *State Prison Expenditure* (Washington, DC: U.S. Government Printing Office, 2001).

30. Hallett, *Private Prisons in America: A Critical Race Perspective.*

31. Byron Eugene Price, *Merchandizing Prisoners: Who Really Pays for Private Prisons?* (Westport, CT: Praeger Publishers, 2006).

32. Benson, "Do We Want the Production of Prison Services to Be More Efficient?"

33. Savas, *Privatization and Public-Private Partnerships.*

34. Corrections Corporation of America, Form 10-K for the fiscal year ended on December 31, 2006. Filed with the United States Securities and Exchange Commission, Washington, DC.

35. Corrections Corporation of America, 2006 Form 10-K.

36. Hallett, *Private Prisons in America: A Critical Race Perspective.*

37. Price, *Merchandizing Prisoners: Who Really Pays for Private Prisons?*

38. Kevin Pranis, "Doing Borrowed Time: The High Cost of Backdoor Prison Finance," in *Prison Profiteers,* ed. Tara Herivel and Paul Wright (New York: W.W. Norton and Company, 2007), 36–51.

OTHER INTERESTING STUDIES

Dyer, Joel. *The Perpetual Prison Machine.* Boulder, CO: Westview Press, 2000.

Chapter 11

Privatizing a Lottery: The Case of Illinois

New Hampshire was the first state to institute a lottery, in 1964. It gave the lottery the name "sweepstakes" and affiliated it with horse racing to circumvent federal antilottery laws. The state sold the first tickets on March 12, 1964, prompting New York to follow in 1967 and New Jersey in 1970. In 1974, Illinois introduced its own lottery with the motto "Have a ball!" Ever since, the lottery has provided the government with an important source of revenue. Initially, this revenue was not set aside for any particular purpose; however, in 1985, a law was enacted mandating that all proceeds from the lottery be contributed to the State of Illinois Common School Fund (CSF), which helps finance K–12 public schools across the state. Today, the lottery generates about 9 percent of the state's contribution to education.[1]

BACKGROUND

Financial Information

In 2007, the Illinois Lottery reported total assets of approximately $94 million. It maintains a highly liquid balance sheet, with current assets making up close to 98 percent of total assets. In 2006, the lottery earned $611 million on sales of $1,687 million, and in 2007, it earned $622 million on sales of $1,856 million. Operating represented approximately 3 percent of total revenue, while vendor fees and commissions were about 7 percent. Net cash flow was $607 million in 2006 and $613 million in 2007. The lottery, because of its nature, is and will continue to be an enterprise driven by a high cash flow.[2] (For more detailed financial information, refer to Tables 11.1, 11.2, and 11.3.) Illinois accounts for 4.4 percent of national lottery sales.

Table 11.1   Illinois Lottery Fund Statement of Net Assets, June 30, 2007

Assets

Current Assets

Cash and cash equivalents	$ 46,247,012
Accounts receivable	7,373,959
Due from Common School Fund	36,762,021
Due from Deferred Prize Winners Trust Fund	710,543
Investments in prize annuities, current portion	129,926
Deferred agent commissions	116,051
Inventories	1,611,335
Total current assets	92,950,847

Noncurrent Assets

Investments in prize annuities	1,102,875
Capital assets, net of accumulated depreciation	698,797
Total noncurrent assets	1,801,672
Total Assets	94,752,519

Liabilities

Current Liabilities

Annuity prizes payable, current portion	129,926
Accounts payable and accrued expenses	14,134,217
Deferred revenues	2,970,201
Accrued prizes payable	
Pick 3 game	4,551,847
Pick 4 game	297,114
Lotto game	1,632,519
Little Lotto game	5,131,436
Mega Millions	873,043
Extra and Numbers Now	11,908
Other games	24,865,566
Total current liabilities	54,597,777

Noncurrent Liabilities

Compensated absences	1,066,159
Annuity prizes payable	1,102,875
Total noncurrent liabilities	2,169,034
Total Liabilities	56,766,811

Net Assets

Investment in capital assets	698,797
Restricted for Common School Fund	37,286,911
	$37,985,708

Source: State of Illinois Lottery, http://www.illinoislottery.com.

Table 11.2   Illinois Lottery Fund Income Statement, June 30, 2007

Operating Revenues	Amount	Percentage of Revenue
Ticket Sales		
Instant games	$878,831,189	47.4%
Pick 3 game	1 307,244,446	16.6
Pick 4 game	168,351,803	9.1
Little Lotto game	130,479,728	7.0
Mega Millions	192,597,726	10.4
Lotto game	29,330,106	7.0
Lotto subscription game	2,206,036	0.1
Little Lotto subscription game	1,295,902	
Numbers Now 3	2,873,156	0.2
Numbers Now 4	1,137,002	
Total ticket sales	1,814,347,094	97.8
Unclaimed prizes	37,709,108	2.0
Other operating revenues	4,074,633	0.2
Total revenues	1,856,130,835	100
Operating Expenses		
Prizes		
Instant games	548,166,994	29.5
Pick 3 game	164,932,640	8.9
Pick 4 game	86,192,419	4.7
Mega Millions	105,512,020	5.7
Little Lotto game	69,259,318	3.7
Lotto game	66,489,153	3.6
Numbers Now	1,712,307	0.1
Numbers Now	628,421	
Total Prizes	1,042,893,272	56.2
Commissions and fees		
Agents	91,879,142	5.0
Independent contractor	34,209,202	1.8
Distributors	4,491,123	0.2
Total commissions and fees	130,579,467	7.0
Other operating expenses	61,092,376	3.3
Total prizes, commissions and fees, and other operating expenses	1,234,565,115	66.5
Net Operating Income	621,565,720	33.5
Interest Income	640,360	
Net Income Before Transfers	622, 206,080	33.5

Source: State of Illinois Lottery, http://www.illinoislottery.com.

Table 11.3   Illinois State Lottery Statements of Cash Flows, June 30, 2007

Cash Flows from Operating Activities	
Cash received from agents	$897,844,180
Cash prizes paid	(195,472,840)
Cash paid to vendors and employees	(93,370,801)
Other operating receipts	4,074,633
Net cash provided by operating activities	613,075,172
Cash Flows Used in Noncapital Financing Activities	
Transfers to other funds	(614,303,782)
Cash used in noncapital financing activities	(614,303,782)
Cash Flows From Capital and Related Financing Activities	
Fixed asset acquisition	(158,426)
Cash used in capital and related financing activities	(158,426)
Cash Flows From Investing Activities	
Interest from short-term investments credited to Common School Fund	576,590
Interest from short-term investments	63,770
Cash provided by investing activities	640,360
Net increase (decrease) in cash	(746,676)
Cash, beginning of the period	46,993,688
Cash, end of the period	$46,247,012

Source: State of Illinois Lottery, http://www.illinoislottery.com.

Products, Marketing, and Distribution

The state of Illinois has several offerings in terms of lottery games: the Mega Millions, Lotto, Little Lotto, Pick 3, Pick 4, Pick n' Play, and instant ticket games. The biggest sellers are typically games that reveal prizes instantly or take a relatively short time to do so. In 2007, instant tickets, Pick 3, and Pick 4 were the biggest sellers with 49 percent, 17 percent, and 9 percent of total sales, respectively.

In 2007, the state spent approximately $18 million (low for a company its size) on various forms of advertising.[3] Its marketing channels included multimedia advertising, consumer magazines, direct marketing to consumers, daily newspapers, outdoor marketing, point-of-purchase marketing, spot radio, and spot television.[4] There are 7,800 statewide distributors for the

Illinois Lottery, including gas stations, grocery stores, convenience stores, liquor stores, bars, and restaurants.

Why Privatize the Lottery?

Rod Blagojevich, the ill-fated then-governor of Illinois, unveiled a proposed new fiscal year 2008 budget of $49.1 billion for his state. The funding was to rely on $16 billion in debt in the form of general obligations, $2.6 billion from a new business tax, and $10 billion from the privatization of the state's lottery. When asked about the privatization of the lottery, the governor stated, "It will allow us to fund our pensions, removing this long-created threat to our fiscal health."

An objective of this new budget proposal is to fund the state's pension plan. Illinois's pension plan is currently underfunded by $41 billion, and Governor Blagojevich aimed to decrease this by $2 billion in 2008. He also planned to eventually maintain a fully funded pension plan by the year 2045. In addition, the governor planned to undertake extensive health care and education reforms. A plan has been proposed to expand health care coverage for those without insurance, and this would cost $2.1 billion in three years. A new reform program also proposed spending $6 billion in the four years beginning in 2007 to fund K–12 education.[5]

So why privatize the lottery? Obviously, the state needs cash. Issuing more debt is not an option, as Illinois already relies heavily on debt. The state has chosen the alternative of taking an asset that generates steady cash flows over many years and selling it off in exchange for a large amount of cash today. The lottery is therefore an ideal choice for privatization. It has produced a steady revenue stream in the past, but advancements in gaming technology and in customer expectations are starting to affect the gambling industry, and the state does not feel that it is readily equipped to keep up with it. John Filan (Illinois's chief operating officer) commented:

> Our main motivation is reducing the risk that the lottery will lose profits. . . . The gaming industry is intensively competitive and reliant on high-tech advances. The state is not equipped to manage such retail business. We are in the business of health, public safety, and education. We want to pass that risk from the state to private industry.[6]

The sale of the lottery is aided by the fact that the lottery is a proven asset with consistent revenue streams, which helps its valuation. Filan described it as "a mature asset with a history of growth." The government, which currently plans to make $10 billion from the lottery deal, plans to invest

$6 billion in education and reinvest the remaining $4 billion in an annuity that will generate approximately $650 million a year until the year 2025 (essentially replacing the lottery's lost revenue). In addition, the government will also continue to make money from the lottery in the form of taxes on the new owner's income. As Filan said, a private owner would probably be better suited to operate the lottery and would increase its profitability, meaning that the state would continue to benefit from the success of the lottery.[7]

Illinois's riverboat casinos and other gaming organizations already provide the government with a large stream of steady income. Unlike the lottery, riverboat casinos are privately owned and operated and therefore are much better adapted to keep up with the advancing gaming industry. The government currently taxes them at about 50 percent, which is much higher than the ordinary corporation. It is not yet known how much the government plans to tax the new lottery, but it seems likely that a less extreme tax rate will be used. The privatization of government-run operations to provide cash needed for short-term use has already been done successfully. The Chicago Skyway was leased to private investors for $1.83 billion, and the state of Indiana privatized its highways for $3.8 billion (and for a period of 75 years). And while lotteries have never been privatized in the United States, the Greek government successfully sold off 16 percent of its national lottery in an initial public offering (IPO).[8]

PART I: THE ECONOMICS OF PRIVATIZATION

Efficiency

Many observers contend that government-run agencies are typically less efficient than private enterprises. From an economic perspective, the price system establishes clear incentives for firms to minimize their costs. If they do so, they have the ability to increase profits. If the firms do not minimize costs, they run the risk of going out of business. Government officials usually have little to no incentive to reduce costs, except when there are political ramifications. On the other hand, private organizations often base their compensation on the performance of their employees. This creates incentive for employees to reduce costs and perform more efficiently. Government agencies also typically pay employees less than private firms do, and thus provide less financial incentive. In fact, one could say that government officials are more inclined to *increase* their costs. The higher the costs, the larger an agency's budget must be. Typically, agencies with higher budgets command the most power and influence.[9] If an agency fails to complete a task assigned to it, such as lowering the crime rate, then its budget for the next year is likely to be increased, whereas a successful agency that does its job under budget is likely to receive budget cuts at the end of a year. This encourages many agencies to go on spending sprees near the end of their fiscal year. But in the private sector, bankruptcy weeds out inefficient firms, so all firms must be cost-conscious.[10]

It is also difficult to judge the efficiency of a government agency, especially when it is a monopoly (see Part III below for more regarding the lottery's monopoly power). This can create a vicious circle, as government officials, falsely believing that their agency is running efficiently, cannot make changes to improve its efficiency, and therefore maintain the status quo (inefficiency). For example, how does the Environmental Protection Agency know whether it is operating efficiently? Because it is so difficult to measure the EPA's output and because there is no standard to compare it against, this question is a very difficult one to answer. Missing also are signals from the capital markets. When a corporation announces a new strategy that investors believe will not work, the stock price drops. There is no such mechanism in the public sector for government agencies to use.[11]

In addition, government-run agencies tend to be very bureaucratic. A clearly defined authoritative chain exists, and each person must report to his or her supervisor before taking action. This creates a lot of "red tape" and wasted time, which results in a very slow, tedious operation. Bureaucrats have more freedom to pursue narrow goals and interests without a strong regard for controlling costs relative to the benefits derived for the public.[12]

Specialization

The government cannot specialize in every industry. As the state of Illinois has come to realize, technology advances quickly, and the government cannot keep track of every changing aspect of every business. Rather, it must rely on certain private organizations (publicly owned corporations or private enterprises) to conduct the research necessary to develop the expertise in a certain field. Privatization, in this sense, is a clear manifestation of economic rationalism on the behalf of the privatizing government. Rather than being the direct provider of the goods or services, the government is delegated to a regulatory role. Its responsibility therefore becomes supervising the provision of the goods or services, a task that it is much more equipped to handle. As we have seen here in the United States (and as mentioned in the introduction), the upkeep and maintenance as well as the organization and administration of public highways are increasingly being contracted to private firms that have more expertise and can perform the same function more efficiently. These roads then become private tollways, which, being cleaner and in better condition than public roads, can charge higher tolls. While this might result in less equality in society, it certainly does make the toll operator more profitable. Health and education have been moving in the same direction. Private schools in general tend to produce graduates with better educations and therefore can charge a higher price on average than public schools. Specialization and efficiency tend to run hand in hand, as firms with expertise in their field are usually aware of the most cost-efficient methods of doing business.

PART II: WHY WOULD ANYONE BUY THE LOTTERY?

For a private investor or group of investors, buying the lottery should be regarded as an investment. What benefits, then, can the lottery offer to an investor seeking to make a profit? There are three qualities of the lottery that make it a worthwhile investment: income stability, profitability, and potential for improvement.

Income Stability

The lottery's revenue stream is very stable, for a number of reasons. It has a very loyal customer base. In a survey of 13,151 adults aged 18 and over, 29 percent of all respondents admitted to playing the lottery once a week or more, and 58 percent admitted to playing at least once a month.[13] Also important is that the lottery is a monopoly. Typically, a company's earnings fall when a competitor introduces a better product or when consumer tastes shift. Since there is no direct competition with the lottery, however, potential investors do not need to worry about losing sales to competitors and can instead focus on retaining customers and organically growing the business.

In general, very few external factors can influence the lottery's success. Unlike large manufacturing companies that require constant shipments of various raw materials, which can fluctuate in prices, the lottery has a very limited supply chain. The lottery is a self-contained, controlled system with little room for unanticipated error. This allows for easy planning of short- and long-term objectives.

Profitability

The Illinois Lottery is a very profitable enterprise. In 2006 and 2007, it reported net profit margins of 36.5 percent and 33.5 percent, respectively.

This is about the national norm for lotteries. In comparison, the margin for Harrah's Entertainment was 8 percent in 2006 and 3 percent in 2007,[14] and the rest of the gaming industry reported margins of about 9 percent on average.[15]

As a monopoly, the lottery has full control over every aspect of its business. It is free to increase or decrease ticket prices, jackpots, payout ratios, and vendor commissions with absolutely no regard to how its competitors would respond. Whereas casino gamblers might feel cheated and go to a different casino if gaming becomes "unfair," lottery players will continue to play regardless because they have no basis for comparison due to the lottery's monopoly status. Expenditures for marketing and advertising are also lower because of the lack of competition through substitute products.

Potential for Improvement

The lottery is essentially a government-operated gaming company with no direct competition and few costs. While this really is a great basis for a private company, there is still plenty of room for improvement. Government agencies typically are not as cost-efficient and cost-aware as private companies. The lottery could be made more efficient by a private firm with expertise in handling what is essentially a retail business. For the purpose of this chapter, a benefit to the lottery will be defined as any factor that increases its profitability. Since the lottery is being sold to private investors who will undoubtedly make changes in its operation, anything that makes the lottery more profitable will help it boast a higher price tag, which is in Illinois's best interest.

Based on the factors previously discussed, the Illinois Lottery would benefit from making certain strategic moves and initiatives in three main areas: efficiency, specialization, and marketing and distribution.

Efficiency

The lottery's private owners should almost immediately go through an intense restructuring campaign upon purchasing the lottery from the state of Illinois. They would probably organize the lottery's structure like that of a large corporation, and they would also likely move toward incentive-based compensation. Cutting the number of agents while increasing the amount of incentive-based compensation as a percentage of total compensation should reduce costs and increase productivity. This strategy would help to increase bottom-line earnings by reducing general and administrative expenses. Obviously, there are political repercussions to an "efficient" lottery (many people don't think of a lottery as something that they'd like to see become more efficient). Efficiency can come in two ways: cost efficiency, as just mentioned, or sales efficiency. Current retailer commissions are at 5 percent of sales.[16] Increasing their commission to between 6 and 7 percent, as some states have already done, would give retailers extra incentive to sell lottery tickets and would also increase the sales efficiency of existing retailers.

Specialization

As John Filan was quoted saying: "This [gambling] is fundamentally a retail business, and governments are not equipped to manage retail businesses. . . . Gaming is getting so competitive around the world that we're worried our revenues could go down unless there is retail expertise."[17] Along with their restructuring effort, the new owners should, and probably would, bring in new senior management. As gaming is a highly retail industry, a new CEO should have experience in that industry. This would help establish the new corporate governance needed to keep up with the highly dynamic retail industry. A veteran CEO who has experience working in highly competitive free-market industries would probably be best suited for the job. This would compensate for the fact that, since its existence, the lottery has essentially been a government-run monopoly with no direct competition.

In addition to hiring new senior management, the new private owners should either create a group with the goal of modernizing the lottery's technology or outsource that task completely. Since the gaming industry is becoming increasingly reliant on technology, it is crucial that the lottery maintain its competitiveness by introducing new forms of gaming through research and development. The California, New York, and Florida lotteries are already operated by a company named GTECH, which is based in Providence, Rhode Island, and specializes in the development of gaming technology.[18] This company currently runs Illinois's online games (non-instant tickets), but Illinois could do more to introduce new games and reduce the costs involved with running these games. Technological advances continue to make the lottery more cost-efficient to operate; investment in technology should therefore have a positive impact on profits, especially in a business where costs are highly variable.

Marketing and Distribution

There are vast opportunities in the marketing department. Retail businesses often expertly use marketing to create sales, and the introduction of new management would surely lead to significantly higher marketing budgets. As with technology, marketing can be done in house or out-sourced, as many businesses opt to do.

Currently, R. J. Dale Advertising and Public Relations manages the marketing for the Illinois Lottery. This company's other customers include the Chicago Department of the Environment, Coca-Cola, Harris Bank, the Illinois Department of Commerce and Economic Opportunity, Jewel-Osco, and Osco Drugs.[19] Most of these are rather dull, uninteresting companies or agencies, with Coca-Cola being the clear exception. Even then, in order to meaningfully boost sales, the lottery's new owners should find a company with more experience in selling a product similar to the lottery. People do not buy Coke and lottery tickets for the same reasons. Given that most customers play for the thrill of the game, the lottery could advertise in the same way that the McDonald's, Monopoly, or Six Flags theme parks do.

Currently, the lottery advertises through multimedia, consumer magazines, direct marketing to consumers, daily newspapers, outdoor marketing, point of purchase, spot radio, and spot television.[20] While this list is fairly comprehensive, a private firm could significantly expand marketing in terms of media and its intensity of advertising. A study of a large collection of annual reports from companies in various fields would show that the average firm's marketing expense as a percentage of sales ranges from 5 to 25 percent.[21] In comparison, the Illinois Lottery's 2003 marketing expense of $18 million represented only about 1.13 percent of its $1.58 billion of sales.[22] It is likely that boosting marketing budgets would yield a positive return on investment.

Alliances with major sports leagues such as the NFL, MLB, and NBA are a possibility, with the winning numbers announced at halftime or the seventh-inning stretch. The Massachusetts Lottery has had great success in the past selling $5 "Red Sox" instant tickets, which it plans to reintroduce after it proved to be among the most profitable tickets in lottery history.[23] The lottery could also make its magazine advertising more widespread: it could even go as far as packaging $1 lottery tickets with certain magazines, depending on who is identified as being the largest regional purchaser of tickets in a given locale.

New games should be introduced with a particular consumer base in mind and aggressively marketed to that consumer. The 18- to 24-year-old age group shows the largest opportunity for growth. In a survey, 37 percent of those aged 18 to 24 admitted to having purchased lottery tickets in the last 12 months, versus an average of 51 percent for all age groups combined.

Surveys showed that 61 percent of those aged 18 to 35 said they only played the lottery when they heard that the jackpot was getting really big, compared with an average of 45 percent for the other groups (35 and over).[24] The introduction of a new lottery game with a significantly higher jackpot but more uneven prize distribution could be very successful if it were properly marketed. Similarly, the lottery could introduce a new game with smaller jackpots and far more even prize distribution. Marketing for this game could target those in the 65 and up age bracket, as only 37 percent of respondents claimed to play only when the jackpot was high. Young people also tend to be the most frequent buyers of instant tickets. A new effort could be made to market these instant games to other age groups, as well as develop new instant games for those who already purchase them.

An effort should also be made to make distribution more widespread. There are many places with high potential for sales that the government does not currently exploit. Nelson Rose, a professor at Whittier Law School in Costa Mesa, California, who studies gambling and has advised the Illinois Gaming Board in the past, believes that political tension between the Illinois Lottery directors and the rest of the state government is the cause of this problem.[25] In a recent interview, he said: "Right now, states don't sell Lottery tickets in adult book stores, or next door to welfare offices, because Lottery directors know that they can be fired by politicians. . . . You won't see such hesitation among private companies. Those are great places to sell."[26]

Currently, Illinois Lottery tickets are not sold in strip clubs or on college campuses. Although these would undoubtedly be excellent locations to sell, government officials in charge of maintaining the state's image would never allow it. Private investors, given the freedom to do so, would certainly attempt to exploit these and other markets.

In addition to increasing distribution through conventional, existing methods, the advancement of technology will allow new distribution channels to develop. For example, the Internet has already emerged as a new distribution channel for lottery products. In the near future, people may be able to play the lottery using a cell phone or PDA (if legislation is passed to allow this, as it is currently restricted).

PART III: RISKS

Legal Issues

Currently, the state cannot be sued by gamblers who claim to have become addicted by the lottery. This provides a layer of protection from the many legal cases that the state would have to face if suing were permitted. However, this could change with privatization. A privatized lottery would have to be treated as an ordinary corporation, and would therefore be vulnerable to legal claims against it. The state of Illinois, in an attempt to increase the Illinois Lottery's selling price, could legally grant the lottery protection against such claims. However, if Illinois does not do so, the new owners would need to hire a team of lawyers to reformulate the lottery's terms of use in a manner that best protected it from lawsuits from compulsive gamblers.

There are also risks that the government would maintain very tight control over the lottery through regulation. Although potential investors would probably lobby against such action, if the government imposes heavy restrictions on advertising and distribution (as are currently in effect), then it could prove very difficult for the lottery to meaningfully increase its sales and profit. It is also unknown whether the government would want to leave the lottery as a privately owned monopoly. In a worst-case scenario for the new lottery operators, the state could pass legislation allowing for the creation of other independent lotteries that would compete with the current lottery. The government could also choose to split up the lottery, possibly geographically or by product segment.

Legitimacy

One major issue that the Illinois Lottery will have to face, and a possible threat to its earnings, will be the question of its legitimacy. Since 1985, its primary beneficiary has been the State of Illinois Common School Fund. Now that the lottery is being placed into the hands of private owners, consumers will no longer have the security of knowing that their money is being put toward education. A 2003 poll showed that 61 percent of lottery ticket buyers believe that the lottery benefits government programs that would otherwise be short on funding.[27] A private lottery has the potential of alienating customers who believe that their dollars should go toward good causes while also providing them with entertainment. Customers will also begin to question the motives of the new lottery owners and whether they will try to cheat players to boost profits. After all, for a private investor, higher revenue means more money in the bank. Dave Mizeur, a former deputy director of finance for the state of Illinois, commented on this issue: "The fact that the lottery is state-owned gives it a certain level of legitimacy with the public. They know that the games will be operated fairly. I'm not sure if they would view a privately operated lottery the same way."[28]

The new owners could mitigate these risks through the establishment of charitable foundations or through donations to existing ones. Tobacco and alcohol companies have dealt with similar issues in the past. They spend millions of dollars every year on everything from breast cancer research to domestic violence shelters in order to help them appear as good corporate citizens. In 1999 alone, Phillip Morris spent $60 million dollars on charity in an effort to combat the bad press it received in connection with a series of lawsuits. That same year, it also spent an estimated $108 million on advertising to tell the world about its goodwill. A privatized lottery could use similar methods to maintain its legitimacy. The new owners could promise to donate a percentage of revenue to the Common School Fund (since that is the current beneficiary) or to a variety of local charities. At the same time, the lottery would need to launch an advertising campaign aimed at informing the public of its corporate social responsibility.

PART IV: WHAT IS THE LOTTERY *REALLY* WORTH?

While the lottery does possess many great qualities as an investment, the asking price must still be considered. Is $10 billion too much? A cash-flow analysis reveals that the fair value of the Illinois Lottery may be slightly higher than that figure. Table 11.4 estimates potential investors' cost of capital and the lottery's future cash flows and growth rate, based on several key assumptions.

Cost of Equity: As lotteries are government-run agencies and do not have market data to support a beta calculation, (the rate of return versus the market rate of return where a beta greater than 1 shows that the stock is riskier than the market) a beta of 2.4 was used to reflect the average beta in the gaming industry. This average included Harrah's Entertainment (HET), Boyd Gaming Corporation (BYD), MGM Mirage (MGM), and Trump Entertainment (TRMP).[29] While this may not accurately reflect the risk involved with a lottery as opposed to casinos, there is currently no better comparison. Hence, the current risk-free rate of 5.25 percent and a historic risk premium of 7 percent were utilized. The capital asset pricing model, cost of equity = risk-free rate of return + measure of risk (market return − risk-free rate of return) gives a cost of equity of 22.05 percent.

Cost of Debt: To come up with a cost of debt of 7 percent, the going yield on the average BBB-rated corporate bond was used.[30] According to Standard & Poor's, "an obligation rated 'BBB' exhibits adequate protection parameters. However, adverse economic conditions or changing circumstances are more likely to lead to a weakened capacity of the obligor to

Table 11.4 Cash Flows with Standard Corporate Tax Rate

2005	2006	2007	2008	2009E	2010E	2011E	2012E	2013 Onward
$613,075,172	$643,728,931	$669,478,088	$702,951,992	$843,542,391	$927,896,630	$1,020,686,292.70	$1,071,720,607.33	$13,480,762,356
			($281,180,797)	($337,416,956)	($371,158,652)	($408,274,517)	($428,688,243)	
			$421,771,195	$506,125,434	$556,737,978	$612,411,776	$643,032,364	$13,480,762,356
			0.9279	0.8610	0.7989	0.7413	0.6879	0.6383
			$391,362,341	$435,775,086	$444,792,237	$453,995,974	$442,326,967	$8,604,530,052

Fair Value
$10,772,782,657

Implied Growth

| | | | 5% | 20% | 10% | 10% | 5% | 3% |

Beta	2.40%
Risk-free	5.25%
Risk premium	7.00%
Cost of equity	22.05%
Cost of debt	7%
Tax rate	40%
After-tax K_d	4.2%
Equity %	20%
Debt %	80%
WACC	7.77%
Long-term growth rate	3%

Source: Author's calculations

Table 11.5 Cash Flows with 51% Corporate Tax Rate

	2005	2006	2007	2008	2009E	2010E	2011E	2012E	2013 Onward
	$613,075,172	$643,728,931	$669,478,088	$702,951,992	$843,542,391	$927,896,630	$1,020,686,292.70	$1,071,720,607.33	
				($358,505,516)	($430,206,619)	($473,227,281)	($520,550,009)	($546,577,510)	
				$344,446,476	$413,335,771	$454,669,349	$500,136,283	$525,143,098	$12,641,865,614
				0.9332	0.8709	0.8128	0.7585	0.7079	0.6606
				$321,449,947	$359,986,502	$369,547,709	$379,362,861	$371,736,943	$8,351,429,964
				Fair Value					
				$10,153,513,926					
				Implied Growth					
				5%	20%	10%	10%	5%	3%

Beta	2.40%
Risk-free	5.25%
Risk premium	7.00%
Cost of equity	22.05%
Cost of debt	7%
Tax rate	51%
After-tax K_d	3.4%
Equity %	20%
Debt %	80%
WACC	7.77%
Long-term growth rate	3%

Source: Author's calculations

meet its financial commitment on the obligation."[31] Given its high level of cash inflow, the Illinois Lottery's ability to pay interest on its debt would only be weakened by some adverse macroeconomic event, and so a BBB rating is appropriate. A corporate tax rate of approximately 40 percent yields an after-tax cost of debt of 4.2 percent.

Debt to Equity: Given the low cost of debt as compared to equity, it would be in any investor's best interest to use as much debt as possible in financing the acquisition. Leveraged buyouts typically have a 70 percent debt, 30 percent equity structure, but the percentage of debt can be as high as 90 to 95 percent.[32] A slightly higher-than-average level of debt, 80 percent, was used. This can be defended given the below-average amount of risk in the cash flows.

Growth: Cash-flow growth of 5 percent was forecast for 2009. This is based on historic data and the fact that the new operators will not have had enough time to implement any changes to the lottery's operations. For 2010, a 20 percent growth in income was predicted, based on several factors. The lottery has steadily been growing throughout the past. A 5 percent growth plus an additional 15 percent from the restructuring, described in Part II (efficiency, specialization, and marketing and distribution) seemed reasonable. Forecasts for 2011 and 2012 were a more moderate growth rate of 10 percent, and for 2013, 5 percent growth was assumed. Over time, the lottery's ability to grow will be more and more limited by how large it already is. Finally, for the years after 2013, a 3 percent long-term growth rate was used.

This analysis yielded a fair value of $10.8 billion, indicating that the current asking price is a reasonable one. Even if the tax rate increased to 51 percent, the current tax rate for casinos, the fair value would remain nearly unchanged, at $10.2 billion. Because debt constitutes such a large percentage of the financing for these types of transactions, the decrease in cash flows is offset by the extremely low cost of debt (3.4 percent after tax; see Table 11.5).

CONCLUSION

The privatization of the Illinois Lottery in some ways makes perfect sense for the state. In its current form, the lottery is probably less profitable than it would be in the hands of private investors. This privatization would allow the state to capitalize on the private lottery's future profits in two ways. First, it would provide Illinois with more money today than the fair value of the asset being traded (the lottery), and it could use this money to increase the funding of its pension plan and to undertake major educational reforms. Second, it would allow the state to continue to benefit from the lottery's success, as it collects approximately 40 percent of the lottery's yearly revenue. For investors, the lottery would provide a stable, profitable investment opportunity with plenty of room for long-term growth. The current asking price is very reasonable, and therefore the deal should attract many potential customers.

Casinos will probably be the biggest opponents of the lottery privatization and will likely demand an equal level of taxation. Private lottery owners are much more of a threat to casinos because even though the two do not compete directly, good marketing can shift some customers. Even if this happens, the fair value of the lottery remains mostly unchanged, with a 51 percent tax rate (as shown in Part IV), and the transaction is still a good deal for the both the state and the purchaser.

The most important thing to consider, then, when examining this transaction, is the amount of regulation and taxation that the government will impose on the new lottery. From a social perspective, a profitable, efficient lottery is not in the government's best interest. However, from a monetary point of view, the state really should allow the lottery to increase its efficiency and profits. While the government would ideally like to maintain the same regulation it does now, if it grants the lottery more freedom, it can sell it for more money. Ultimately, selling the lottery will generate cash that the state desperately needs now. Decreasing the amount of regulation allows Illinois to sell for $10 billion an asset that is probably worth much less today. Therefore, major changes in regulation will not pose a direct threat to the lottery in the future.

UPDATE

The privatization of the Illinois Lottery was not the only way Illinois hoped to help fund a construction program to bring more schools, bridges, and roads to the state. At the end of May 2008, the Senate approved a bill that would lead to major gambling expansion, making Illinois a competitive player in the casino gambling industry.[33] The Senate approved the plan that would allow slot machines on racetracks and a new casino in downtown Chicago, by a 32–18 vote. With such a response, it is not surprising that the bill to privatize the state lottery was also approved. Both bills will face much more opposition in the House.

Many other states have moved to privatize their lotteries, including large players such as California, Texas, Indiana, and Florida. New York has also sought advice from J. P. Morgan and other banks about what privatization might offer the state.[34] The issue has drawn support from both political parties, as mainly Democratic Illinois and Republican-dominated Indiana and Texas have all made formal proposals to privatize their lotteries from 2006 to 2008.[35] Although all of these proposals have failed, they look to be resurrected again with the display of strong interest in the idea. In April 2007, Indiana governor Mitch Daniels said that 10 companies, mostly American firms, made nonbinding offers for its lottery, with many exceeding the state's initial estimate of $1 billion, including two "well over twice as big" as this estimation.[36] Such strong interest exemplifies the continued effort in these states to gain support for privatization, and Texas and California have begun laying the groundwork for the 2009 legislative session.

NOTES

1. State of Illinois Lottery, http://www.illinoislottery.com/ (accessed June 25, 2009).

2. State of Illinois Lottery, 2008 Annual Report, http://www.illinoislottery.com/subsections/PR/FY08AnRpt.pdf (accessed June 25, 2009).

3. Mintel Reports, U.S. Lotteries Mintel Report, http://reports.mintel.com/ (accessed June 25, 2009).

4. Advertising Red Books, http://www.redbooks.com/Nonsub/index.asp (accessed June 25, 2009).

5. Yvette Shields, "Illinois Governor Sets $49 Billion Operating Budget," *Bond Buyer* 359 (March 8, 2007).

6. Yvette Shields, "Illinois Governor to Submit Lottery Plan This Spring," *Bond Buyer* 359 (January 24, 2007).

7. Yvette Shields, "Trading Lotto for Schools," *Bond Buyer* 358 (December 20, 2006).

8. Colleen Marie O'Connor, "Maybe a Private Sale, But How About a Public One?" *Investment Dealers' Digest* 72 (June 19, 2006): 6–8.

9. Edwin Mansfield, *Economics,* 7th ed. (New York: W.W. Norton, 1974).

10. James Gwartney, Richard Stroup, Russel Sobel, and David A. Macpherson, *Economics, Private & Public Choice* (Mason, OH: Thomson South-Western, 2006).

11. Mansfield, *Economics.*

12. Gwartney et al., *Economics, Private & Public Choice.*

13. Mintel Reports, U.S. Lotteries Mintel Report.

14. State of Illinois Lottery, 2008 Annual Report.

15. Yahoo! Finance, http://finance.yahoo.com/ (accessed June 25, 2009).

16. State of Illinois Lottery, 2007 Annual Report, http://www.illinoislottery.com/subsections/PR/FY07AnRpt.pdf (accessed June 25, 2009).

17. Charles Duhigg and Jenny Anderson, "Illinois Is Putting Lottery on Block for Quick Payoff," *The New York Times Online* (January 23, 2007).

18. Duhigg and Anderson, "Illinois Is Putting Lottery on Block for Quick Payoff."

19. Advertising Red Books.

20. Advertising Red Books.

21. Kathy Waters, "Marketing Expenses in Various Industries," Carroll School of Management Working Papers, fall 2007.

22. State of Illinois Lottery, 2007 Annual Report.

23. The Commonwealth of Massachusetts, Office of the State Treasurer, "Lottery and Red Sox Team Up for New Instant Ticket," http://www.mass.gov/?pageID=trehomepage& L=1& L0=Home& sid=Ctre (accessed April 1, 2009).

24. Mintel Reports, U.S. Lotteries Mintel Report.

25. Duhigg and Anderson, "Illinois Is Putting Lottery on Block for Quick Payoff."

26. Duhigg and Anderson, "Illinois Is Putting Lottery on Block for Quick Payoff."

27. Mintel Reports, U.S. Lotteries Mintel Report.

28. Scott Reeder, "Critics Skeptical of Lottery Plan to Sell It to Private Company," *The Kankakee Daily Journal* (February 6, 2007).

29. Yahoo! Finance, "Beta for Gaming Companies," http://finance.yahoo.com/ (accessed June 25, 2009).

30. Yahoo! Finance.

31. Standard and Poor's, "Understanding Rating Definitions," http://www2.standardandpoors.com/spf/pdf/fixedincome/Understanding_Rating_Definitions.pdf (accessed June 25, 2009).

32. Wikipedia, http://www.wikipedia.org (accessed November, 2, 2007).

33. Larry Rutherford, "Major Gambling Expansion Coming to Illinois after Senate Approval," Casino Gambling Web, http://www.casinogamblingweb.com (accessed May 31, 2008).

34. Nelson D. Schwartz and Ron Nixon, "Some States Consider Leasing Their Lotteries," *The New York Times* (October 14, 2007).

35. Schwartz and Nixon, "Some States Consider Leasing Their Lotteries."

36. Lottery Post, "Indiana Lottery Privatization on Hold," http://www.lotterypost.com (accessed April 23, 2007).

OTHER SOURCES OF INTEREST

Stilwell, Frank. *Political Economy, the Contest of Economic Ideas*. South Melbourne, Australia: University of Oxford Press, 2006.

The Illinois Lottery Annual Reports from 2003 to 2008 (online).

Part Five

Conclusion

Chapter 12

General Motors and the Government Bailout: The Hybrid Privatization

This final chapter will discusses one of the more recent controversial public policy measures, the rescue of General Motors (GM) by the federal government. For free-market advocates, it represents "nationalization" of the U.S. auto industry, while others advocated the complete takeover of the industry in order to preserve jobs. This example summarizes the various issues facing policy makers when they attempt to either privatize or nationalize a firm or industry. The case of GM is particularly fruitful in illustrating all of the economic and political forces that needed to be "satisficed" to come to any resolution. The resulting compromise between GM and the federal government does not satisfy either left- or right-wing ideologues but does illustrate all of the conditions that are needed to have a "successful" privatization or nationalization.

A BRIEF HISTORICAL ACCOUNT

For the nearly eight decades from 1931 to 2008, General Motors maintained its stature as the world's largest car manufacturer.[1,2] Founded in 1908 by a high school dropout named William "Billy" Crapo Durant, the General Motors Corporation originated as a holding company and grew in its early years by acquiring Oldsmobile, Cadillac, Oakland (later renamed Pontiac), and Chevrolet. These acquisitions positioned Alfred P. Sloan Jr.—a Massachusetts Institute of Technology educated engineer—to continue to grow GM's market share over the 23 years he served as chief executive officer, beginning in 1923.

Sloan steered the corporation to massive success under the guiding strategy that GM should offer "a car for every purse and purpose."[3,4] Synergizing with the traditional perception of "the American dream," Sloan directed GM to link a "ladder of success" with its brands so that as consumers moved up the income ladder, they could simultaneously upgrade their automotive status by transitioning to a higher-end brand still within the GM family. At the base of the ladder, GM offered Chevrolet, its most affordable brand. Next came Pontiac and Oldsmobile, and of higher quality and greater luxury still were Buick and Cadillac.[5]

Sloan left GM's helm in 1946, and soon after, in the 1950s, GM held 46 percent of the U.S. auto market. Ford and Chrysler, its closest competitors, held a combined 44 percent of the market, and all remaining competitors clutched a total share of 10 percent. GM's market share peaked in 1962, when it was responsible for 51 percent of car and truck sales in the United States[6] and the government debated using antitrust laws to split the company.[7,8]

But GM's place at the pinnacle of the automobile industry was to be short-lived. The automaker's success had depended on distinguishing its products from each other in strategically distinct design and positioning. It stumbled, however, in the 1980s, when it strayed from this strategy and, with the objective of cutting costs, began sharing basic designs in new products across brands. With distinctiveness among its brands blurred and increasing competition from foreign automakers, GM sought to diversify by creating a new brand, Saturn, which cost billions of dollars to launch, and by purchasing Saab and Hummer. Through the 1990s, with its finances stretched thin across its many brands, the company struggled to develop innovative models for each. For those new models that GM did bring to market, it practiced a strategy of "launch and leave," in which it introduced new products to the market at huge upfront costs and then left them without the support of adequate advertising. At the same time, Toyota and Honda, with fewer models to support, enjoyed successful sales as a result of their careful and committed development and marketing of the Camry and Accord.[9]

The 1990s, partially as a result of the era's low gas prices, also saw the advent of sport utility vehicle (SUV) popularity. In this arena, too, GM failed to innovate; it trailed Ford and Chrysler by five years in introducing a successful SUV model. In 1998, GM acquired Hummer, whose cars were even bulkier and offered even worse fuel economy than typical SUVs. But when gas prices began to increase in 1999, GM proved reluctant to move from high-margin SUVs to lower-margin, smaller cars.[10]

Hurt by less-than-desirable sales in many of its brands and by generous sales incentives that had trimmed margins, in 2005, GM reported a loss of

$8.65 billion.[11] Its gross profit continued to plummet in the following years[12] amid high gas prices and eventually the sweeping financial crisis that forced many potential consumers into economic retreat. Even prior to that, between 2003 and 2007, Hummer, Saab, and Saturn combined had average annual pretax losses of $1.1 billion per year.[13] When Rick Wagoner, GM's CEO until 2009, had assumed control of the company's North American operations in 1994, it held a 33.4 percent share of the U.S. auto market. In February of 2009, GM's share stood at 18.8 percent.

GM's first-half sales for 2008 had fallen 20 percent from the year before. In July of 2008, it announced plans to idle factories that had been producing SUVs and pickups and to add additional shifts at plants that had been building smaller cars. The transition proved too little and too late, especially in the midst of the declining industry sales that resulted from a receding general economy. In mid-September of 2008, GM's CEO, Rick Wagoner, joined the heads of Chrysler and Ford to "fly" to Washington, DC, to petition the federal government for $7.5 billion in relief.[14]

The heads of the "Big Three" were granted the funds they requested, but a continuing collapse in industry-wide sales brought them back before Congress just a couple of months later, this time requesting $25 billion in aid. Republicans in the Senate prevented a "bailout" bill from passing, but President George W. Bush exercised his executive power to extend $13.4 billion to GM and Chrysler. The government told the automakers that in order to receive further funding, they would have to present plans for long-term profitability that incorporated "concessions from unions, creditors, suppliers, and dealers."[15]

In February of 2009, GM returned to Washington with its plans for restructuring. Though its plan included painful, large scalebacks and massive job cuts, GM would still require many billions of dollars from the government to avoid bankruptcy. President Obama's task force on the auto industry agreed to provide taxpayer funding to keep GM out of bankruptcy for 60 days, while the firm would have to devise a plan for further cost-cutting. One of the conditions for this extended lifeline of funding was that Rick Wagoner resign from his post as CEO. He soon did, and the position was turned over to the COO, Fritz Henderson.[16]

GM returned again in April with a revised plan that called for $11.6 billion more in government funding and that would require—if GM were to stay out of bankruptcy—significant concessions from its bondholders. GM would need at least 90 percent of its bondholders to accept a trade of $414 of stock for every $1,000 in bonds that they held. By May 26, GM did not receive the concessions it needed, and on May 31, 2009, it filed for Chapter 11 bankruptcy in New York.[17]

This was a filing of massive proportion and importance. For 77 years, until 2008, when it relinquished its position to Toyota, GM—the 101-year-old company—had been the world's largest automaker. In the years preceding its bankruptcy filing, GM had been producing annually 9 million cars and trucks in 34 countries. As *The Economist* reported at the time of its Chapter 11 filing:

> It [had] 463 subsidiaries and employ[ed] 234,500 people, 91,000 of them in America, where it also provide[d] health-care and pension benefits for 493,000 retired workers. In America alone, it [spent] $50 billion a year buying parts and services from a network of 11,500 vendors and [paid] $476m in salaries each month.

It also owned $172 billion in liabilities and only $82.2 billion in assets. GM's crash had been the largest industrial bankruptcy in history.[18]

GM's demise was a painful blow not only for company executives, shareholders, and bondholders, but also for a number of other stakeholders, many of whom had no formal connections to the fallen behemoth. The Center for Automotive Research in Ann Arbor, Michigan, estimated that

> the folding of GM could result in over 200,000 jobs lost due to the disruption of supply chain to U.S. plants owned by Ford and some foreign car makers; 460,000 jobs lost at firms that supply goods and services to auto and auto-parts makers; and almost 660,000 jobs lost as a result of reduced spending by laid-off workers.[19]

Clearly, GM was not the only player in the arena that would be profoundly impacted by a permanent crash into bankruptcy and nonexistence.

The U.S. government faced a serious dilemma. In little time, President Obama, his auto task force, and his Treasury would have to decide whether to intervene further in the fate of the private corporation and use taxpayer funds to resurrect GM from bankruptcy, in the process effectively becoming the corporation's largest, and controlling, shareholder. The government faced on one hand the almost certain economic devastation that would result if GM were allowed to become entirely extinct. On the other hand, it had to contend with the prospect of violating central principles of neoliberal economics; risking what could be called misuse and abuse of taxpayer money; possibly negatively and unfairly—especially to Ford—interfering with competition in the auto industry; and improvidently disrupting the evolution of U.S. industry.

The Obama administration found itself in the middle of a game it never wanted to play: a question of whether to take a *laissez faire* approach and let the market forces run their destructive, and hopefully regenerative, course, or to intervene by providing national support to private enterprise. Should the government leave GM to crash and burn as a privatized corporation, or should it nationalize it in some way?

Some spectators who would have been sitting in the section of the arena usually reserved for the political far left called for a total nationalization of GM.[20] Others screamed, from their seats in the far right of the arena, for the government-referee to "just let them play" and, at all costs, to refrain from entering the game as a player, which would violate what they shouted were the inherent rules of the game.[21]

Indeed, the government found itself wedged between opposing pressures from both sides and many stakeholders. Vehement cries from around the arena threatened riot if the government chose either extreme: to idly permit GM to sink into extinction, or to take total charge of the corporate titan that had failed to survive in the market.

THE DECISION

Ultimately, the government decided that it would be best to help resurrect GM through a short-as-possible Chapter 11 restructuring. In order to return GM to functioning form, the U.S. government would have to authorize a major restructuring and become the corporation's largest shareholder.

On top of the previous $20 billion, the U.S. Treasury would provide $30.1 billion in financing. In return, it would receive $8.8 billion in debt and preferred stock and 60.8 percent of the new GM's total equity.[22]

The governments of Canada and Ontario would provide $9.5 billion in return and receive $1.7 billion in debt and preferred stock and 11.7 percent of the equity in the new corporation.[23] Canada has a much stronger precedent of government-owned business than does the United States. Its "Crown corporations" include the Canadian Broadcasting Corporation and Atomic Energy of Canada.[24] The decision to nationally own shares of GM may have been a less controversial one in the minds of Canadian taxpayers, for whom nationalized businesses are not so unusual.

Joining the U.S., Canadian, and Ontario governments as shareholders would be the United Auto Workers (UAW) and GM's bondholders at the time it entered bankruptcy. Both groups would have to make important concessions. Health care benefits for retired GM employees would now be paid for from a newly established trust that would hold 17.5 percent of the new GM's equity. Bondholders who held 54 percent, or nearly $15 billion, of GM's unsecured debt would trade in their bonds for 10 percent of the equity in the new GM.[25]

The restructuring plan intended for GM to emerge from its Chapter 11 proceedings after only three months, by September 2009, and to be much leaner and more competitive. In the restructuring process, GM would lower its breakeven point from one that required an annual domestic market of 16 million car sales to one that requires only 10 million. In order to do this, GM would not only need these concessions from the UAW and its bondholders, but would also have to downsize its plant operations, closing 11 plants and idling another 3,[26] closing 2,400 dealerships, and cutting "21,000 hourly-paid jobs and 8,000 white-collar jobs."[27] Still, these job losses are mild compared to what would result without the government's intervention.

Along with the shares of equity owned by the Canadian government and the UAW, each group received the right to appoint a director to the board of the new GM, and the U.S. government—the largest shareholder— would appoint all of the remaining directors.[28]

But the question remains: How much authority would the U.S. government exercise in its role as majority shareholder? To help answer this question, President Obama commissioned an interagency task force informally named "The Government as Shareholder," headed by Diana Farrell, the deputy director of the National Economic Council who previously headed the McKinsey Global Institute. Under Farrell, "The Government as Shareholder" agency published four core principles that it said would guide U.S. governance of such national investments as GM, American International Group (AIG), Citigroup, and other banks the government had bailed out.[29]

As a self-described "reluctant equity holder but careful steward of taxpayer resources," the U.S. government's first principle of ownership is that, while it aims to "promote strong and viable companies that can quickly be profitable and contribute to economic growth and jobs without government involvement," it desires to own equity in companies no longer than necessary.[30] Similarly, the UAW and the Canadian government also announced that they intended to sell their shares as soon as possible.[31]

The second principle notes that for companies that require substantial financial assistance, as in the case with GM, "the government will reserve the right to set upfront conditions to protect taxpayers, promote financial stability and encourage growth." The third principle states that once these upfront conditions are in place, the government will "protect the taxpayers' investment by managing its ownership stakes in a hands-off, commercial manner" and that it "will not interfere with or exert control over day-to-day company operations." Further, "no government employees will serve on the boards or be employed by these companies." Finally, the fourth principle holds that the government, as shareholder, will only vote on core governance issues.

While the United States intends to sell its equity stake in GM as soon as possible, there is some question about how soon and how successfully it will be able to do so. *The New York Times* reported that Obama's own auto task force warned him that "the faster the government sells its stake to private investors, the less it is likely to recover its investment of more than $50 billion in the company." The other side of the danger is that the longer the government owns its sizable stake in GM, the more pressured and tempted it will be to intervene in the company's operations.[32]

Skeptics argue that the government's political interests are inevitably at odds with GM's economic interests, and that "hands-off" ownership by the government is impossible, and perhaps already violated. They point to the replacement of Wagoner with Henderson as CEO, the government's pressure on bondholders to concede their holdings for prorated equity, and its requirement that GM produce small, fuel-efficient cars.[33] Critics of the U.S. government's involvement worry especially about this last point: that the government will mandate GM to produce small, fuel-efficient "green" cars for which there may not even be adequate consumer demand.[34, 35, 36] Concerns have also been raised about how the U.S. government will handle profit-oriented decisions to produce at lower costs in Asian countries and forego job creation in the United States.[37] Any number of other stumbling blocks could arise as GM's fate unwinds, and the U.S. government could easily find itself faced with further conundrums of intervention versus inaction. Its competing interests as GM shareholder, steward of taxpayer interest, protector of U.S. economy and social welfare, and creator of political and legal precedent could again come at odds.

Still, given the definition of a successful nationalization or privatization as one that benefits all stakeholders in the short run and the long run, the government's purportedly temporary national investment in, and resulting control of, GM does seem—at least at this early stage—to fulfill the requirements. President Obama stated that in the restructuring process all stakeholders would be expected to sacrifice and that none would receive special treatment,[38] yet all of them seem to benefit from the government's intervention.

For the UAW, current and retired employees had to concede certain health and retirement benefits, but the union escaped the loss of hundreds of thousands of jobs. For the UAW, the government's intervention was surely preferable to a more striking demise of their employer.

Bondholders were bound to lose big in this affair no matter what. At least with the government's rescue through the Chapter 11 resurrection process, the bondholders will end up with some equity; though less than the value of the debt they were owed, it is better than the nothing they might have received if GM were not able to get back on its proverbial feet.

The general taxpaying public has contributed to an investment whose return is still not guaranteed, but their dollars did help to prevent a permanent collapse of GM, which would have hurled the U.S. economy deeper into its current woes, furthering unemployment and initiating a ripple effect outward from the influential auto industry into much of the rest of the U.S. economy.

For suppliers, obviously, the government's intervention was their only hope of sustaining a critical and—in many cases—preeminent source of revenue.

Competitors, especially Ford, may be hurt by what could easily be deemed preferential treatment of GM by the government. Conversely, Ford might benefit in some ways in that it will still have its many suppliers who might have been dropped out of business if a customer as substantial as GM discontinued all its orders. Still, competitors probably made out the worst in the affair, especially in the eyes of neoliberals, who doggedly endorse a survival-of-the-fittest economic mentality.

Overall, it can be concluded that the outcome—at least at this stage—is not ideal for any stakeholder, though it is also far from the worst possible scenario for any. This middle-of-the-road outcome for stakeholders results from what was a middle-of-the-spectrum decision by the government: to intervene by investing public finances but to refrain from complete or overly active control of the new GM. Indeed, it is likely that this partial and intended temporary nationalization of sorts—a moderate course of action given the extreme options for complete nationalization or sustained privatization—was the only reasonable outcome that the nation's bipartisan politics and public would permit.

FINAL THOUGHTS

The GM situation (along with the other chapters) provides the background for a few concluding comments about the three essential conditions for privatization.

1. *Market Ideology*: Privatization depends on a political and economic environment that is conducive to private ownership as well as a legal system that will enforce the right to private property. In the United States, the GM case illustrates that completely nationalizing a previously private firm is politically unacceptable. Meanwhile, in Venezuela, it would be equally unacceptable to privatize the oil industry. In other examples, such as the lottery, the market ideology makes privatization acceptable, but it appears that there is not sufficient market ideology to make the privatization of public transportation a possibility. The following second necessary condition might explain why ideology alone is not a sufficient condition to make a privatization possible.

2. *Economic Viability*: The Obama administration's contention that GM was still an economically viable enterprise but in need of assistance was the focus of this chapter. As of May 25, 2010, GM turned a profit in the first quarter of 2010, but it is far too soon to declare that the government bailout was a success. In three of the cases that we studied (a cigarette firm, a lottery, and state liquor stores), these enterprises would certainly be profitable, which has made their possible privatization much more of a realistic option. Meanwhile, attempts to privatize port facilities and public transportation are considered at best economically risky, and private firms would continue to demand public funding of these enterprises or certainly substantial public investment in these facilities before they would take over operations of these suspect economic enterprises. Finally, in the case of the oil industry, there seems to be a tug of war between nationalization and privatization. While this industry would certainly be profitable to an oil firm, it points to the final factor that needs to be accounted for in the privatization scheme, namely, is the firm or industry a reliable source of revenue for government?

3. *Source of Revenue*: The odds of a government entity being privatized are much greater if a government is in need of short-term revenue. This has clearly been the case with the oil industry. These firms are nationalized when government takes the stance that this industry can provide the funds for long-term economic change. Oil firms are privatized when governments have immediate revenue needs. Meanwhile, there is a great deal of hesitation to privatize a nationalized cigarette firm or a lottery that has been a fairly stable source of revenue. Hence, if these firms are privatized, the question becomes, what is the appropriate tax rate that will ensure (1) that this stream of revenue will continue but also (2) that the private firm will be able to reinvest in the enterprise for its long-term viability? The revenue needs of government change with

economic circumstances, and the attractiveness of privatizing a firm or industry also changes with economic winds of fortune.

FINAL CAUTION

None of the three above "parts"—market ideology, economic viability, or source of revenue—are necessary or sufficient to ensure that a privatization will take place or, for that matter, that government will nationalize a firm or industry. In the end, the economic, political, and social implications of a privatization are of equal importance, and none of the factors "trump" the other factors. The "game" of privatization as it was defined in Chapter 2 is one that involves many stakeholders who have all kinds of different economic, political, and social agendas. Hopefully, this book with its numerous and varied examples will enable the reader to forecast what government entities might be proposed for privatization, identify the groups that would challenge any effort to privatize a government entity, and finally project the revenue needs of government with any privatization. There is no one "successful" privatization strategy, and in any potential privatization, sacrifices must be made by all the various stakeholders.

NOTES

1. John D. Stoll, Kevin Helliker, and Neal E. Boudette, "A Saga of Decline and Denial," *The Wall Street Journal* (June 2, 2009).

2. "General Motors Corporation," *The New York Times*, http://topics.nytimes.com/top/news/business/companies/general_motors_corporation/index.html?scp =1-spot& sq=gm& st=cse (accessed June 16, 2009).

3. "General Motors Corporation."

4. Stoll et al., "A Saga of Decline and Denial."

5. Stoll et al., "A Saga of Decline and Denial."

6. "General Motors Corporation."

7. "General Motors Corporation."

8. Stoll et al., "A Saga of Decline and Denial."

9. "General Motors Corporation."

10. "General Motors Corporation."

11. Stoll et al., "A Saga of Decline and Denial."

12. Financial Information: General Motors Financials, *Hoovers*, http://www .hoovers.com/general-motors/--ID__10640,target__financial__information--/free-co-samples-index.xhtml (accessed June 6, 2009).

13. Stoll et al., "A Saga of Decline and Denial."

14. "General Motors Corporation."

15. "General Motors Corporation."

16. "General Motors Corporation."

17. "General Motors Corporation."

18. "A Giant Falls," *The Economist* (June 4, 2009).

19. Justin Lahart, "Filing Has Potential to Lift Economy in Long Term," *The Wall Street Journal* (May 31, 2009).

20. Robert Weissman, "GM Nationalization: The Path Not Taken, Choices Still Ahead," *The Huffington Post* (June 3, 2009).

21. "The Obama Motor Co," *The Wall Street Journal* (June 2, 2009).

22. "The Obama Administration Auto Restructuring Initiative General Motors Restructuring," *The White House Briefing Room*, http://www.whitehouse .gov/the_press_office/Fact-Sheet-on-Obama-Administration-Auto-Restructur ing-Initiative-for-General-Motors/ (accessed June 23, 2009).

23. "The Obama Administration Auto Restructuring Initiative."

24. Micheline Maynard, "G.M.'s Chief Promises Full Details of Restructuring," *The New York Times* (June 3, 2009).

25. "The Obama Administration Auto Restructuring Initiative."

26. "The Obama Administration Auto Restructuring Initiative."

27. "A Giant Falls."

28. "The Obama Administration Auto Restructuring Initiative."

29. "The Obama Administration Auto Restructuring Initiative."

30. "The Obama Administration Auto Restructuring Initiative."

31. "GM Goes Bust: Bankruptcy, at Last," *The Economist* (June 1, 2009).

32. David E. Sanger, "Obama's Test: Restoring GM at Arm's Length," *The New York Times* (June 1, 2009).

33. "The Obama Motor Co.," *The Wall Street Journal* (June 2, 2009).

34. "The Obama Motor Co."

35. "A Giant Falls."

36. Sanger, "Obama's Test."

37. Sanger, "Obama's Test."

38. "The Obama Administration Auto Restructuring Initiative."

Index

About the Author

RICHARD A. MCGOWAN, SJ, is a professor with a joint appointment in the Economics Department and the Carroll School of Management at Boston College, where he has won numerous teaching awards. He is the author of six books on the interactions of business and government.